ROBERT KILWARDBY O.P.
ON TIME AND IMAGINATION

Introduction and Translation

AUCTORES BRITANNICI MEDII AEVI · IX(2)

ROBERT KILWARDBY O.P.

ON TIME AND IMAGINATION

PART 2

INTRODUCTION AND TRANSLATION

BY

ALEXANDER BROADIE

Published *for* THE BRITISH ACADEMY
by OXFORD UNIVERSITY PRESS

Oxford University Press, Walton Street, Oxford OX2 6DP
Oxford New York Toronto
Delhi Bombay Calcutta Madras Karachi
Kuala Lumpur Singapore Hong Kong Tokyo
Nairobi Dar es Salaam Cape Town
Melbourne Auckland Madrid
and associated companies in
Berlin Ibadan

Published in the United States
by Oxford University Press Inc., New York

© *The British Academy, 1993*

All rights reserved. No part of this publication may be reproduced, stored in a retrieval system, or transmitted, in any foirm or by any means, without the prior permission in writing of the British Academy.

British Library Cataloguing in Publication Data
Data available

ISBN 0–19–726121–3

Typeset by Alden Multimedia
Printed in Great Britain
on acid-free paper by
the Alden Press,
Oxford

Contents

Acknowledgements	vii
Introduction	1
(i) Kilwardby's career	1
(ii) On Time	2
(iii) On Imagination	10
(iv) Appendix: Questions concerning time, from Kilwardby's *Commentary on the Sentences of Peter Lombard*	17
(v) Conclusion	19
On Time	21
On Imagination	65
Appendix	149
Bibliography	167
Index	171

Acknowledgements

Anthony Kenny and Christopher F.J. Martin provided invaluable help in the preparation of this volume. They coaxed sense out of Latin passages that had perplexed me, and also suggested, to the benefit of my translation, many stylistic changes. I am grateful to them.

A.B.
Glasgow 1992

Introduction

(i) *Career*

The British philosopher-theologian Robert Kilwardby, contemporary of Albert the Great and Thomas Aquinas, taught arts at the University of Paris for about eight years from *c*.1237 to *c*.1245.[1] He taught grammar and logic, including *Priscianus minor*, *De accentu*, the *Barbarismus Donati*, Aristotle's *Organon*, the *Isagoge* of Porphyry, the *Liber divisionum* of Boethius, and the anonymous *Liber sex principium*. In addition his commentary on the first three books of Aristotle's *Nicomachean Ethics* (these being the only books of the *Ethics* available in Latin *c*.1240) bears witness to a course on that text also. In *c*.1245 Kilwardby entered the Dominican Order and then or thereafter began to study theology. Evidently however he remained close to developments in arts subjects, for his *De ortu scientiarum* ('On the rise of the sciences'), a major work testifying to Kilwardby's wide reading and formidable intellectual powers, was composed *c*.1250, probably at Blackfriars, Oxford.

Kilwardby was a regent in arts at Oxford from *c*.1256 to *c*.1261. In 1261 he was elected prior provincial of the English Dominicans, an appointment which did not however foreclose his philosophical and theological studies, as is evidenced by the fact that in 1271 the master of the Dominican Order, John

---

1. For discussion of Kilwardby's career, see: Daniel A. Callus, O.P. 'The "Tabulae super originalia patrum" of Robert Kilwardby, O.P.' in *Studia Mediaevalia in Honorem R. J. Martin*, Bruges 1948, 243-52.

    Albert G. Judy, O.P. (ed.) *Robert Kilwardby, O.P., De Ortu Scientiarum* (Auctores Britannici Medii Aevi IV), Oxford University Press for the British Academy, 1976.

    P. O. Lewry, O.P. 'The Oxford Condemnations of 1277 in grammar and logic' in *English Logic and Semantics from the End of the Twelfth Century to the Time of Ockham and Burleigh: Acts of the Fourth European Symposium on Medieval Logic and Semantics*, Leiden-Nijmegen, 23-27 April 1979, ed. H.A.G.Braakhuis, C.H.Kneepkens, L.M. de Rijk, Ingenium, Nijmegen, 1981, Artistarum Supplementa 1, 235-278.

    P. O. Lewry, O.P. 'Robert Kilwardby on meaning: A Parisian course on the "Logica Vetus"' in *Sprache und Erkenntnis im Mittelalter*, ed. A. Zimmermann, De Gruyter, Berlin-New York, 1981 (Miscellanea Mediaevalia, 13/1), 376-384.

    P. O. Lewry, O.P. 'Robert Kilwardby on imagination: The reconciliation of Aristotle and Augustine' in *Medioevo*, 9, 1983, 1-42.

    P. O. Lewry, O.P. (ed.) Robert Kilwardby O.P. *On Time and Imagination: De Tempore, De Spiritu Fantastico* (Auctores Britannici Medii Aevi IX), Oxford University Press for the British Academy, 1987, xiii-xvii.

of Vercelli, sought his answers (as well as those of Albert the Great and Thomas Aquinas) to forty three questions ranging widely across philosophy and theology. In 1272 he was elevated to the Archbishopric of Canterbury, and five years later, on 18 March 1277, instigated the condemnation at Oxford of a set of propositions, some philosophical, some theological. Most especially Kilwardby was opposed to doctrines of Thomas Aquinas on privation and on the unicity of form. The firm base of Kilwardby's opposition to Aquinas was the work of St Augustine or was at least thirteenth century Augustinianism. The great depth of Augustine's influence on Kilwardby is plain from the treatises translated in this volume. In 1279, and by then a cardinal, he died in papal service at Viterbo.

It is not known when the two treatises translated in this volume were composed, though in *On Time*, at least, there is the confident deployment and manipulation of complex theological as well as philosophical material, suggesting a composition by a mature theologian. In the next two sections I shall comment upon the structure of the two treatises as well as focusing attention upon some of their main doctrines.

(ii) *On Time*

Kilwardby begins by investigating whether time is one of the things (*de entibus*) outside the mind. It is perhaps surprising that he starts with that question, rather than with his second question, 'What is time?', for the answer to the first will certainly depend upon that to the second. However, he starts where he does and we shall follow his ordering. The term 'thing', my translation here of *ens* (also = 'being' and 'entity'), should be carried lightly at this stage. *Ens* as applied to time implies that time has a mode of being but leaves it entirely open what that mode might be; in particular it leaves it open as to whether time is outside the mind or inside. It seems not to make sense to ask *when* time exists, but Kilwardby thinks that we can ask *where* it is. Of the two possibilities that he airs, the one he associates with Aristotle is that it is outside the mind, and the one associated with Augustine is that it is inside. These contrasting views are a chief formal feature of the treatise, and, as we shall see, the counterpoint between the two philosophers is pursued with even greater persistence in the treatise on the imagination.

The question whether time is outside the mind calls for elucidation. What is it for something to be outside the mind, or to be inside it? Should we think of something as inside the mind if it is a mental act, an act of conceiving, imagining, perceiving, and so on, or a mental skill or ability, and as outside the mind if it is none of these things but is instead a physical object, or an attribute of a physical object, or a relation between two or more such objects?

It quickly becomes clear that the thought that time is outside the mind is prompted by the way Aristotle links time to a certain aspect of physical objects (para.3), and that the thought that time is in the mind is prompted by Augustine's doctrine that 'time is a certain extension, not of something outside the mind, but of an affection of the mind present to itself and left behind in it by things passing by' (para.4).

For the moment I should like to concentrate upon the fact that Kilwardby's contemporaries would readily have slotted into their metaphysical preoccupations the form of his question, whether time is outside the mind or inside it. For they had a particular interest in locating universals or common natures. Should we say that the universal cathood, the common nature shared by all cats, is in each and every cat and is not in any way dependent upon mind for its existence, or should we say that it is a concept, a mental act, under which all individual cats can be brought? Or should we say indeed that it is neither of these things but is instead the very word 'cat', the word which is truly predicable of all cats? This dispute regarding universals is closely matched by the corresponding question about the location of time, a question which can evidently be expressed as a metaphysical one concerning mode of existence. Thus we might adopt a realist position to the effect that time is outside the mind and does not depend upon a mind for its existence. And we might instead adopt a conceptualist position (which can be thought of as nominalist, in so far as concepts are to be thought of as mental nouns — *nomina mentalia*), to the effect that time is either a mental act or at least is dependent for its existence upon such an act. There are many intermediate positions between the extremes of realism and nominalism in respect of the mode of existence of time. And several of the positions are to be found in Kilwardby's treatise.

Why hold a non-realist view about time? *On Time* opens with an argument in support of a non-realist view. Time has parts — days are parts, so are weeks, years, and so on. Many things outside the mind, perhaps all, also have parts. However, whereas in the case of every external thing some or all of its parts exist at the same time, this cannot be true of time, for its parts succeed each other and cannot be simultaneous. Hence time cannot be outside the mind. But against this (para.5) there is Aristotle's doctrine that time is a cause of decay of natural objects, at least in so far as things mature and die in temporal sequence. But if we think of time as causal in this way, it is difficult to see how it can be located in the mind; it must surely be a feature of external things. Yet if this is right, how do we deal with the argument that since at least some parts of any external compound exist simultaneously whereas no parts of time exist simultaneously, time cannot be anything external? Kilwardby's short answer is that though some external things, those that exist 'in a permanent and fixed way', have parts which are simultaneous, it does not follow that all external things do. In particular, there are things which 'exist essentially in a successive and transient way'. Time and motion are such things — by their nature their parts exist successively and never simultaneously.

All this of course is not to say what time is, but it does at least provide part of the conceptual framework necessary for the answer to the technical question 'What is it?' (*Quid est?*) which seeks a real definition *per genus et differentiam*. Aristotle's definition, to which Kilwardby immediately attends (para.11) is this: 'Time is the number of motion in respect of the earlier and later'. The phrase *numerus motus*, which I have rendered as 'number of motion', is not easy to translate. Perhaps 'reckoning' or 'counting (or even "countability") of motion' would have been better. Heavenly bodies move in a regular way. The sun passes across the heavens and it does so again and again. There is today's passage, and the one before, and the one after. Because they are perceived as successive these various passages are countable despite the fact that they are, merely as passages of the sun, mutually indistinguishable. This numberedness or countability of motion in respect of the earlier and later is, according to Aristotle, what time essentially is.

But 'number of motion' (*numerus motus*) is difficult to translate as much because of the term *motus* as because of *numerus*. 'Change' might do as well as 'motion', and is preferred by many. In any case we are dealing with a technical term in scholastic philosophy, and should deal with it on that basis. I shall translate *motus* as 'motion' throughout. 'Change' might be thought to be just as appropriate, but whichever term were chosen what would matter would be its systematic use.

Even if time is defined in terms of motion, why should it be defined in terms of number of motion and not simply in terms of quantity of motion? Thus it might be argued that any unit of time could be defined in terms of such a quantity. For example, a day is one revolution of the earth about its axis, and a year is one revolution of the earth about the sun. Hence instead of speaking about a day we can speak about a revolution of the earth about its axis, and similarly we can speak not about a year but about the earth's revolution round the sun. Hence if each nameable unit of time is definable in terms of a particular quantity of motion, then indeed why not define 'time' as 'quantity of motion'?

This suggestion however ignores the fact that we use time for measuring. 'Time', as Kilwardby puts it, 'has been imposed as the name of a measure *tout court* in so far as it is a measure of motion. And specific nouns, for example, "year" and "day", have been imposed to designate partial measures. For "time" is the name of a quantity of motion simply and universally, but "day", "month", "year", and such like are names of partial, distinct, and limited quantities of motion' (para.24). These examples take us to the heart of the matter. Had Plato written a dialogue on time he might well have begun by putting into Socrates' mouth the question ' What is time?', and into the mouth of a pupil the reply 'A day is a time, so is a month, and so is a year', to which Socrates would have replied 'What you say is true, but these are only instances or examples of time. What is time itself?'. We might almost say that what Plato would be seeking is the form of time, though no doubt that would be a tendentious way of phrasing his question. At any rate the question might well be pursued by asking what a day, a month, and so on, have in common. And the answer is that they are all units of measurement, units which measure motion or change in respect of the earlier and later.

Why, then, not define 'time' as '*measure* of motion in respect of the earlier and later' rather than as '*number* of motion *etc.*'? Kilwardby's answer is: 'the concept of measure applies to every quantity, but only a discrete quantity or a continuous quantity which can in some way be made discrete can be measured numerically. But it is in this latter way that time is a measure...namely as both a continuum and something discrete' (para.26). Moreover Kilwardby adds that while 'measure' implies that a determinate quantity is made manifest, 'number' implies this and implies also the arithmetical nature of the quantity (para.27). In a strict sense arithmetic is here being envisaged as the science of time.

Given that time is the number of motion, what motion is here being spoken about? Is it motion without qualification, or some motion in particular? On this matter Kilwardby takes issue with Averroes, who holds that in speaking about the number of motion, the motion in question is the diurnal first circular motion, which we can think of as represented by the passage of the sun from one sunrise to the next. Of course, as Averroes knew, time measures every motion, but time is attributed to the diurnal first circular motion and through that motion it is attributable to every other motion also. This appears to amount to the view that a day is *the* unit of time, and that all other motions are measured in terms of their relation to this unit. Thus time is not the measure of the first diurnal circular motion in the way in which it is the measure of all other motions. To mark this special case Averroes speaks of time as measuring that motion as a form measures what it in-forms, rather than as a number measures what is numbered.

Kilwardby, however, registers his unease at this doctrine (para.36). For people regard the diurnal circular motion as itself to be numbered in terms of hours. And it is the diurnal motion, already measured as lasting for so many hours, that is then itself used as the measure of other motions. Of course, as Kilwardby grants, Averroes might have been expressing, even if inadequately, the doctrine that though time is to be thought of as measuring the first diurnal motion in the way that a form measures what it in-forms, it is also to be thought of as a number measuring what is numbered. And in that case Kilwardby withdraws his objection. If Kilwardby is here saying that though a day can be measured in terms of hours, nevertheless we reach the concept of an hour by dividing up the day, so that, considered as a unit of measurement, the day has primacy in relation to the hour, then there seems no serious disagreement of substance between Kilwardby and Averroes.

Kilwardby is particularly clear about the advantage of treating the diurnal circular motion as basic. It is, quite simply, that that motion is known by all people and is regular. It is a motion 'which has a perfect equality always and in relation to the same things', it is 'best known and most regular', and is therefore 'the regular motion assumed by art and human industry' (para.49). So we mark it out as a unit, then mark its quarters, mark the thirds of each quarter, and mark the halves of each third. Each of these halves is an hour, one twenty fourth part of the diurnal motion. It is to be noted that since this is how Kilwardby understands the concept of an hour, he must hold that the concept of the diurnal motion is no less a part of the definition of 'hour' than it is of 'day'. Which is not, of course, to deny that in one sense the day has primacy, as a unit of measurement, over the hour, and perhaps over every other unit of time also.

At the start of *On Time* Kilwardby enquires whether time is one of the things outside the mind, and then focuses on Aristotle's 'scientific' view of time which appears to require an affirmative answer to the question. But even if time is outside the mind it might nevertheless be so dependent upon the mind as only to exist if a mind does, for if the unit of measurement of motion has, as Kilwardby argues, two termini which are each a now, one earlier and the other later, then surely the existence of time presupposes the existence of a mind. For there cannot be a now except in relation to someone for whom it is now.

Kilwardby adopts a compromise position on this matter. A distinction has to be made, between time existing as unlimited and undetermined and as limited and determined (para.77, and *cf.* paras.46–9). The point is that defining a measure of motion, say, a day or an hour, requires a mental act. Before a day is defined, there was, on this view, no day, that is, a determinate unit of measure of motion. Yet in an obvious sense there were days before there was a defined measure. But they were, in Kilwardby's language, unlimited and indeterminate, and hence do not presuppose the existence of a mind. A parallel distinction can be (and is) made regarding units of land measurement, such as feet, perches, and miles. Until a perch (a twenty foot rod) is marked and defined, there are no definite and determinate perches. But Kilwardby adds: 'if [a perch] be considered simply as something shared, and in respect of an existence which is not fixed, and is unlimited and indeterminate, it is then in all elements, and in all things composed of elements, whose length comes to twenty feet' (para.48). A perch, unlimited and indeterminate, does not presuppose the existence of a mind. When Averroes (para.75) says that time presupposes the existence of a mind, he is thinking of time as limited and determined, and in that case he is not contradicting Aristotle when the latter says, or at least implies, that time does not presuppose the existence of a mind (para.73).

Did time have a beginning? This is a question in which Kilwardby the theologian would have a deep interest, but here he approaches the matter as a philosopher rather than as a theologian, and in particular does not ask how time stands in relation to the creator God. Instead he suggests an approach on the basis of the fact that if time passed into existence it did so (i) in eternity or (ii) in time, or (iii) in an indivisible now (para.79). The first alternative is not plain sailing. The obvious thing to say about it is that only what is eternal is in eternity. But eternal things cannot have a beginning, and hence, as Kilwardby puts the point: '"to begin to exist" signifies "not to be eternal"' (para.79). But he is not happy with this position; it is too crude. Revealing something of his Augustinian predilection, he argues that there is more than one way of being in eternity (para.84). Eternity is the proper and essential measure of some things; in this sense God is in eternity. But other things are in eternity in the sense of participating in it, much as we are to think of mundane things participating in the Platonic forms which they exemplify. We are here close to the Platonic concept of time as the moving image of eternity. In a suggestive but difficult passage (para.84) Kilwardby affirms that time does indeed begin in eternity but 'as in a common measure which is transcendent and not entirely coequal'.

As regards the suggestion that time begins in time, Kilwardby's first move is to set up a dilemma (para.80). If time does begin in time then does it begin in a coeval time or in an antecedent time? If the former then we have to ask when that coeval time came into existence, and hence nothing is explained by invoking a coeval time. If the latter then we have to ask when that antecedent time passed into existence, and additionally we are faced with the absurdity of supposing that a time existed before time. Yet Kilwardby wishes to hold, all the same, that time can be said to begin in time, but not to begin in either a coeval or an antecedent time; the time it can be said to begin in is itself (para.84). We can suppose there to be a first motion, and time as the measure of motion begins when that motion does.

Finally, as regards the suggestion that time began in an indivisible now, this might seem to imply the absurdity that a continuum existed in something indivisible (para.81). But Kilwardby thinks that sense can be made of the suggestion, for we are not required to suppose that any period of time is contained in something indivisible. Instead we are merely required to think of the indivisible now as the initial terminus of time (para.84). That first now is in time but it does not take, or 'take up', time.

This consideration prompts Kilwardby to attend to the concept of being in time. On this matter he remains close to the spirit of Aristotle. For motion to be in time is just for motion and its existence to be measured and counted by time (para.85). Of course, not everything is in motion but even things at rest can be measured by time. In that case, Kilwardby holds, a distinction should be brought into play between being essentially (or by nature) and being accidentally in time. For time essentially measures motion and the existence of things in so far as they are in motion, and it accidentally measures things at rest and things in motion in so far as they simply exist, that is, without regard to the fact that they are moving (para.87).

However, not everything is either in motion or even able to move, at least spatially. And since time is the measure of motion, a question arises as to whether there is some measure other than time but analogous to it which is applicable to the other kinds of being. In particular what is at issue here are spiritual beings, especially God and angels, which are capable of what may be termed spiritual motion though not physical. Now, more than before, Kilwardby speaks as a theologian. He focuses on the point that corresponding to the time in which physical things are in motion or at rest, there is the eternity in which God exists, and, between time (conceived of here as successive duration) and eternity (which is durationless) there is the everlastingness of angels (where everlastingness is conceived of as stable duration). A hint of this development is already to be found in para.72 where Kilwardby suggests that in some respect a corporeal being might, even if secondarily, exist in everlastingness, and a spirit might, even if secondarily, exist in time — 'even though less truly and less intelligibly'. He adds that Augustine would say this, and that Aristotle would have said it if he had posited motion in spirits. The appeal to Aristotle is customary with Kilwardby, but it is not plain upon what he here bases his confident assertion about what Aristotle would have said.

Given the distinction between eternity, time, and everlastingness, for Kilwardby the latter two of these have more in common with each other than either has with eternity, for the latter two belong to the created order, and there is no greater conceivable metaphysical divide than that between the uncreated and the created. But Kilwardby is not so set upon stressing the transcendence of God as to deny His immanence. On the contrary, following Anselm of Canterbury he argues that God is immanent in His creation, and in particular that God is in all time. This is a hard doctrine to grasp. I shall here spell out Kilwardby's argument.

If God exists in all time then He does so either simultaneously or distinctly. As a first move, to say that He is simultaneously in all time is to say, at least, that while existing in the present He exists in the past and future; not that He now also has a past and a future (for that is true of us humans), but that His past and future are simultaneous with His present. However, it surely follows that the past and future are in the present (para.134). But this seems absurd. To take the other alternative, to say that God exists distinctly in all time is to imply that His existence today is distinct from His existence yesterday and is distinct from His existence tomorrow. And this is plainly incompatible with standard teaching on the absolute unity of God, teaching which implies that God is in no way separated from Himself, as He would be if His past existence were other than His present or future existence.

Should we say therefore that God does not exist distinctly in all time? Kilwardby answers this on the basis of a distinction (para.137). What does the term 'distinctly' qualify? If it qualifies God's existence then the answer is no, for no part of the divine existence is distinct from any other part. One cannot indeed speak meaningfully about 'parts' of God's existence. But if 'distinctly' qualifies the parts of time in which God exists then the answer is yes, for the parts of time in which God exists are distinct from each other.

It is not easy to penetrate this teaching. If God does indeed exist in different parts of time, that is, if He exists now, and also existed in a time past in relation to this now, and will exist in a time future in relation to this now, then how can these temporal qualifications not qualify His existence, as they qualify the existence of familiar objects? And if they do qualify His existence then must we not say that He exists distinctly in all time? If it is replied that God does not exist distinctly in all time because He remains the same through time, then why can I not reply by pointing out that the same is true of me? I am today who I was yesterday; in Frege's phrase I am 'the same again'. But though it is the same 'I', I have nevertheless changed in many respects since yesterday, and Kilwardby would say that since yesterday God has not changed in the least in any respect whatever. It is God's nature to be changeless, and therefore not to have a history, somewhat as it is the nature of the natural numbers to be absolutely changeless and therefore to lack a history. But to speak in this way about numbers carries the implication that they do not exist in time, not in any time and therefore not in all time either. Kilwardby does not explain why the same should not be said about God. If he means that everything that occurs in time is present to God in a durationless now, then he does not say this, and in any case such a doctrine is beset with logical difficulties.

If God does not exist distinctly in all time, does He exist simultaneously in all time? As with 'distinctly', a distinction has to be made regarding the use of 'simultaneously' (para.139). Does it qualify the eternal existence of God, or does it qualify times? If it qualifies the former alternative, then what is being said is that God's existence is a simultaneous whole in all time, and hence His existence is not divided by partitions of time. Kilwardby assents to this position.

But if 'simultaneously' qualifies times rather than qualifying God's existence, then a further distinction has to be made. For 'simultaneously' qualifies times either according as they exist in God's providence, or according as they exist in their successive nature. Kilwardby argues that taken in the first sense God is simultaneously in all time, for in His eternal providence nothing is past or future, but the concepts and causes of all times exist there simultaneously. The situation, according to Kilwardby, is comparable to the way in which a person has in his memory a plan he has formed of an action which was to unfold in reality over a period of years. On the other hand, if 'simultaneously' is taken to qualify times (para.140), then it is false that God exists simultaneously in all time, for that would be to imply that the different times exist simultaneously in God, which is impossible for nothing can be both simultaneous and successive.

Although *On Time* can in many ways be regarded as a commentary on Aristotle and in particular on the sections concerning time in *Physics* IV, it is plain that there is much in what Kilwardby says that owes little or nothing to Aristotle, but is instead best read in the light of the Patristic and most especially the Augustinian tradition. Kilwardby's debt to St Augustine is even more striking in *On Imagination* to which I shall now turn.

(iii) *On Imagination*

As with *On Time* there are here problems of translation, starting this time with the very title of the treatise. I have translated *spiritus fantasticus* as 'imagination', and could equally have chosen 'imaginative soul'. In my translation of the treatise, *spiritus* is translated as 'soul'. 'Spirit' might have done as well but there is a long tradition of speaking about intellect, imagination, and sense, as parts of the soul rather than of the spirit, and I have fallen into line with that tradition. In any case, it does not greatly matter which of these English terms is employed so long as it is employed systematically. Kilwardby himself starts by pointing to terminological problems. Above the faculty of sense there is a cognitive power which has an upper and a lower part, the upper being the intellectual and the lower the imaginative or fantastic, and the mind as a whole and also the intellectual part and the imaginative part separately can be termed 'soul'. I think that in general Kilwardby uses 'soul' in all the ways just indicated and that he does so with no more ambiguity than he is prepared to tolerate.

Kilwardby employs a faculty psychology inherited from Aristotle, in particular from the *De Anima*, and on Kilwardby's interpretation the soul is hierarchically organized with the imagination intermediate between sense and intellect. But in his view the difference between sense and imagination is a difference not of essence but of function, by which he means that it is one and the same part of the soul which functions as a sense when a sensible object is present, and which functions as an imagination when, in the absence of sensible objects, it attends to images of sensible things.

Images, often also referred to as likenesses, phantasms, or even species, are in the imagination. The first question which Kilwardby raises concerns the time of their acquisition. Is the imagination endowed from its origin with images of sensible objects, or does it acquire them later? It might be argued that it acquires them later. One argument, an ancient one which has had a very long run, is that there are things that we cannot imagine till after the use of our senses (para.7). Thus those who from birth are deprived of a particular sense faculty are unable to imagine qualities appropriate to that faculty. It might be replied that exercise of the sense faculty is not the means by which the images are acquired but rather is the means by which the images are roused (para.9). But against this Kilwardby in effect wields Ockham's razor. For if the images innate within us were roused by the images acquired by sensing, there would be a duplication of images. Why not say instead that we do have images in us after sensing and these are indeed acquired by the act of sensing? Furthermore, in the same spirit of parsimony, it can be argued that if images are in the mind from the beginning and are merely roused by sensing, this implies that there are in the mind as many images as there are corporeal objects, and that this is indeed infinitely wasteful since 'in this life the mind would not succeed in imagining all corporeal things, and after this life the mind would not need such images naturally inherent in the imagination' (para.12). There is in addition an important argument from authority. The potential intellect is at a worthier level of creation than is the imagination. Yet according to Aristotle the former is at the start like a bare tablet, and therefore how much more must this be the case as regards the imagination.

The matter is not straightforward since there are proof-texts to be considered, particularly by Boethius, which appear to suggest that the mind has from the beginning images which are duplicated by those we acquire via the senses (paras.17–22). But, relying on proof-texts by Aristotle and St Augustine, Kilwardby draws the conclusion that 'the imaginative part of the mind entirely lacks images of corporeal things until a man uses his senses' (para.23). He acknowledges (para.17) that a man can imagine something that he has never seen, but again invokes St Augustine, this time to the effect that though the mind has innately a power to diminish, increase, change, and compound, such power is exerted upon images brought in by the senses (para.24).

Granted that images of corporeal things are not endowed from the beginning but are acquired later, a question arises as to the means by which they are acquired, and here two possibilities are considered, one that they are acquired by sensing, the other that they are acquired by intellectual acts. Kilwardby's conclusion is that strictly speaking the imagination 'acquires images of sensible and corporeal things only by sense where there is a corporeal seeing' (para.36), though he allows that there is an intellectual seeing by which imagination acquires images of intelligible and spiritual things.

This prompts a question concerning what it is from which imagination acquires images of corporeal and sensible things. Imagination acquires images of sensible things from sense, but how does sense come by them? Kilwardby, following ancient tradition, thinks of the images as impressed upon sense, and his immediate question concerns the identity of the causal agent by which those images are thus impressed. He thinks that there are just four possible candidates for this role, and his argument is stated as if it were an argument by elimination. The eliminated candidates are intellect, imagination, and body, and this leaves sense itself as what impresses the images upon sense. Intellect has to be ruled out (paras.43–44). One reason for this is as follows. The sensory soul of a beast receives images of sensory objects, and yet beasts do not have an intellect. Furthermore the mode of sensing in ourselves is essentially the same as that in beasts. It follows that if no image in the sensory soul of a beast is supplied by the intellect, then neither is any supplied in us by our intellect.

The second candidate, imagination, has to be ruled out also (paras.45–46). One reason is as follows. If it is indeed imagination that impresses images upon the senses then imagination has the images before the sensory soul does. But this possibility has already been rejected.

The third candidate, body, is ruled out next (paras.47–50), this time on the basis of an Augustinian principle which makes itself felt at many points in this treatise. Augustine affirms: 'It is not sensible to think that a body can make something in a soul, for a soul does not stand in a matter-relation to a making body. For that which makes is in every way more excellent than the thing out of which it makes something' (para.47). St Augustine here employs the metaphysical doctrine that soul never stands to body in the relation of matter to form. From which it follows that a body cannot impose anything, and therefore not an image, upon a soul. It quickly becomes plain (see especially the important para.57) that Kilwardby is operating with a concept of the universe as a hierarchically arranged system in which the direction of government is from the more perfect and more excellent to the less perfect and less excellent. He refers to God the creator, the first, most perfect, and most excellent being in the universe, who acts upon everything, and who himself is entirely impassible, and refers also to angelic souls, human souls and dead matter, with angels governing human souls and humans governing dead matter. Within such a system the lower, of course, cannot act upon the higher. Suppose it did. Kilwardby is horrified at the very thought: 'What could be more dreadful than that?' (para.49).

It is not in doubt that when a sensory soul senses, an image of a sensible thing begins to be impressed upon that soul. Since, as we have now seen, neither the intellect, nor the imagination, nor even the sensed body, can be the efficient cause of the impression duly made, it follows that it is the sensory soul itself that forms in itself the image of the sensible thing. And this conclusion finds support in a number of statements by St Augustine (paras.64–7), for example the statement that: 'it is not the body that produces its own image in the soul, but the soul which produces the image in itself with wondrous speed, a speed unutterably far removed from the slowness of body' (para.64). St Augustine's words are however not absolutely unambiguous on this matter, and Kilwardby devotes many paragraphs to discussion of the pros and cons of various interpretations, before returning (para.97) to the central issue of whether or not the sensory soul produces within itself images of sensible things.

There is a view according to which the sensible object has an effect upon the medium (that is, upon what is intermediate between the sensible object and the sense organ), and, through its effect upon the medium, has an effect on the sense organ, and the sensory soul is changed by the duly affected sense organ, the change in the soul being the acquisition of an image of the sensible object. On this view, the first mover of the sensory soul is the sensible object and the immediate mover is the sense organ.

Kilwardby tentatively ascribes this doctrine to Aristotle, but he is not tentative in ascribing a contrary doctrine to St Augustine with whom he sides, asserting that 'St Augustine was much more sublimely enlightened than Aristotle, especially in spiritual matters' (para.98). The Augustinian account presented (and endorsed) by Kilwardby involves regarding the sense organ as a passivity acted upon by the sensible object, much as Aristotle maintained, and regarding the sensory soul, not as acted upon in its turn, but as itself an active principle going forward to meet the organ of sense. The images in the soul are due to the soul's attending to the organ, and in particular to the effects produced in the organ by the sensible object. The degree of attention will be greater or less according as the affecting of the organ by the sensible object is greater or less. On this view, sensing is 'this more attentive act of the soul by which it goes forward to meet the passivity of the body' (para.102). Thus in the order of nature, if not of time, the sensible object acts on the sense organ and then the sensory soul acts on the duly affected organ — first the passivity of the organ and then the activity of the soul. In none of this is there any room for the concept of the organ acting on the soul. The image in the organ is indeed a necessary condition of the image coming into existence in the sentient soul, but it is not an efficient cause of this, because, as Kilwardby puts the point, 'the action of the sensible thing or of its image ⟨in the organ⟩ does not rise beyond the limits of the corporeal nature. But once it has reached the innermost part of the sense organ it stays there' (para.103). Once in the innermost part it is itself acted upon by the sensory soul in the way Kilwardby describes, and this latter activity produces an image, not in the organ but in the sensory soul. There are thus two images, with the one in the soul able to remain when the one in the organ has ceased to exist.

The doctrine which thus emerges is of sensing as the product of two motions which come together as if from opposite directions (para.112), one from the sensible object to the innermost part of the sense organ, the other from the sensory soul to the passivity produced in that innermost part. But Kilwardby does not let the matter rest at this point for there are numerous objections to be dealt with. For example it might well be said that the image in the sense organ is indeed the efficient cause of the image in the sensory soul, for the former image is the means by which the latter is effected. And here attention might be drawn to Kilwardby's own illustration of the mechanics of sensing (see para.103) where he speaks of an image in the sense organ as like a seal, and the sensory soul as like wax. In that illustration the seal is surely the efficient cause of the figure duly impressed on the wax, and so the image in the sense organ is surely the efficient cause of the image in the sensory soul.

Kilwardby replies to this by making a distinction between two senses of 'efficient cause'. Something can be an efficient cause (i) properly speaking and by its nature, or (ii) commonly and by accident. Thus, for example, properly speaking and by its nature it is the person who impresses the seal on the wax who is the efficient cause of the figure on the wax; the seal itself is not such a cause of the figure. However, commonly and by accident the seal is indeed the efficient cause of the figure because by means of the seal the figure is effected. Likewise in sense (ii) the image in the sense organ is the efficient cause of the image in the soul. But in sense (i) the efficient cause is the sensory soul 'which applies to itself the image found in the sense organ and co-mingles that image with itself, makes itself like that organ and makes in itself an image similar to the one in the organ' (para.117). Kilwardby returns to this central doctrine in para.123: 'For the act of the artificer is essentially the cause of the statue, but the adze is the accidental cause as the necessary instrument by means of which the art is exercised. Likewise, the mind going out to meet the passivities of the body is essentially the cause of cognition; the sensible things and the sense organ are an accidental cause like an instrument or instruments used by the mind in order to become informed.'

All this accords well with St Augustine's teaching that the images of external bodies are made in and from the mind, for 'it cannot by itself bring those bodies inside as into the realm of incorporeal nature' (para.67). Thus the matter of a mental image is itself mental. But it has now been shown that the sensory soul is the efficient cause of the image in the sensory soul. Does it not follow that the soul is therefore both the efficient cause and the matter of the image in the sensory soul? And yet does not Aristotle think that though the final, efficient, and formal causes coincide, matter does not coincide with them? In that case Aristotle and St Augustine are here at odds. Kilwardby sets up this problem (para.80) and later deals with it (paras.129–34).

He begins by noting that it is possible for one thing to be the efficient cause of another and also to pass on its matter to that second thing. It is in this way that one human being generates another. 'This', declares Kilwardby, 'seems commonly true in those things which generate by the separating of seed' (para.129). But, as he notes, it is open to Aristotle to say that the matter of things which are generated by means of the separating of seed does not coincide with the efficient cause, for that which is separated is not the matter of such a thing except after the separation, that is, when there is actual seed, and then it is not the same as the efficient cause for it differs in genus, species, and number. In any case it may be that when Aristotle discusses the relation between the various kinds of cause he intends his discussion to be applied to things which come into existence by a physical motion, whereas it is not in this way that images come to exist in the soul (para.133).

Kilwardby's account of the sensory soul fully prepares the way for his discussion of the imaginative soul. His basic position is that the 'two' souls are substantially the same, that is, are the same in respect of their substance. In the act of sensing, the sensory soul acquires images, and after that act has ceased the soul retains those images. The soul which has those retained images is the imaginative, and that soul is 'the very same in substance' as the sensory soul which first acquired the images. Kilwardby is not saying that that which is acquired by the sensory soul begets the image in the imagination. His point is that it is one and the same image which produces a sensation when the knower is in the presence of the sensible object and produces an imaginative act when that sensible object is absent. This position is supported by numerous proof texts from Aristotle and St Augustine (paras.143–149).

Problems are then raised concerning mental or imaginative seeing. For example, we must ask by means of what nature the soul retains images which have been received, and how it can retain them (para.161). The answer Kilwardby gives is in terms of a 'vitalizing sensory soul' which by its nature (i) is assimilable to sensible things, (ii) can preserve this assimilation, and (iii) can show this assimilation to itself while it (the soul) is contemplating itself. The power thus manifested is that of memory, the power of the sensory soul by which it assimilates itself to sensible things outside, and brings back from outside, and retains, a sensible image which is to be shown to its own eye at another time in the absence of the sensible thing (para.206). It is to be noted that Kilwardby does not invoke a 'memorative soul' to deal with the fact that we remember things. Remembering, like imagining, is a function of the sensitive soul. The relation between imagination and memory is simply stated: 'there can be no imagination without memory, since imagination is the contemplation of the image of an absent sensible thing which is represented within by the memory' (para.207) . Of course, as Kilwardby knows, this story requires augmentation, if only to take account of the possibility of imagining what has never been sensed. But memory is always in play for, even when imagining what has not been sensed, the matter which is re-formed by the imagination is itself a set of memories; because I remember what men and horses look like I can imagine a centaur.

A further problem concerns the relation of images or species to desire. We often have simultaneously a multitude of images of things to be desired and of things to be avoided. Why does this multitude not confuse desire (para.162)? Kilwardby's reply starts from the fact that the mere presence, in memory but unattended to, of the image or species of a desirable thing is not enough for a motion prompted by desire. A determinate imaginative act must be performed. But suppose that we simultaneously desire several distinct and mutually exclusive things. Will desire not then be confused? Kilwardby's first reply is that it is common for distinct desirable things to be imagined successively rather than simultaneously; and the successiveness of this multitude saves the desire from confusion. But in addition a person (at this point Kilwardby focuses on beasts but what he says applies equally to humans) — a person will not act at the prompting of desire unless he imagines there to be an opportunity to gain the object of desire. Thus even if several desirable things are imagined simultaneously, the person might not imagine there to be an opportunity to gain them, or any two of them, simultaneously. So no confusion there. Suppose, however, that a person did imagine simultaneously several equally desirable things, and simultaneously imagined there to be an opportunity to attain each of them. Then, agrees Kilwardby, the motivating power would be somewhat confused by the imaginative acts, and a deliberative act might be required to dispel the confusion (para.210). While, in his discussion, he does no more than hint at the form that practical reasoning, or deliberation, might take, his discussion has an immediate bearing on matters to do with deliberation in so far as he points to some of the ways in which the imagination might play a role in the process.

In the final part of the treatise Kilwardby turns to a 'secondary topic', the identification of the organ of common sense. Here he rehearses and weighs, with frequent recourse to authoritative texts, arguments concerning the role of the brain and the heart in the exercise of common sense. This section of the treatise, though of less philosophical interest than the preceding sections, has its own value as a mine of information concerning the state of the art of

INTRODUCTION 17

physiology in the mid-thirteenth century. Aristotle and St Augustine loom large in this final discussion, but despite Kilwardby's attachment to the Augustinian tradition the pull of Aristotle is never plainer than in this final discussion. The tone adopted at the start of the last paragraph is unmistakable: 'We have therefore discussed these points about the organ of the common sense, by displaying, without any rash assertions, the agreement which obtains between things said by Aristotle and by others. At the same time, reader, note that we have squared the words of Aristotle with those of the others, because it is unlikely that all the ancient doctors and their modern imitators have made a mistake in claiming that the organs of the proper senses arise in the brain and converge in the same place in the one organ of the common sense' (para.315). There is much in Kilwardby's treatise on imagination which is clearly Augustinian in tone, but the Augustinianism is grafted onto a firm Aristotelian stock.

(iv) *Appendix: Questions concerning time, from Kilwardby's Commentary on the Sentences of Peter Lombard.*

Kilwardby's *Commentary on the Sentences* includes several questions concerning time. Fr. Lewry's edition of those questions is translated in the appendix of this volume; the translation is appended to facilitate comparison with the doctrines in the treatise *On Time*.

First Kilwardby discusses the relation or order between the non-existence and existence of the created world. Is there such a relation or order? Surely there must be, for first the world did not exist and then it did exist. There is therefore between the non-existence and existence of the world a relation of earlier to later. But there are several kinds of 'earlier', and the kind here at issue is the earlier of eternity (para.1) as when God is said to be earlier than all things. And Kilwardby's briefly stated reason for adopting this position is that while the existence of the world is in time, its non-existence is in eternity. Something of what he means by this gnomic statement emerges in the course of his discussion.

That discussion, conducted, as always, somewhat in the manner of a disputation, proceeds by objecting to the claim that there is an order or relation between the non-existence and the existence of the world. For a relation relates two things; it is of something to something. But non-existence is not something, and therefore nothing can be related to it (para.2), nor indeed in respect of non-existence does there seem to be an 'it' to which the world's existence can be related. However, Kilwardby rejects this argument (para.5), for though non-existence, considered without qualification, is just that — non-existence — nevertheless it is existence in a way, at least in the sense that the world, which previously did not exist in reality, existed in the foreknowledge of God for He intended to create the world and knew through His intending that it would exist. On that basis, believes Kilwardby, it is possible to speak about a relation or order between the non-existence and existence of the world, and it is that relation that is compared to the relation between eternity and time. Why eternity? The answer is that the world in so far as it exists as an idea in the mind of God must possess the same mode of existence as God, and God exists eternally.

It might, however, be objected that the existence of the world cannot stand in any relation or order to its non-existence, for this reason: 'The world exists' and 'The world does not exist' cannot both have been true at the first instant, and therefore must have been true at different instants. But if true at different instants, then an intermediate time must have existed between the instant when this is true: 'The world does not exist' and the instant when this is first true: 'The world exists'. The reason why there must be an intermediate time between those two instants is not spelled out here by Kilwardby, but he may be relying on the common doctrine that no two instants are so close together as to be adjacent, just as no two points on a line can be so close together that there is no point between them — two adjacent points would be one point, just as two adjacent instants would be one instant. If, therefore, there is an intermediate time between the instant when 'The world does not exist' is true and the first instant when 'The world exists' is true, there must have been a time antecedent to the first instant of time, which of course is absurd (para.3).

Kilwardby does not deny that the conclusion is absurd, only that it does not follow from his premisses. Certainly between any two instants in time there falls an intermediate time, but Kilwardby has already stated that the 'earlier than' relation in which the non-existence of the world stands to the existence of it is not a temporal relation, for the non-existence of the world is a non-existence in eternity, not a non-existence in time (para.6).

Later in his *Commentary on the Sentences* Kilwardby discusses the nature of angels. These we can, for the present, think of as pure spirits and in particular as lacking a corporeal nature. The mode of existence of such creatures is clearly different from ours in fundamental ways, and from Kilwardby's perspective one way in which they must be different concerns their relation to time. For in so far as he follows the Aristotelian teaching presented in *On Time*, Kilwardby can be expected to deny that incorporeal beings are temporal. A chief consideration here is that only beings capable of physical motion can be measured in units of time, and of course pure spirits are not capable of such motion. Kilwardby, following St Augustine, allows that there is such a thing as spiritual motion, but that it is metaphysically a very different kind from physical motion, and certainly not a kind that is countenanced by Aristotle. Hence here, as in *On Time*, Kilwardby invokes the concept of everlastingness which he treats as a measure intermediate between time and eternity; intermediate because eternity is the measure of God who is immutable without qualification, and time is the measure of beings which not only can change by nature but actually do change, and between these two categories there is everlastingness which is the measure of beings who by nature can change though by grace they are not changed (para.16).

One distinction between time and everlastingness quickly emerges — time falls under the heading of quantity more than everlastingness does (para.25). Kilwardby's reason for making this distinction is that a quantum is something which has a part next to or outside another part. Thus a passage of time is a quantum for it includes a part which is outside another part, each part distinct from the other in respect of existence, though they are related to each other by the relation of successiveness. Everlastingness, on the other hand, does not include first one existence and then another. On Kilwardby's account of the matter there is an unchangeable duration of the one existence, and hence there is not one part outside another, and in that sense, a basic one, everlastingness strictly should not be brought under the category of quantity.

There follows a discussion of the kinds of things, in particular, pure spirits and separated spirits, which can in one respect or another be measured by everlastingness, and then a discussion of the way they are in everlastingness. There is, next, an account of the difference between everlastingness and an instant of time, a difference of which some account has to be given, since everlastingness and a temporal instant are crucially alike in that neither has temporal duration. And finally a question is addressed concerning what it is of which everlastingness is the essential measure.

To many who are attuned to modern ways of philosophizing, this discussion must seem odd. But there is merit to attending to the material presented in the Appendix, for, quite apart from the worthwhileness of understanding how the world looked to a metaphysician of the high middle ages, there is no doubt that Kilwardby is addressing problems which are still on the agenda of philosophers, even if those problems are now addressed in a very different idiom from one with which Kilwardby was familiar. For example, the mode of existence of disembodied spirits and the nature of non-temporal existence are both live issues.

(v) *Conclusion*

No doubt parts of the treatise on imagination, for example, the description of the brain, nerves, heart, and blood vessels, are now of merely antiquarian interest. It may be also that it is only such an interest that is now served by parts of the more specifically philosophical discussions. Nevertheless, Kilwardby is addressing problems which are familiar to present-day students of the philosophy of mind, such as the nature of imagination, the relation between sensation and imagination and between imagination and desire, and he leaves us a detailed record of one man's struggles in these deep waters.

Likewise in the treatise on time Kilwardby makes a close examination of questions which can be expected to engage the interest of present-day students of time, questions such as how time is to be defined, whether time is independent of mind, wherein lies the unity we suppose time to have, whether it makes sense to speak about a beginning of time, and whether we can make sense of an analogue of time in the life of pure spirits. Kilwardby brings an acute philosophical intellect to bear upon these various topics, and an investigation of the treatises here translated might yet yield up insights which could advance present-day discussions on the foregoing questions.

In the course of preparing this volume I appropriated a large number of references recorded in the Latin edition of the late Father Osmund Lewry. I have also included in my footnotes translations of a number of key passages which appear in the footnotes of his edition. '⟨. . .⟩' indicates an addition by the translator.

ON TIME

Index of Questions in *On Time*

1. Is time one of the things outside the mind? (paras.1–9)
2. What is time? (paras.10–12)
3. In what way is motion continuous? (paras.13–14)
4. Why does Aristotle speak only of local motion? (paras.15–18)
5. Why is 'time' not defined as 'quantity of motion'? (paras.19–24)
6. Why is 'time' not defined as 'measure of motion in respect of the earlier and later'? (paras.25–29)
7. What number is time? (paras.30–34)
8. What is motion which is the subject of time? (paras.35–36)
9. What is this that Averroes says, that 'what is numbered is not involved in the definition of "number"'? (paras.37–38)
10. In what way is time the same for everyone if it is only in the motion of the heavens? (paras.39–43)
11. On the unity of time. (paras.44–51)
12. A doubt concerning the unity of determinate time. (paras.52–53)
13. A doubt concerning the unity of indeterminate time. (paras.54–72)
14. Could there be time if there were no mind? (paras.73–77)
15. When or in what way did time come into existence? (paras.78–87)
16. Concerning the now and the when of time. (paras.88–100)
17. On the relation between time and everlastingness (paras.101–110)
18. Is everlastingness prior in nature to time? (paras.111–119)
19. Is there a measure between everlastingness and time? (paras.120–127)
20. On the existence of the eternal God in time. (paras.128–132)
21. How God is in all time. (paras.133–141)
22. Are 'God always exists' and 'God exists in all time' the same? (paras.142–143)
23. Why is there not a fourth thing which is measurable and a fourth measure? (paras.144–151)

Treatise on Time

⟨*Question One. Is time one of the things outside the mind?*⟩

1. It seems that time is not one of the things outside the mind. When something[1] is composed of parts, either all of its parts exist at the same time or some of them do. This is not true of time, though time is composed of homogeneous parts.

2. Moreover, if time exists, some time exists. But, against that, neither past time nor future time nor present time exists, but only an instant does. Therefore no time exists.[2]

3. Moreover, time is the number of motion in respect of the earlier and later.[3] Therefore where time exists, there the earlier and later of motion exist, and where earlier and later do not exist, neither does time. But earlier and

---

1. Strictly 'something' should be 'something outside the mind'. Kilwardby's argument can be expressed syllogistically as: 'Every composite existing outside the mind has at least some parts which exist at the same time as each other. Time is a composite no two parts of which exist at the same time as each other (since the parts, e.g. the days of the year, are successive). Therefore time is not a composite existing outside the mind.' Obviously what is at issue here are not simply parts of time, say, a day and the week which contains that day, but parts of time which are mutually exclusive. Any external thing has at least two parts which are mutually exclusive and exist at the same time, but no period of time has two parts which are mutually exclusive and yet exist at the same time. Kilwardby's reply (para.7) will in effect attack the major premiss of the syllogism. For why not allow that there can be an external thing, such as a period of time, which is essentially successive and transient, in the sense that, by its nature, of any two parts one succeeds the other?
2. See the preceding footnote. Here Kilwardby does not state the required conclusion, *viz.* that time is not one of the things outside the mind. But that conclusion certainly follows from the conclusion that he does state, *viz.* that time does not exist at all. With this argument Kilwardby proves more than he requires. He will reply that the argument has a false premiss, since the present does exist (para.8).
3. *Cf.* Aristotle *Physics* iv, 11 (220a24–25); *U* fol.51ᵛ and Aquinas's comment: 'We determine that there is time when we take one part of motion and another, and we take a medium which is intermediate between those two parts. For when we grasp the diverse extremes of an intermediary, the soul says that there are two nows, this one earlier and that one later' (*In octo libros Physicorum*, lib.IV, lect.17). See the Introduction p.4 for comment on the difficulties in translating *numerus* and *motus*. I suggest 'reckoning' as a possible alternative to 'number', and *motus* is commonly translated as 'change'. The point of the term *numerus* emerges as the treatise develops. 'Motion' covers local motion (or locomotion), change in size, change in quality, and substantial change (as when a person dies). See para.9 for the reply to the argument.

later do not exist anywhere except where they exist together, since where only one of them exists they do not both then exist there. But they exist nowhere at the same time except in the mind. Therefore they do not exist anywhere unless it be in the mind. Therefore neither does time exist anywhere.

4. For these and similar reasons Augustine[4] stated that time exists only in the mind,[5] and according to him time is a certain extension, not of something existing outside the mind but of an affection of the mind present to it and left behind in it by things passing by. In that affection a present intention of the mind causes an expectation of future things to pass into a recollection of past ones.

5. But, against this, according to Aristotle[6] time is by its nature a cause of decay, even if not primarily, and it could not be such a cause if it existed in the mind only.

6. Moreover, the same arguments, and similar ones, which have been advanced in connection with time could be advanced in connection with motion. But since no one doubts that motion is something outside the mind, it should therefore be said that time is a real thing outside the mind.

7. In reply to these objections it should be said that some things, such as time and motion, exist essentially in a successive and transient way; others exist essentially in a permanent and fixed way. Hence as regards the first objection (para.1) it should be said that all or some of the parts of every permanent composite thing exist at the same time. But a transient and successive thing has parts which are only transient and which therefore exist successively and not at the same time.

8. In reply to the second objection (para.2) it should be said that some time does exist, namely the present, and time is not some simultaneous whole but, rather, exists successively and in a transient way.

9. Likewise as regards the third objection (para.3), the earlier and later in a motion do exist somewhere since they exist in the motion. But they are in

---

4. *Confessions*, xi, 26, 33, in *CCSL* 27, p.211 (19–21): 'Hence it has seemed to me that time is just an extension, but I do not know of what, and I am wondering whether it is of the mind itself'; *Conf.* xi, 27,27; in *CCSL* 27, p.213 (65–67): '..while the present intention relegates the future to the past, with the past increasing as the future decreases, until the future is consumed and all is past.'
5. Since Kilwardby has been working towards the Augustinian doctrine that time exists only in the mind, para.2 seems particularly out of place, since the conclusion of that argument is incompatible with Augustine's doctrine.
6. *Physics* iv, 12 (221b1–2); *U* fol.53^v. It is idiomatic to speak about the action of time, and the effect of time. But such expressions have to be unpacked in terms of factors internal and also external to the substance. Living organisms have a natural span, an internal principle of growth, maturation, and decay, and it is this principle that is the primary cause of the gradual disintegration of a healthy organism. The process takes time, of course, but how long a time it takes does not depend on time itself, but upon those internal factors (as well as external ones).

it in act not simultaneously but successively. And for the existence of time and motion no more is required as they are successive and transient. Hence as regards such things, it is false that they do not exist anywhere except where they exist in act simultaneously. But this is true as regards the parts of permanent things.

⟨*Question Two. What is time?*⟩

10. If time exists, what is it? What it is according to Augustine has already been stated (para.4). But since this view of Augustine's seems somewhat metaphysical,[7] let us see what time is according to the physical view of Aristotle, who said that time is the number of motion in respect of the earlier and later.[8]

11. For an explanation of this and for the solution to doubts which arise, note that in essence time is, formally, just the existence of a movable thing,[9] an existence which is changing without interruption. Hence in the case of local motion, what is in motion in space is always the same in the whole motion, but if it were always transient it would be different in every part of space. Hence its existence is renewed and changed continuously and without interruption with respect to position in space or to a part of space. Hence local motion is just taking up a new local position in that which moves in space continuously and without interruption. Likewise in the case of qualitative change, when someone changes from being sick to being healthy he changes continuously and without interruption acquiring more and more of the quality of health. Hence qualitative change is just the existence of something which has continuously changed, progressing through successive dispositions towards that to which the motion is directed. And so on for other kinds of change. Hence it is clear that motion is just the existence of a movable thing, made different and renewed without interruption.

12. But since the existence of a thing in motion is first thus and then so, in such existence there is one part outside another part, and hence there is a quantity; and since that existence alters uninterruptedly and without inter-

---

7. One reason, which will emerge later, for saying that it is metaphysical rather than physical is that Augustine's concept of time leaves room for the possibility of applying temporal categories to the actions of pure spirits (see paras.71–72).
8. *Cf. Phys.*, iv, 11 (220aa24–25); *U* fol.51ᵛ
9. I have translated *mobile* throughout as 'movable thing'. The English 'mobile' carries the implication of being in motion. The Latin *mobile* carries the implication of being capable of being in motion. For that reason Kilwardby speaks later about a *mobile* which is at rest. This is an important point to hold in mind. Only a *mobile* can be in time. Something can be at rest and in time, only in virtue of being a *mobile*, and not in virtue of being at rest. We shall later meet the point that time measures motion essentially (*per se*) and measures rest accidentally.

mission, it is a continuum. For just as a natural form which informs matter makes a quantity by making one part outside another part, so also it makes a continuum by making two parts so adjacent to each other that there is no distance between them and nothing intervening. This is how the natural form makes the accident of a continuous quantity, and this is how it is above. And just as in the latter case there comes to be in the substance a continuous quantity which measures that substance, so also in the former[10] there comes to be a continuous quantity in a motion which measures that motion. And just as, as regards the existence of a substance, there is its matter and its form, and in the conjunction of these a continuous quantity comes into being through the action of the form on the matter, so here, as regards the substance of that motion, there is the power of the cause of motion which is in the movable thing, and there is the existence which is continually altered, and in these things which are conjoined in motion the continuous quantity comes to be through the action of that power of moving upon the thing which is moved or upon its existence. Hence it is obvious that continuous quantity is an accident of motion and is caused essentially by motion. Continuous quantity by which motion is measured is of this kind, but not every continuous quantity is of this kind, only that by which motion is measured; and it is clear how this comes about.

Question Three. ⟨*In what way is motion continuous?*⟩

13. But there seems now to be a doubt about this. For according to what has just been said (para.12) any motion, of itself and essentially, *qua* motion, is continuous. But according to Aristotle, motion is continuous because magnitude is continuous.[11]

14. It should be said that motion *qua* motion has in itself the continuity of altered existence. But this continuity in local motion is from the continuity of magnitude. For the renewal of the existence of the movable thing is only through the renewal of the position and of the part of space, and hence the contiguity of the altered existence is from the contiguity of the parts of the magnitude and of space. Hence it should be noted that local motion *qua* motion has continuity of existence; and *qua* local it has that continuity through the continuity of magnitude. And it is of such motion, *viz.* local, that

---

10. *sc.* that of time
11. *Physics* iv, 11 (219a12–13); *U* fol.51ʳ

Aristotle there speaks, as is obvious from what he adds in the same place: 'The earlier and later apply primarily in respect of place.'[12]

Question Four. ⟨Why does Aristotle speak only of local motion?⟩

15. But then one can ask (i) why Aristotle speaks there of local motion only. Moreover (ii) what makes for continuity of existence in other motions?

16. As regards the first question (para.15–i) there are two reasons. One is that local motion is first and therefore time applies to it first. The other is that local motion is the best known of motions as regards the continuity of existence through the earlier and later.

17. As regards the second question (para.15–ii), in every movable thing there is some magnitude, whether of mass or of power, from whose divisibility there arises quantity in motion and from the unfolding of whose parts, each part contiguous with the next, there arises continuity. Hence just as in the case of local motion there is a local magnitude which is of a mass, so in the case of other motions there is the magnitude of a power. Hence if in the sentence by Aristotle which has just been cited (para.13), *viz.* 'Motion is continuous because magnitude is continuous', 'magnitude' were taken generally for the magnitude of a mass and of a power, the sentence could be understood generally to be about all motion. But in truth Aristotle did not mean it that way, as can be seen in the same place, and I do not see how there could be continuity in other motions except by way of the magnitude of a power.

18. It is therefore sufficiently obvious that motion has, in and of itself, both causally and essentially, continuous quantity of which the motion itself is both the subject and the cause; and it is by that continuous quantity that the motion is measured, just as every quantum[13] is measured by its quantity. It is also obvious that quantity of magnitude and quantity of motion are not the same thing; one is the cause of the other, and the one is permanent and the other transient.

---

12. *Ibid.* (219a14–15); *U* fol.51ʳ. Kilwardby was heir to a tradition that saw the earlier and later in place in cosmic terms. There is a natural ordering of the four elements, earth, water, air, and fire. And there is a natural ordering of the heavenly bodies. Since there is a natural and irreversible direction of rotation in, for example, the passage of the sun across the sky one point is by its nature earlier than another, for the sun cannot reach the second point except by passing through the first one.

13. 'quantum', *i.e.* 'thing to which the answer to "How big?" applies'.

Question Five. ⟨*Why is 'time' not defined as 'quantity of motion'?*⟩

19. There is next a question as to why 'time' is not defined as 'quantity of motion'.

20. Reply. Though the quantity of a quantum is both a quantity and a measure, they are not so in the same ways. It is a quantity because quantity by its nature and primarily is what has extension. It is a measure because a measure as applied to another quantum reveals the quantity of that quantum. For example, by its nature an ell[14] is a quantity, and as applied to a piece of cloth it is a measure. That is, on account of its extension an ell has quantity, and because it has been prepared or marked out for measuring cloth or is in fact being applied to cloth, it is a measure. Therefore since 'time' marks out a quantity of motion, not in virtue of being that quantity but in virtue of being a measure of it, 'time' is not defined as 'quantity of motion' but as 'number of motion', for 'number' is the name of a measure.

21. Hence in support of the premisses I argue as follows. If time is the quantity of motion it is also its measure, for a quantity of anything whatever measures that of which it is a quantity. And conversely, if time is the measure of motion, which is plainly Aristotle's meaning,[15] then it is the quantity of it. For it is the property of a quantity to measure that of which it is the quantity, and anything whatever which has a quantity is measured by its own quantity as its own measure.

22. There are many examples of the foregoing kinds of case. For the spaces occupied by the elements and by the things composed of elements, seas, fields, the walls and towers of cities, and so on, have in common a permanent continuous quantity and are measured by that quantity. But in so far as this quantity of theirs has the character of a measure it takes on the names of measures, such as 'inch', 'foot', 'yard', 'perch', 'furlong', and so on. Likewise the lengths of cloth have their quantities by which they are measured, and in so far as that quantity is a measure it takes on the names of determinate measures, such as 'ell', 'cubit', and such like. Likewise in the case of those things, whether liquid or dry, which are measured by volume, there is a proper quantity which measures such things. And so far as it is a measure it takes on the names of different measures, for example, in the case of dry things, 'peck' (a measure of corn), 'bushel', and such like; in the case of liquids, 'pint', 'gallon', 'firkin', and such like. Likewise in the case of heavy things, for weight has its own quantity, and heavy things are measured by that quantity according to their weight. But that quantity, so far as it

---

14. An ell is a forearm and, derivatively, the length of a forearm; hence 'by its nature'.
15. *Cf. Physics* iv, 12 (220b32–221a1); *U* fol.52[v.]

measures or is a measure, has names of different measures, and is called 'ounce', 'pound', and such like.

23. So, just as in these cases, so also transient motions are measured by their own quantity; and that quantity, so far as it is a measure of time, is called 'day', 'hour', 'week', 'year', and such like. It is obvious therefore that quantity is a measure of all quanta, and quantity as a measure takes different names, in virtue of human convention, according to the difference between materials which are measured, as where quantity of length is a perch, a furlong and so on, and quantity of weight is a pound, a stone, and such like. And so on for the remaining cases. And likewise, as has been said, in the case of motion its quantity is in terms of a measure with determinate names, such as 'year', 'month', 'day', 'week', 'hour' and such like.

24. But there is a difference here. In the remaining cases no generic name of a measure is posited, but names of specific and determinate measures are clearly used. For example, in the case of length, 'foot', 'yard', 'furlong', 'mile', league', are partial and distinct measures of distances, and there is no noun which is common to measures of distances as such. For the noun 'measure' is common but is not more applicable to distances than to weights or to other quanta which are measured by volume, or are measured in any other way. Likewise in the case of weights, there is no common name for the measures, although 'weight' is used, though improperly, of such a measure. Instead names such as 'pound', 'ounce', and such like, are given to special measures. Likewise in the case of liquids and dry things which are measured by volume; and likewise in the case of cloths which are measured by yardsticks. But the situation is different in the case of motion. For in that case a common noun, 'time', has been imposed as the name of the measure *tout court* in so far as it is a measure of motion. And specific nouns have been imposed to designate partial measures, for example, 'year', 'day', and such like. For 'time' is the name of a quantity of motion simply and universally; but 'day', 'month', 'year', and such like are names of partial, distinct, and limited quantities of motion.

Question Six. ⟨*Why is 'time' not defined as 'measure of motion in respect of the earlier and later'?*⟩

25. Given these points, I think that it is sufficiently obvious, both from the arguments and from the examples, that time is a quantity of motion considered as a measure. But in that case why is 'time' defined as 'number of motion in respect of the earlier and later' rather than as 'measure of motion in respect of the earlier and later'?

26. In response to this it could easily be said that in the definition

'number' stands for 'measure'. But I think that more is meant by the noun 'number' than by 'measure'. For the concept of measure applies to every quantity, but only a discrete quantity or a continuous quantity which can in some way be made discrete can be measured numerically. But it is in this latter way that time is a measure, as will now be obvious, namely as both a continuum and something discrete, and it is for this reason that 'number', rather than 'measure', appears in the definition of 'time'. For 'number' implies what 'measure' does and more besides.

27. Moreover, 'measure' implies nothing absolutely except that a determinate quantity is made manifest. But 'number' implies this and implies also the arithmetical nature of the quantity. For this reason it is more appropriate that 'number' be in the definition of 'time' than that 'measure' be. For when a motion is to be measured in respect of its quantity, first a small quantity of a slight motion is determined, and on the basis of that the whole quantity of the large motion is exhibited. For example, it is decided that a given quantity of motion makes a minute or an hour. And then on the basis of that hour the remaining hours are measured. And when the quantity of a day has been determined, on the basis of that quantity other days are measured. Hence Aristotle says: 'Time measures the whole motion by determining the motion which will measure the whole'.[16]

28. But this determination is made of the first small part of motion in this way: when the earlier instant and the later instant and the motion intermediate between these instants are taken, this quantity which is thus taken between the two instants is then a number, first because it is the measure of the motion occurring between the two instants, and secondly because this measure is defined in terms of the pair of instants. But when, after the first part ⟨of the motion⟩ has been determined, the other motions are measured in terms of a motion equal to that first part, that measure is then the number of the partial quantities succeeding each other, of which one quantity is earlier and another is later, as is the case with the parts of the motion. And this whole quantity is called the 'number of motion', both because it is a measure, and because it numbers the earlier motion and the later motion. There are likewise two ways of measuring in the case of the other kinds of measure mentioned above (paras.22–24). On account of this arithmetical way of measuring, 'number' rather than 'measure' is rightly used in the definition of 'time' and of other similar measures.

29. On the basis of the foregoing paragraph we can answer a question which could be raised, namely: What is implied by the phrase 'the earlier and

---

16. *Ibid.* 12 (221a1–4); *U* fols.52^v–53^r: 'Time measures motion by fixing a motion which will measure the whole motion, just as the cubit measures length by fixing a magnitude which will measure the whole magnitude.'

later' in the definition of 'time'? For in defining the first measure by which the other things are measured, the earlier and the later are the two nows terminating the motion at the start and at the end. But in measuring the other parts of a motion by the part which has now been defined, earlier and later are two times or motions. And each of these things is clearly implied in the passage in Aristotle before the definition,[17] where he presents the explanation on the basis of which he infers the definition. And because the earlier and later can stand for now or for a time, as has been said, it is fittingly said in the definition that time is the number of motion in respect of the earlier and later, and what that earlier and later are is not determined.

Question Seven. What number is time?

30. At last we can ask about what Aristotle says in the explanation of his definition, namely that time is not the number with which we count but is that which is counted.[18] For it is obvious that time is the number of motion just as a thing's own quantity is the number of that in which the quantity is. It counts itself reflexively, as Aristotle teaches, and this is an inseparable characteristic of quantity, namely to count and measure itself.[19]

31. Reply: The reason why Aristotle says that time is not the number with which we count, is not that time does not count either itself or something else, but that it is not such that it would only count and would not be counted by something else. For the number with which we count is a discrete number, which is a discrete quantity, and with such a number we can count both the number itself and other things, in such a way that we do not count that number with something else unless perhaps accidentally. Now time, however,

---

17. *Ibid.* 11 (219a2–220a23); *U* fol.51^{r-v}
18. *Ibid.* 12 (220b8–9); *U* fol.52^v. Kilwardby is relying here upon a distinction between (i) numbers, 2, 3, 4, and so on, with which we count things, and (ii) number *in actu*, where we can also speak about a numbered number, ten men, ten horses, and so on. A number *in actu* is a number which is in fact applied to things. Time cannot be the number with which we count or number things. Aquinas's comment is: 'If time were number simply, then the same time would be the time of a past change and of a future one. For number, simply, is one and the same in different numbered things, for example, it is the same hundred in a hundred horses and a hundred men. But a numbered number is different in different things. For a hundred horses are something other than a hundred men. And since time is the number of the earlier and later in motion, and those things in motion which are related to the earlier and later as already past are different from those things which are related to the earlier and later as future, it follows that past time is different from future time.' (*In octo libros Physicorum*, lib.IV, lect.19).
19. *Ibid.* 12 (220b14–18); *U* fol.52^v: 'Not only do we measure motion by time, but also time by motion, since time and motion are defined in terms of each other. For a given time fixes a motion since it is the number of it, and a motion fixes a time.'

is counted by something else, since, as Aristotle teaches (para.30) it is counted by motion but this is rather a case of counting accidentally.

32. Moreover, since time is a continuum, it is counted only through the discreteness of some things, as has been said (para.26); and these discrete things are counted with a number which is a discrete quantity, according to a mental apprehension. And so time is counted with a number which is a discrete quantity.

33. Moreover, as Aristotle teaches, in numbers there is something which is without qualification a minimum which is entirely indivisible.[20] In continua there is nothing which is simply a minimum which is entirely indivisible, though there is a minimum which is posited. Hence in time there is no minimum simply but there is one which is posited. But every such thing, in so far as it is divisible, is countable. Hence if it is infinitely divisible, it is infinitely countable.

34. For three reasons therefore (paras.31–33) time is said to be a number which is counted and not a number with which we count. This is the point of the definition, that time is a quantity of motion so far as it measures motion with numbers in respect of a now which is earlier and a now which is later, or in respect of a motion which is earlier and a motion which is later, or a time which is earlier and a time which is later — these last two amounting to almost the same thing. It is also obvious what the genus is in this definition and what the differentia. For 'number' is in it as the genus. 'Of motion' is there as the material differentia according as the subject should be understood in an accidental definition; 'the earlier and later' are in the definition as the formal and complete differentia. For the number of motion in respect of the simultaneous does not make time; what it makes, rather, is a number of many motions. This seems to be Averroes' judgment about this passage.

Question Eight. What is motion ⟨which is the subject of time?⟩

35. It is usual to ask what that motion is which is the subject of time. That is, is it just motion, or is it some particular motion? In reply to this Averroes[21] says that the subject of time is the diurnal first circular motion, and such motion is understood in his definition. For he says that though time is the measure of every motion, it is nevertheless attributed to some motions in priority to others, so that it is attributed first to the motion of the first heaven. And it is that motion which is posited in the definition of 'time', and time measures it, not in the way that a number measures what is numbered, but

---

20. *Metaph.* x, 1 (1052b36–1053a2); ed. Venetiis, 1574, fol.252^{rA}: '...for they posit a unit which is entirely indivisible'.
21. *Cf.* Averroes *In Phys.* iv, 14 (223a29–223b12); ed. Venetiis, 1562, text.132, fol.$^{rD-E}$.

in the way that a form measures the thing in which the form is.²² But time measures other motions in the way in which a number measures what is numbered, and these motions are not understood in the definition, because 'what is numbered' is not involved in the definition of 'number'.

36. This is his opinion, but it is certainly a dubious view. For first, his claim, that time does not measure this whole first diurnal motion in the way in which a number measures what is numbered, seems extraordinary. For that motion is primarily numbered by everyone in terms of the passing of the hours, and it is in terms of that motion, already measured and numbered, that other motions are measured and numbered. If perhaps Averroes meant that time is not in the motion of the heavens only as a number is in what is numbered but as a form is in the subject, then that is another matter according to him, but he expresses inadequately what he means. For as the quantity of a substance is in the substance as both form and measure — as form in so far as it is inherent in it, and as measure in so far as it indicates the quantity of the substance — that seems to be what he ought to say about time and the motion of the ⟨first⟩ heaven to those who say that that motion is by its nature the subject of time.

Question Nine. ⟨*What is this that Averroes says (para.35), that 'what is numbered' is not involved in the definition of 'number'?*⟩

37. Secondly, there is a question concerning what Averroes means when he says (para.35) that 'what is numbered is not involved in the definition of "number"', for number is an accident and hence ought to be defined in terms of its subject as such, and that is in terms of what is numerable or in terms of what is numbered primarily by number.

38. But he means that not everything which is numbered is involved in the definition of number, but the first thing is. This is true but inadequately stated.

Question Ten. ⟨*In what way is time the same for everyone if it is only in the motion of the heavens?*⟩

39. Thirdly, Averroes' statement (para.35) that the motion of the first heaven is the subject of time and is involved in the definition of 'time', seems contrary to the express word of Aristotle. For he says in the chapter on time

---

22. The language is not wholly unidiomatic. We do enquire how far a given thing *measures up* to the form which it embodies, for example, whether a given cat is a well-*formed* cat, that is, a cat which is good of its kind.

that time is at the same time everywhere and for everyone.[23] But in what way is it the same for everyone if it is only in the movement of the heavens as in the subject?

40. He says further on that if a man is in darkness and undergoes nothing bodily, but he imagines a motion in his mind, then suddenly at the same time a certain time seems to come into existence, and vice versa.[24] It seems from this that, since motion can be imagined without imagination of the motion of the heavens, time follows upon motion simply rather than only the motion of the heavens — I mean, as its subject.

41. Furthermore, as was said (para.3), when later he defines 'time' he says that it is the number not of circular motion but of motion simply. This would be an inadequate statement, if Averroes was right about the motion which is the subject of time.

42. Moreover, Aristotle later asks of what kind of motion time is the number, and he replies that it is the number of every kind of motion, so that in so far as a motion exists, time is its measure. Hence, time is the number of motion simply and not of some particular kind of motion.[25] He could have been more explicit on this matter.

43. On this matter there are also many other statements by Aristotle to the same effect. By reason of these statements it can be said that, in holding to the aforementioned definition of time, it seems in general that Aristotle means that motion simply, in so far as it is such, is the subject of time by its nature and primarily, and that it is that motion which is involved in the definition of 'time'.

⟨Question⟩ Eleven. ⟨On the unity of time⟩

44. But then a difficult question arises concerning the unity of time. For if the subject of time is motion without qualification, and an accident is multiplied in respect of the multiplication of the subject, then just as motion is multiplied in respect of species and individuals, so also is time, or so it seems, even though it is commonly said that time is numerically one in all temporal things. However when Aristotle says that there is one time of all motions and temporal things existing simultaneously, he does not add 'numerically',[26] but that is added by men who do not take much trouble to look for what he has in mind.

45. There is an easy answer to this question if we rely on Averroes. For

---

23. Aristotle *Physics* iv, 14 (223b10–12); *U* fol.55ᵛ.
24. *Ibid.* 11 (219a3–10); *U* fol.51ʳ.
25. *Ibid.* 14 (223a29–30); *U* fol.55ʳ⁻ᵛ.
26. *Ibid.* 14 (223b10–12); *U* fol.55ᵛ.

he would say that time is numerically one in respect of the numerical unity of one subject, *viz.* the motion of the first movable thing, and this is indicated by a remark of Aristotle's towards the end of the chapter on time, where he says that it seems that time is the number of the motion of the sphere, because it is by that number that other motions are measured.[27]

46. But in that same chapter there are many explicit statements which are contrary to the foregoing judgment, as was said in the previous question (question 10, para.43). It should therefore be said that it is possible to consider time so far as it is known and limited and defined by fixed termini, and to consider it simply, so far as it is unlimited and undefined and not yet denoted by fixed termini. According to the first way of considering time, time is numerically one simply from the unity of a subject which is numerically one. According to the second way it is one through the unity of essence and of definition and by the essential unity of the subject, one not in respect of number but of essence.

47. For example, as was said above (para.22), distances which are permanent continua are measured by a continuous quantity in them. Assume therefore that all the distances of roads, fields, waters, cities, and such like, had to be measured in perches, and that a perch is a length of twenty feet exactly. Moreover, assume that no perch had yet been cut up and prepared for measuring distances. If, then, it is asked whether a perch exists at the start, the reply is that none does.[28] For since men are not accustomed to call every length of twenty feet a perch, but to call a perch something twenty feet long which has been made determinately, knowingly, and precisely twenty feet long, so that it can be applied to other lengths of twenty feet which have to be measured, marked, and defined, it is therefore replied that at first no perch exists. This is not because none exists simply and with an undefined being, but because there is none which is definite and determinate.

48. Let there then be prepared a length of wood which can be carried easily by hand and can be applied to distances which have to be measured in a regular way. There is now a definite and fixed perch, and this perch is a measure of a length of twenty feet, not a measure which applies more to land than to air or to water or to some other body, but simply a measure of length whatever the matter may be. Since therefore a perch is a length of twenty feet, if it be considered in respect of a fixed, limited, and definite existence it is only in that piece of wood which has been prepared for measuring other bodies. But if it be considered simply as something shared, and in respect of an existence which is not fixed, and is unlimited and indeterminate, it is then in

---

27. *Ibid.* 14 (223b21–23); *U* fol.55^v.
28. P.O.Lewry *On Time and Imagination*, p.20, lines 2–3 (Cum...longitudines) seem out of place. I have placed my translation of them at the start of the last sentence in para.47.

all elements, and in all things composed of elements, whose length comes to twenty feet. And taking 'perch' in the first sense, a perch is numerically one from an individual subject which is numerically one. Taking 'perch' in the second sense, a perch is one only as a length which is in permanent continuous existing distances. Hence, just as a length in all these distances is one in definition and in essence, so also a perch, considered in that way, is one. 'Ell', 'gallon', 'peck', 'pound', and all such measures and weights can serve as examples in the same way.

49. The situation seems just the same as regards time. For from its beginning right up to now every motion has something which is its earlier and something else which is its later, and so it has its quantity and measurable continuity which is what I said time was. But it was not immediately after the beginning, from which there was motion and its measure, that that measure was limited and defined by fixed termini by which the quantity of every motion could be known with certainty. But nevertheless there was a quantity of motion which was, though indefinitely, a measure of motion. In order, therefore, that a fixed and definite quantity of every motion be recognised, a fixed measure was prepared by which all motions could be measured. Since a more suitable motion for this is a common one known by everyone and regular rather than a motion which is known by some people and not by others, the regular motion assumed by art and human industry is the motion which is most common to all people, is best known and most regular. For all other kinds of motion have an intensity and remission[29] in respect of their beginning, middle, or end, but not circular local motion, especially the circular local motion of the first movable thing, a motion which has perfect equality always and in relation to the same things, and has the same velocity. And so this motion has been appropriated in which these fixed definite quantities of motion should be marked out by which are measured in the first instance the motion of the heavens, and next and secondarily the other motions. Hence this motion has been marked by quarters, the quarters by thirds, and the thirds by halves, and these last mentioned quantities, the halves, are called 'hours'. The hour is the twenty fourth part of the diurnal motion, that is, of the motion of the first heaven, and hours themselves are

29. The doctrine of *latitudo formarum*, the *intensio* and *remissio* of forms, is central to medieval physics (see M.Clagett *The Science of Mechanics in the Middle Ages, passim*). Here the distinction is applied to motion. The brightness of a flame intensifies as you approach it and weakens as you withdraw; likewise the loudness of a sound as you approach or withdraw from the source of the sound. Similarly a motion can be faster (more 'intense') or slower (more 'remiss'). But a motion which is not stable is less useful as a measure than is a stable motion. Nothing is more stable than the circular motion of the first heaven, which suffers neither acceleration nor deceleration. It is upon this that our measures of motion are based; any other motion is either a fraction or a multiple of that motion.

divided into minutes, seconds, and such like. The quantities of the motions of the stars are next measured by these fixed quantities measuring that motion, and finally all the motions of the lower world, such as work, writing, speech, and such like, are said to be of an hour, since they last for one hour of the motion of the heavens. And so on for like cases.

50. And so a motion of the heavens has been limited and determined by marks and fixed periods, and when these are applied to other motions we know their determinate quantity. And from what Aristotle says[30] this demarcation and determination of quantities in the motion of the heavens seems to have been made by astronomers. For when he speaks of such measures, he says that among continua there is no minimum simply, only a minimum by an act of positing. It is a minimum because nothing can be added to it or subtracted from it without it being noticed at once. And he says that men use this kind of measure in the case of simple and very fast motion because it lasts little time. And therefore in the computation of the stars, that is, in astronomy, that minimum is the starting point and the measure. For it has been laid down by astronomers because the motion of the heavens is uniform and is also the fastest, and they judge other motions in terms of it.

51. It is obvious therefore that if time be considered in respect of limited and determinate existence it is numerically one from the unity of an individual subject, *viz.* from the motion of the first movable thing, and time is in that individual as in a subject. And this is what Aristotle means when he says that time seems to be the number of the motion of the sphere, for other motions are measured by it.[31] He says 'seems to be' because he has in mind not every kind of every motion of the sphere but every motion of the sphere with respect to an existence which is limited and determinate for the purpose of measuring other motions. But if time be considered without qualification and with respect to its unlimited and indeterminate existence then it is one in essence and definition like the changed and contiguous existence which is in every motion. Considerered in this way, time is one in the way in which its subject by its nature is one. As regards this kind of time, the definition of 'time' was given above (para.3). For taken generically 'time' is the name of a measure not narrowed or specified by the fixing of termini. But 'hour', 'day', 'year', and such like, are names of a definite and limited time, and are partial and definite measures of parts of motion. It is time considered simply, aside from every definition of a fixed measure, that the aforementioned words (para.3) of Aristotle are about. And it is of time considered simply that Aristotle speaks for almost the whole of the chapter on time. And it is to time considered in this second way, *viz.* as common and indeterminate, that

---

30. *Cf.* Aristotle *Metaph.* x, 1 (1053a1–12); ed. Venetiis. 1574, fols.252rD, 253rE.
31. Aristotle *Physics* iv, 14 (223b21–23); *U* fol.55v.

Aristotle's example about number corresponds, *viz.* the number as being the same whether we are speaking about ten men or ten sheep.[32]

⟨*Question Twelve. A doubt concerning the unity of determinate time*⟩

52. But there is still a doubt about the unity of time. For since time is of two kinds, one being determinate and ⟨limited, the other unlimited⟩ and indeterminate, as has been said (question 11, para.46), there is a doubt about the first of these. For it was said (para.51) that the former kind of time is numerically one with the unity of an individual subject. Let determinate time, which is in the motion of the heavens, be applied, therefore, to some other motion which has to be measured, for example, to one day's writing.[33] The time and motion of one day's writing will therefore be determinate. Likewise, if it is applied to another motion the time of that other motion will be determinate. For this reason, since many, or almost all, motions which exist at the same time could be determined definitely at the same time by a measure, many determinate and limited times could exist by nature at the same time.

53. My reply. None of all these times is definite and limited except accidentally. For only time which measures what is determinate in its relation to that time and limited, in order that it may determine and limit the time of other things, is determinate by its nature. It is only through that time that the other times are determinate and limited.

⟨*Question Thirteen.*⟩ *A doubt concerning the unity of indeterminate time*

54. Next there is a doubt about the unity of indeterminate time. For it has been said that such time is one in essence and definition (para.51). Therefore, either this is because its essence is one which is not divisible into essences, but is a most specific species which is not divisible into essential specific differences; or because it leads back causally to one essential source which, in the aforesaid way, is one in essence. But the first alternative seems wrong because (i) time is divided into the present, the past, and the future, and these seem to be its species.[34]

55. Also (ii) since that which is by its nature a subject and that which is an accident of it by its nature are alike in respect of unity and diversity,

---

32. *Ibid.* iv, 12 (220b10–12); *U* fol.52ᵛ: 'It is one and the same number which is the number of a hundred horses and the the number of a hundred men; but the things of which it is the number are different — horses are different from men'.
33. The number of pages that a scribe would write in a day.
34. In para.60 Kilwardby will deny that past, present, and future are species of time.

because motion is by its nature the subject of time it seems that time is divided into the same different species as is motion.[35]

56. Moreover, the second alternative (para.54) seems wrong. For since an accident leads back causally to what is by its nature its subject, it seems that time leads back causally to motion. And this has been shown above (para.12). Since therefore motion neither is nor is said to be one in essence, since it is divided into specific differences,[36] neither will time be one in essence. Alternatively, if time is one in essence, then so also is motion; and hence motion is not divided into species.

57. Someone might perhaps say that the source, one in essence, to which time leads back, is matter, which is one in essence in all changeable things. It is because something has possibility and mutability that it changes from existence to existence, and this is only on account of its matter. So time leads back to matter.

58. But this is not different from what has just been said (para.56). For motion is in something entirely because of matter which is the principle of potency. Hence 'motion' is defined as 'an act of a being in potency in so far as it is in potency'.[37] But time is not in something except by means of the motion of the thing. So time leads back first to motion as an intermediary, and then, by means of motion, it leads back to matter. Hence to lead time back to matter is nothing but to lead it back to motion. And then the earlier objection reappears, that if time is said to be one by the unity of matter, then the same thing should be said of motion. And since motion is divided into species which are caused by matter, and motion causes time, not only is time not one in essence, neither is matter, as can be seen.

59. Reply. Time is one in essence in both ways (para.54). For time can be considered in two ways. (a) It can be considered as what it is in itself, and in that case it is a most specific species of accidents[38] and is not divided into further species. (b) It can be considered in respect of its existence, namely as it concerns the subject that it has by nature, and in that case though time is one in essence just as its subject is, it is many things as regards existence just as its subject is. This will be come clear later (para.62).

60. As regards the first point (para.54), it can be said that the present, the past, and the future are neither species of time nor specific differences but are

---

35. In para.62 Kilwardby will distinguish between formal and material aspects of motion, and will argue that, considered formally, motion is not divisible into formal specific differences. Neither therefore, we are left to conclude, is time.
36. In para.63 Kilwardby will deny that when considered formally time is divisible into specific differences.
37. *Ibid.* iii, 1 (201a10–11); *U* fol.27^v.
38. That time is here classified as an accident is not surprising, for earlier (para.37) it was stated that number (which time is) is an accident of the numerable.

rather parts of continuous time, named in respect of their relationships. For it is the 'present' [= *praesens*] since it is *prae sensu* (= 'in front of sense'),[39] and the future and the past are spoken of in relation to the present.

61. Someone might object that 'when' of the present and 'when' of the past and 'when' of the future are specific differences of 'when' itself, but this is no objection. For when is not a continuum as time is, but a sort of boundary, and specifically different boundaries can be caused by different parts of continuous time. For example, a perpendicular line is not divided by species into an upper part and a lower part, and yet the up and the down in those parts are specifically different.

62. As regards the second point (para.55) it should be said that motion can be considered (i) formally and without regard to the particularization or adjunction of the form in which it exists, or (ii) materially, by having regard to the form towards which it is directed. Averroes makes this distinction.[40] Taken in the first way, motion is no more than a route to completion; that is, motion is here taken as the very alteration or change not separated from existence itself. Taken in the second way, motion always involves the form with the motion, something of the form always being acquired by the motion, in such a way that motion is the same thing as the acquisition of successive parts of the form towards which the motion is directed. In the first way, motion is one in essence and definition; it is not something divided into formal specific differences but is only divided in respect of the different existence in different motions. And in this way motion is a cause of time, as was shown above (paras.44–51). And in this way motion is by its nature the subject of time, and they are thus like each other in unity and difference. In the second way, motion is divided into species in virtue of the different kinds of forms towards which something moves.

63. It is now obvious what should be said about the third point (para.56). For motion is divided into species according as it is considered materially in respect of the division of the species towards which motion is directed. However it is not divided into species according as it considered formally, but, considered formally, motion is only divided in respect of the different existence in different things.

64. But what was said about matter (para.57), *viz.* that time leads back, via motion, to matter as to a radical source or a radical cause, agrees well with this, and especially according to those who say that matter is one in essence.[41]

---

39. For example, a visible object is present to me in virtue of being in front of my eyes.
40. *In Phys.* v, 1 (225a34–b9); ed. Venetiis, 1574, text.9, fol.215^{rB}.
41. Cf. Robert Kilwardby *De Ortu Scientiarum*, 24; ed. Judy. p.73, ch.188: '...there are two opinions about matter. One of them is that it is numerically one in all things, I mean one in respect of the number of essences and not the number of individuals. The other is that matter is essentially different in different things...'

65. From what has now been said it is fairly obvious how we should reply to the objection (para.58). For motion is from a contrary to a contrary, and therefore that which is in motion is at the start dissimilar in act ⟨*sc.* to what it will become⟩, though it has a potency to be like what it is going to be. Hence the fact that unlikeness is present in the thing moved in act comes from the actual form which it has, while the fact that there is in it the possibility of likeness comes from its matter which is in potency to contrary forms; and the motion, formally considered, is from a possibility which is in it on account of matter, as is obvious from the foregoing. Hence motion, considered formally, leads back to matter, and that is how it is defined in the definition 'an act of being in potency in so far as it is in potency'.[42] For the act of being, in so far as it is simply of that kind, seems to be nothing but an uninterrupted change of existence itself. But motion, considered materially or concretely, as it concerns the form to which it is directed, is by its nature from matter actually formed by a form contrary to the form which is to be acquired. And, briefly stated, since what is in motion is something movable which both has a form and also has the possibility of acquiring a contrary form, the movable thing is therefore simply in potency, and hence is a cause of the motion, speaking of motion formally. And it is in so far as it is in potency to a form whose contrary it actually has, that it is a cause of motion, speaking of motion materially. And since that dispositional form which is to be acquired has several modes, motion, materially considered, therefore has several modes or species. And since the possibility of matter is basically one in undifferentiated essence, but gets a different existence in respect of different forms — for one potency is open to contrary forms, but different potencies are in them in respect of existence — motion, formally speaking, is therefore one in essence and is multiple in existence.

66. Thus it is obvious how from matter which is one in essence there is motion which is one in essence, and how from motion which is one in essence there is time which is one in essence. It is therefore obvious how indeterminate time is one in essence, but is many in respect of existence, as has been said, where that many is very closely analogous to motion, materially considered, which is its cause.

67. Some[43] make a different move in assigning a cause of the unity of time.

---

42. Aristotle *Physics* iii, 1 (201a10–11); *U* fol.27ᵛ. Kilwardby speaks of '*actus entis*' (= 'act of being') whereas U has '*endilicha existentis*'. But the disagreement here seems terminological rather than substantial.
43. *Cf.* Alexander of Hales *Summa Theologica* i,1,1,2,4,3,2, *ad sol.*; ed. Quaracchi, 1924, 1, 102ᵃ, no.66: 'If therefore time exists in a similar way to eternity, time will be one, not from the unity of temporal things which are measured by time...but from the unity of the cause, which is an inflowing or a power of duration from eternity, according as things share in eternity...'

They say that there is numerically one time in all things, and they do not find the cause of its unity in the aforesaid way, but say that time is one not from the unity of the temporal thing but from the one inflowing of eternity which makes continuous and preserves the existence of motions and of movable things with respect to the established termini of a beginning and an ending. For according to them it can be said that the first cause flows in one way into all things whether perpetual or temporal, but that since perpetual things receive that cause from closer by, they always remain, whereas temporal things, since they receive it from a greater distance, therefore have a beginning and an end.

68. But I do not see from this how these men can say that because the active inflowing is numerically one, time is numerically one. For in that case all things would be numerically one by the same token, unless perhaps they mean, as is said of everlastingness,[44] that the active inflowing is what is formal in the essence of time, and the duration of motions and of movable things receiving that inflowing is what is material.[45]

69. And then they will say that time is eternity pouring the duration of successive existence which is in temporal things, according as it is the inflowing or inflowings of eternal existence, into those temporal things in order to maintain the continuity of the temporally successive existence of those things.

70. But this is difficult to claim, for according to it eternity, everlastingness, and time would be the same in essence and differ only in thought. Moreover, this seems to be a divergence from the truth and an ignorant equivocation for the causal and natural unity of time could be found equally well in motion itself and in the movable thing, as has already been shown (para.65).

71. But there are some[46] who think otherwise on this matter. They say that there are two times neither of which is reducible to the other. For according to Aristotle and other philosophers, time is a measure of corporeal things, and according to Augustine and other holy men, time applies to the actions

---

44. Everlastingness (= *aevum*, sometimes rendered as 'aeon') is intermediate between time and eternity. See below, questions 17–19.
45. *Cf.* Bonaventure *In Sent.* ii,2,1,1,2; ed. Quaracchi. 1885, 2, 60ª: 'Some have tried to argue that the unity comes from the cause: they have said that the duration of the intelligences is continued and maintained by the divine inflowing, and that since the inflowing is one, everlastingness which is its measure is one.'
46. *Cf. ibid.* 1 ad 6; 2, 57ᵇ: '...just as time is posited in spiritual substances, according to Augustine, with respect to the affections, though Aristotle would not go so far as that, so also a measure is posited as specifically different from other quantities; though Aristotle does not speak about that, for his intention was to settle matters concerning the measures of inferior things.'

of spirits⁴⁷...⁴⁸ where everlastingness is dealt with. And they say that neither is reducible to the other.

72. But I do not see the need to say this. For if time does not measure the existence of corporeal things except in so far as they are in motion, time ought to be present where there is motion. If there is motion in the actions of spirits, it seems to me that time must be there, and the same time which is in bodies, in the same way as that specified above (questions.5–8). Moreover, since perpetual spiritual beings as well as temporal ones exist in everlastingness in some respect, though spiritual beings exist in everlastingness primarily and corporeal ones secondarily, it seems that both corporeal and spiritual beings are in time in some respect. But in some sense it is corporeal things that are primarily in time. For they are at least more intelligibly and also more truly in time, and spiritual beings are in time secondarily. For if some corporeal beings, in respect of some motion, exist in everlastingness, why will a spirit, in respect of some motion, not be in time, even though less truly and less intelligibly, just as perhaps motion also is there less truly and less intelligibly? I think that Augustine would say this, and that Aristotle would have said it also if he had posited motion in spirits.⁴⁹

Question Fourteen. Could there be time if there were no mind?

73. Could there be time if there were no mind distinguishing and counting it?⁵⁰ It seems that there could, for in the chapter on time Aristotle says that time and motion exist simultaneously in respect of act and form, and that if it should happen that there be motion but no mind, then the earlier and later

---

47. Kilwardby here opens up the distinction, made in para.10, between the 'physical' approach which characterizes Aristotle's writings on time, and the 'metaphysical' approach by Augustine and other of the early fathers.
48. Lacuna in Latin text.
49. Kilwardby does not spell out his reasons for thinking that Aristotle would have agreed with Augustine on this matter, nor is it clear what his reasons might have been.
50. In his discussion of this topic Aquinas argues as follows: Just as there can be sensible things though no sense exists, so also there can be numerable things and number though there is no-one who is counting. If there is something which is sensible then it must be possible for there to be something which senses; but the existence of a sensible thing does not imply that there *is* something which senses. And likewise if there is something numerable then it must be possible for there to be something which counts; but the existence of something numerable does not imply that there *is* something which counts. But just as the totality of a motion is fixed by a soul relating an earlier disposition of a movable thing to a later one, so also the totality of a time is fixed by the ordering activity of a soul counting the earlier and later in the motion. Hence even if no soul exists, time and motion exist, but their existence is merely imperfect. (*Expositio in octo libros Physicorum*, lib.IV, lect.23).

are in the motion but there is no mind. But these are times according as they are measurable.[51]

74. On the other hand, he says in the same place that when we think of the extremes of motion and the intermediate motion, and the mind says that there are two nows, the one earlier and the one later, then we say that this is time. For it seems that once a now is determined, there is time.[52] It seems from this that there is no time before the mind determines and counts motion.

75. Averroes' reply[53] to this question accords with the text just referred to. He says that if there is no mind then time is not in a motion except potentially, and that time comes into act by way of a mind which is counting. Thus Averroes says that there will be no time if there is no mind. For according as the earlier and later are counted potentially, time exists potentially, and according as they are counted in act time exists in act. But Aristotle says in the same passage[54] that time is an attribute or disposition of motion, an existing number, which accords with the earlier authoritative texts.

76. Moreover, if time is a quantity which is the measure of motion in so far as it is such a measure, and this quantity is in a motion as soon as the motion exists without any action by a mind which is counting, as was shown earlier (para.21), it seems that time always exists in motion without any action of a mind which is counting.

77. In accordance with what has already been settled, it should therefore be said that time exists without qualification as unlimited and undetermined or as limited and determined, and this first kind of time exists without any action of the mind, and this is the meaning of all authoritative texts which are quoted in favour of this position. Time in the second sense does not exist without the counting and the determining by a mind, and that is the meaning of the authority with which Averroes agrees. Hence in that same place Aristotle says[55] that we know time when we mark off motion, fixing the earlier and later, and we say that time comes into existence when we perceive the direction of the earlier and later in motion. And again in the same place, he says that we determine time when we apprehend first one now and then another, and apprehend also something else which is intermediate between them. Note carefully his words. Aristotle says, not that we 'make' time, but that we 'know' it, by our definition or our counting. And he does not say that time 'comes to be' when we perceive the distinction between the earlier and later, but that we then 'say' that time comes to be. Moreover he does not say that we 'make' time when we apprehend one now and then another, but that

---

51. *Physics* iv, 14 (223a20–23, 25–29); *U* fol.55ʳ.
52. *Ibid.* iv, 11 (219a26–30); *U* fol.51ʳ.
53. *In Phys.* iv, 14 (223a21–29); ed. Venetiis, 1574, text.131, fol.202ʳᶠ.
54. *Physics* iv, 14 (223a18–19); *U* fol.55ʳ.
55. *Ibid.* 11 (219a22–25); *U* fol.55ʳ.

we 'determine' time, as if saying that before we count nows in motion and count motion, time existed, but it was not determined and known by us in respect of fixed and limited quantities of hours and days and such like.

Question Fifteen. When or ⟨in what way⟩ did time come into ⟨existence⟩?

78. When did time come into existence? It seems not to have begun, since if there is something whose first cannot be apprehended, one can never say 'Now it exists for the first time'. But one cannot apprehend the first because of the infinite division of the continuum. It seems therefore that it can never be said of time: 'Now it exists for the first time'. But as regards everything which begins, it is true to say at some time: 'Now it exists for the first time'. For it is in this way that the verb 'begins' is expounded, *viz.* that now it has existence and before this it did not exist. It is therefore not true to say that time began.

79. Moreover, if time began to exist, it began either in eternity, or in time, or in an indivisible now. If we say 'in eternity' then, against that, there is an implicit opposition; for what began to exist is not eternal, but only that which is eternal is in eternity. For this reason, therefore, 'to begin to exist' signifies 'not to be eternal'.

80. Moreover, if time began in time, then either it began in a time coeval with it, or in a time which preceded it. If in a time coeval with it, there are therefore two times, *viz.* one time which was made in another. Moreover, with regard to that other coeval time it is asked when it was made, and we are back with the earlier question. Moreover, there will be an infinite regress, for the reason for saying that this time was made in another coeval time, is a reason for saying that that second was made in a third, and so on. If this time was made in a time which preceded it there are the same unsatisfactory implications as before, plus another, *viz.* that time existed before time.

81. Moreover, if time began in an indivisible now, there is therefore a continuum in something indivisible, and something indivisible contains something divisible, which is not possible.

82. Reply to the first point (para.78). A distinction should be made regarding the sentence 'Of something whose first cannot be apprehended, one can never say "Now it exists for the first time"'. Either that 'first' is taken to stand for the least thing which the resolution of a composite thing reaches in a composition; or it stands for the first now of existence. If it is taken in the first way, then one should deny the first ⟨premiss⟩,[56] and if taken in that way

---

56. *sc.* 'If there is something whose first cannot be apprehended one can never say "Now it exists for the first time"' (see para.78, second sentence).

the second ⟨premiss⟩[57] is assumed. For one cannot apprehend a first of that kind in any magnitude, and yet one may apprehend when for the first time there is a magnitude, and one may say 'Now it exists for the first time', as is obvious in the case of all generated things. If 'first' is taken in the second way, then one should concede the first ⟨premiss⟩ if the second ⟨premiss⟩ is not accepted in that sense. But if the second ⟨premiss⟩ is taken in the same sense as the first, it should be denied. For as regards time one may apprehend the first now of existence and at that moment it was true to say 'Now for the first time time exists', that is, at the initial terminus of time.

83. But you object that it was not then true to say 'Now for the first time time exists', for time does not exist in an indivisible instant. By the same token 'Time now exists' could never be said truly, for only an instant ever exists. But as regards transient and successive things, we say that they exist when they are at their least, and we say this truly on account of the continuity of time or of motion in that least part, or on account of their termination in it. In just the same way, when a sphere touches a plane at a point which is indivisible it is truly said that the sphere touches and the plane is touched, even though the contact is not in continuous space but in its least part in which there is continuity or a termination.

84. Reply to the second point (paras.79–81). Corresponding to the different natures of what time is in, time can be said to begin in different ways. For it begins to be in a first motion or change as in its proper subject. For it begins to be in time as in its proper measure. It is not in another time, however, but in itself. For since time is a measure, it is a measure both of time and also of motion and there is no other measure of it, and likewise with the quantity of everything that has a quantity. Time also begins in eternity as in a common measure which is transcendent and not entirely coequal. And since it is said (para.79) that only the first eternal God is in eternity, that is true speaking of a proper and essential measure, but other things which are not eternal are in eternity as in a common measure and by participation, but not essentially. Time begins to be in an indivisible now as in an initial terminus, not in a measure as the objection claims (para.81), but as has been said (para.83), just as a body is said to touch and to be touched because it is touched or touches at an indivisible point.

85. It is commonly asked what it is to be in time. Aristotle gives a clear reply to this.[58] He says that for motion to be in time is just for motion and its existence (that is, its duration) to be measured by time. But in things other than motion their being in time is not their being measured by time, but their

---

57. *sc.* 'One cannot apprehend the first because of the infinite division of the continuum' (see para.78, third sentence).
58. *Physics* iv, 12 (221a4–7, 9–17, 19–23); *U* fol.53^r.

existence being measured by time. For since to be in time is either to be when time exists, or to be in time as in number, temporal things or any things whatever are not said to be in time in that first way. For if all things which exist when time exists were in time, by the same token all things which exist when a given place exists would be in that place. And so all things would be in everything, and heaven would be in a grain of millet.

86. Moreover, since there are two ways in which something can exist in number, *viz.* (i) as something of a number or as an attribute or a part of a number, or (ii) as something measured or counted by the number,[59] things are said to be in time in this second way.[60] Hence for things to be in time is just for their existence to be measured and counted by time. This is Aristotle's judgment.

87. From this it is obvious what it is for something to be by its nature and primarily in time, and what it is for something to be accidentally in time. For since time is by its nature the measure of motion and would not measure the existence of things except by their motion, it is plain that time primarily and by its nature measures motion and the existence of things in so far as they are in motion. But, except accidentally, it does not measure the existence of things in so far as they are at rest or in so far as they simply exist. Aristotle settles this matter shortly after, and he has several other doctrines concerning things which are, or are not, in time.[61]

Question Sixteen. ⟨*About the now and when of time*⟩

88. Regarding the now and when of time. A question is posed as to what now itself is.

89. Moreover, how is it the same now in all time in respect of substance, but different in respect of existence, as Aristotle says? [62]

90. Moreover, how does the now always follow that which is being moved along, as Aristotle says,[63] since time is in every motion and not only in local motion?

---

59. Even is in four as an attribute of it, and odd is in seven as an attribute of it. Two is in four as a part of four. As regards being in number by virtue of being measured or counted by a number, English idiom comes readily to hand. Thus we say that the disciples were twelve in number.
60. *Ibid.* 12 (221a10–13); *U* fol.53^r.
61. *Ibid.* 12 (221b7–8, 19–20); *U* fol.53^v: 'Since time is a measure of motion it will *per accidens* be a measure of rest...Therefore something which is in motion will be measurable by time not simply in so far as that thing has a given quantity, but in so far as the motion has a given quantity.'
62. *Ibid.* 11 (219b9–11); *U* fol.53^v.
63. *Ibid.* 11 (219b22–23); *U* fol.53^v.

91. Moreover, is the now the whole substance ⟨of time⟩, as some say?[64]

92. Moreover, does the now exist outside the mind or without the mind noticing?

93. Likewise as regards the when of time, what is it, and how does it stand in relation to something temporal, and to time, and to the now of time?

94. Reply to the first question (para.88). Motion considered formally, as has already been shown (para.11), is nothing other than existence which is changed uninterruptedly and which succeeds itself by alteration. But time is the quantity or duration of such existence, measuring it while the future passes continuously through the present to the past. Therefore time is the continuity or continuous quantity of existence, but an instant, it seems to me, is the presentness of the same existence crossing and flowing through an alteration, an existence considered simply and without either succession or passage in the quantum.

95. Reply to the second question (para.89). Just as the existence of a movable object is essentially the same in the whole motion and is continually different through renewal of its modes ⟨of existence⟩, so also the presentness of the same existence is necessarily always the same as regards the thing and different because of the renewal of its modes of existence.

96. Reply to the third question (para.90). Just as the existence of the movable object follows upon the movable object itself, participating in the whole motion, so also the presentness of existence which is attached to that existence follows upon the movable object; and, as has already been said (para.94), that presentness is an instant. And Aristotle says[65] that the instant follows upon that which is carried along, not because it follows only that which is moved locally, but because it is there primarily and is best known there, and through this the existence is determinate and known.

97. Reply to the fourth question (para.91). It does not seem to me that the now is the whole substance of time, although in a way it remains the same in the whole of time. This is because the truth and perfection of time lie in the continuous successiveness and in the numberedness of the earlier and later, and neither that successiveness nor that numberedness has the substance of an instant so far as they are of that kind. For they differ as do simple existence and its extended duration. Hence they are basically the same, namely changeable existence. But, as I have said (para. 94), they are different as being its simple presentness and continual duration.

98. Reply to the fifth question (para.92). In respect of indeterminate existence an instant can indeed exist without a mind noticing. But as regards

---

64. *Cf*. Richard Fishacre *In Sent*., ii,2, *sol*.; MS. Oxford, Balliol Coll. 57, fol.81[va]: '...the flux of time is not prior to the now which is the whole substance of time.'

65. *Physics* iv, 14 (223b18–20); *U* fol.55[v].

its existence as something marked out and noticed and fixed by us it requires mind to mark it out. But in each way it exists outside the mind.

99. Reply to the sixth question (para.93). According to the author of *Six Principles*,[66] the when is a disposition or circumstance of a thing which is in time, a disposition or circumstance left behind in the thing by the addition of time to it. For it is because the thing is in time that it is said to exist as a when, and the when is nothing but existence in time, and it is an accident which differs from time since it is caused by time. And just as, in the *Six Principles*, the where is divided into the simple where and the composite so also the when can be divided into the simple when and the composite. That which is left behind by an indivisibly present now may be called a simple when. That which is left behind by a continuous time, of which there is past time and future time, may be called a composite when. And just as a when left behind by a continuous time is different from that time, so also a when left behind by an indivisible now is different from that now.

100. Let that be enough on this question.

Question Seventeen. On the relation between time and everlastingness

101. Regarding the relation between time and everlastingness it could be said, in accord with a position presented above (paras.67–70), that they are the same as far as the thing is concerned but different as regards the concept. But since a more secure, more certain, and truer position has been considered (para.72), time and everlastingness should be supposed to be essentially different. For time is successive duration, and everlastingness is stable duration; time is continuous and divisible duration, everlastingness is a whole duration which is simultaneous, or such like.

102. Let us now ask about the now of time and the now of everlastingness, which, according to the definitions given of them above (para.101), seem to be different.

103. Moreover the one flows and the other remains; the one unites past and future; the other does not.

104. Against this, each is the simple existence of a created thing. In what therefore do they differ? For if you take away change, what remains of changeable existence except stable existence?

105. Moreover, when a motion exists an angel exists. Therefore in the now in which a motion exists an angel exists. But a motion is in the now of time

---

66. *Liber sex princ.*,4, 33: *AL*, 6–7, p.42 (1): 'The *when* is what is left behind by the addition of time...'

and an angel is in the now of everlastingness. Therefore the same now is a now of time and of everlastingness.[67]

106. The reply to the first question (paras.102-3) is obvious from the definition. For the now of time does not have within itself a continuous and successive flux, but it does have within itself a sudden passing. Hence Aristotle says[68] that a point in a line is different from an instant in time, for one and the same point which joins two lines can be taken twice over as marking the beginning of one of the lines and the end of the other; but one and the same instant which joins two times cannot be taken twice over, once as the beginning of one time and once as the end of the other. But the beginning of the one and the end of the other are taken as different instants, and the cause is the flux of time. However, as regards the substance of an instant in time, it is not a flux unless it is a sudden one. For time has a continuous flux. But an instant of everlastingness has no flux at all. Therefore an instant of time is the presentness of changed existence, and thus it is a measure of change and of that which is changed existence. An instant of everlastingness, which therefore has not undergone a sudden change, remains a stable existence, but that existence is different from changed or changeable existence, and is caused by a different cause. But they agree in this, that they are, as it happens, in one created thing. But this is not absurd, because essentially different existences are in the same subject in respect of different causes and reasons.

107. Reply to the second question (para.104). 'Now', taken as a noun, without doubt has more than one sense, as has been said (para.106); but

---

67. Cf. Alexander of Hales, *Summa theologica*, i,1,1,2,4,4,3, *contra*; ed. Quaracchi, 1924, 1, 109ª, no.70: 'When a motion exists, an angel exists and God exists. If, therefore, the 'when' indicates a simultaneous existence in some now, then the motion and the angel and God exist in the same now. But the now in which the motion exists is the now of time. The now in which the angel exists is the now of everlastingness. The now in which God exists is the now of eternity. Therefore the same now is a now of everlastingness, of time, and of eternity.'
68. *Physics* iv, 11 (220a9–14); *U* fol.52ʳ.

'now', in its adverbial use, prompts a doubt, as Alexander of Hales says.[69] To resolve it he makes a distinction between three kinds of now, the now of eternity, of everlastingness, and of time. The order of these three is this: the now of eternity is prior to, and superior to, the others, and the now of time is posterior to, and inferior to, the others. The now of everlastingness is intermediate. Alternatively these nows should be considered in respect of measurement and coexistence. For superior and prior nows coexist with inferior and posterior ones but are not measured by them, whereas inferior nows are measured by superior ones. For the now of eternity is the measure of the now of everlastingness and the now of time, and the now of everlastingness is the measure of the now of time. But the prior time is not a proper measure, but is a common and surpassing measure, for a proper measure is coequal with ⟨what is measured⟩. And in this way eternity is a measure only of eternal things, and everlastingness is a proper measure only of everlasting things, and time is a proper measure only of temporal things.

108. But that eternity is a measure containing and measuring the other things is said in *On the Divine Names* : '[God] is the everlastingness and origin and measure of being, existing before substance, and before that which exists, and before everlastingness, and the beginning, middle, and end of all things that have been made substances', and further on: 'containing and prepossessing in Himself all origins, all endings of all wholes'; and, in the last chapter: '[God is] everlastingness itself, and existent things, and the measures of existing things, and the things measured through Him and by Him'.[70]

109. On the basis of these points a reply can be made to a further one of

---

69. *Cf.* Alexander of Hales, *Summa theologica*, i,1,1,2,4,4,3,*resp.*; ed.Quaracchi, 1924, 1, 109ª-110ª, no.70: '"Now" is sometimes taken as a noun. And then there was no doubt regarding the question of whether the now of time, of everlastingness, and of eternity are the same now, for it is certain that they are different. "Now" is also taken as an adverb; and then there is room for doubt over whether it is the same now in "God now exists and an angel now exists and a motion now exists"...It should be said that the motion, the angel, and God are said to be in the same now, but it does not follow from this that the now of time, of everlastingness, and of eternity are the same now. The motion, the angel, and God are said to be in the now of time, but to be so in different ways. For motion is in the now of time as in what measures it, and hence it is in that now, properly speaking [= *proprie*]. But the angel and God are in it as in something concomitant; hence they are in the now of time, that is, they are *with* [or 'along with'] the now of time. Moreover, the motion, the angel, and God are in the now of everlastingness, but in different ways. For the motion is in the now of everlastingness as in a common measure, which is not equal to what is measured; the angel is in it as in a proper measure, and God is in it not as in something measuring him but as in something concomitant. That is, when the now of everlastingness exists God exists. Moreover, the motion and the angel are in the now of eternity as in a surpassing common measure. But God is in the now of eternity as in a proper measure, for it does not differ from God.'

70. Ps.-Dionys. *De div. nom.*, 5; transl. Sarraceni ed. Chevallier, 1, 353-354.

the questions (para.105). The following distinction can be made.⁷¹ When this is said: 'When a motion exists, an angel ⟨and God⟩ exist' what is meant is that, in the now in which a motion exists an angel and God exist, not as in a measuring ⟨now⟩ but as in a concomitant ⟨now⟩; similarly when this is said: 'When an angel exists, God exists'. But when this is said: 'When God exists, an angel and a motion exist', the sense is: 'In that now in which God exists as in a proper measure, an angel and a motion exist as in a measure which is not coequal but instead is surpassing'. Likewise when this is said: 'When an angel exists, God and a motion exist', the sense is this: 'In that now in which an angel exists as in a proper measure, God exists, not as in a proper measure but as in a concomitant one, and a motion exists as in a common measure'.

110. From these points it is obvious how to defend his position that the now of everlastingness is not the same as the now of time. But since it seems highly inappropriate to say that something exists in something if it does so only as in something concomitant, a different kind of line can be taken, namely that when and now are relative to each other. This is clear from this inference: 'When a motion exists an angel exists, therefore in the now in which a motion exists an angel exists.' And the relation can be either simple or personal⁷² when this is said: 'When a motion exists, then an angel exists' or 'In the now in which a motion exists, an angel exists'. For a simple relation makes it true and a personal one makes it false, as here: 'She who has damned, has saved', and 'Where the king is, there the queen is'. But when it descends determinately to the now of time and the now of everlastingness it descends personally and becomes a figure of speech, changing the simple supposition or simple relation into a personal one, and a 'what kind' is changed into a 'this something'.

Question Eighteen: Is everlastingness prior in nature to time?

111. As regards their coevality it seems that everlastingness is prior to time, just as stable and fixed existence is prior to mutable and changeable existence. And this can be seen from the words of John of Damascus: 'Some, for example, the theologian Gregory ⟨of Nazianzen⟩, say that angels were generated before all creation. Others say that they were generated after the first heaven was generated. But all admit that they were generated before the creation of man. But I agree with the theologian Gregory, for he said that intellectual substance was created first, and then sensible substance, and that

---

71. Alexander of Hales *ibid.*
72. *Cf.* C.H.Kneepkens, '"Mulier quae damnavit, salvavit": A note on the early development of the *Relatio Simplex*', *Vivarium,* 14 (1976), 1–25.

man was then created from both.' [73] It seems here that, according to Gregory, everlastingness preceded time, just as angels preceded sensible nature. Boethius suggested the same doctrine in *Consolation*.[74]

112. Against that, in Book II of the *Sentences* it is said that angels, prime ⟨matter⟩, and time were created simultaneously.[75]

113. Moreover, Richard of St Victor said: What began to exist, began in time.[76] Therefore everlastingness began to exist in time. Therefore it did not begin before time.

114. Moreover, every change is measured by time; and everlastingness passed from non-existence to existence by a change. Therefore it did so in time. Therefore it was prior to time or simultaneous with it.

115. Reply. Angels were created prior in nature and worth, but were created simultaneously in time as we read in the *Sentences*.[77] So it is obvious what should be said in reply to the first objection (para.112).

116. Reply to the second objection (para.113). 'In time' [*ex tempore*] has two senses, (i) 'after time began', and (ii) 'from the beginning of time, that is, simultaneous with time'. Taking it in this second sense but not in the first sense, everlastingness began in time.

117. Reply to the third objection (para.114). It does not seem absurd to say that in the first instant of time something everlasting was created and the enduring now of everlastingness was co-created, just as it does not seem absurd that in the now of time a mind should pass suddenly from a lesser joy to a greater. For although the everlasting and everlastingness are not in time as in a measure in respect of stable and unchanged existence but only, so they say, as in a concomitant measure, it does not seem absurd that in respect of

---

73. Ioh. Damasc. *De fide orthod.*, 17, 19, ed. Buytaert, p.74 (94–101).
74. Boethius *Phil. con.*, iii, met.9; *CCSL* 94, 51 (1–3): 'O You who guide the world by perpetual reason,/ Creator of the planets and the sky, who time/ From everlastingness did bring...'
75. *Cf.* Peter Lombard. *Sent.*, ii,2,3,1; ed. Grottaferrata, 1971, 1, 2, p.338 (15–16): 'Simultaneously therefore with the making of time were the making of a corporeal created thing and a spiritual creature.'
76. Richard of St Victor *De Trin.*, i,6; ed. Ribailler, p.91: '...everything which exists or can exist, either has existence from eternity or began to exist in time.'
77. Peter Lombard. *Sent.*, ii,2,1,3; ed. Grottaferrata, 1971, 1, 2, p.337 (13–14, 17–19): 'It seems therefore that it should be held that a spiritual creature, that is, an angel, and something corporeal were created at the same time...And yet wisdom was created first of all, for even if it was not first in time it is first in worth.'

the existence of change they exist in time.[78] And I have said this of the creation as of a passion, which, as it happens, has passed from non-existence to existence.

118. However, Alexander ⟨of Hales⟩[79] said that it should not be conceded that something everlasting was created in the now of time as in a measure of that creation, but that something everlasting was created in the now of everlastingness just as a temporal thing was created in the first now of time, and these two nows are simultaneous. Therefore creation of something everlasting, according to this, is in the now of everlastingness as in a measure; it is not so in the now of time.

119. And if it is then asked in what the now of everlastingness was created, it can be said that it was created in itself. For after non-existence it exists first in itself, and for it to be created is nothing other than for it to exist after not existing. Neither is there, on account of such an 'after', an earlier and a later in everlastingness, since that 'after' follows the pure non-existence of the created thing. For prior to that, nothing, whether a potency or an act, of the created thing was in the thing. And if it be said that there between act and nothing is potency, and thus some composition and an earlier now and a later now are there, this can be conceded. But such earlier and later nows are not excluded from everlastingness. What are excluded are what they call a variety with respect to existence in act.

⟨*Question Nineteen: Is there a measure intermediate between everlastingness and time?*⟩

120. There is a question whether there is a measure intermediate between everlastingness and time. And it seems that there is, for Plato says that time is coeval with heaven.[80] Therefore it did not exist before heaven. But before

---

78. Heavenly bodies and angels are everlasting. Heavenly bodies are like eternal beings in respect of the unchangeability of their substance, but are like temporal beings in respect of their locomotion. Angels also are like eternal beings in respect of the unchangeability of their substance, but are like temporal beings in respect of their changeable thoughts and affections. Thus the substance of heavenly bodies and angels, though not in motion, can be said to be accompanied by motion, or to have a concomitant motion. It is this view that leads Kilwardby to speak of everlasting things as being in time 'as in a concomitant measure'. For contemporary discussion of this matter see Aquinas *Summa Theol.* 1,10,5, esp. *corpus, ad* 1, and *ad* 3.

79. *Summa theol.* i,1,1,24,4,4,1 *ad* 1; ed. Quaracchi, 1924, 1, 106a-b, no.68: 'It is not absurd that there should simultaneously be two nows of different kinds. For just as the now of eternity contains the now of everlastingness, so the now of everlastingness contains the now of time. But it should not be conceded that the now which is the beginning of time is the measure of everlasting creation. What measures everlasting creation is the now of everlastingness. But the now of everlastingness began with the now of time.'

80. *Timaeus*, 38B; ed.Waszink, p.30 (15): 'But time is coeval with heaven.'

ON TIME   57

heaven some motion or change of corporeal nature existed, according to those who say that the works of the Six Days were done successively. And that motion did not exist in everlastingness, which is obvious. Therefore an intermediate ⟨between everlastingness and time⟩ is the measure of ⟨that motion⟩.

121. Moreover: 'Then the angel ⟨that I saw standing on the sea and land raised his right hand to heaven, and⟩ swore ⟨by him who lives for ever and ever, who created heaven and earth and the sea and everything in them⟩, that there will be no further time *etc.*'[81] Therefore at some time time will cease. But there will be perpetual motion in the punishment of the reprobates: 'They will cross from the snow waters ⟨to excessive heat⟩.'[82] And it is clear that that motion will not exist in everlastingness. Therefore there will be some intermediate measure.

122. Some people[83] concede this. They say that 'an age' [*seculum*] is the intermediate measure, from the word *sequitur* [= 'follows'], since in an age one now follows another now but not in time. For they say that outside eternity there are three kinds of now. One is stable and non-flowing, neither succeeding ⟨something⟩ nor joining ⟨things⟩, and that is the now of everlastingness. The second kind of now does succeed ⟨something⟩ but does not join ⟨things⟩, and that is the now of the age. The third kind is the now which succeeds ⟨something⟩ and joins ⟨things⟩, and that is the now of time. And

---

81. *Apoc.*10, 5–6
82. *Job* 24, 19; cf. Alexander of Hales *Summa theol.* i,1,1,2,4,4,2, *arg*.5; ed. Quaracchi, 1924, 1 107ª, no.69: 'The punishment of hell is variable, for as it is said in *Job* 24, 19: "They will cross from the snow waters to excessive heat". From this it follows that the measure of [such a punishment] will not be everlastingness.'
83. *Cf.* Alexander of Hales, *ibid. ad* 5, p.108ᵇ, no.69: 'But it has seemed to others, on the contrary, that a measure should be posited between everlastingness and time, which would be called 'an age' [= *saeculum*] from 'following' [= *sequendo*], because it would have one now following another now, but without the mediating continuity of motion, just as time has one now following another, but with the mediating continuity of motion. And in accordance with this view they claim that outside eternity there is a now or a present which remains, but is neither successive nor continuous; and it is in this way that the now of everlastingness exists. And there is a now which flows, and which is both successive and continuous; and it is in this way that the now of time exists; it is in this way that a point on a line both begins a line and terminates a line, and is also the point which joins the one line [to the other line]. And, again, there is a now which succeeds a now but is not continuous with it; and now exists in this way in the measure which is called 'age'. For one now follows another, although there is no mediating continuity in the dimension. And in accordance with this view they say that outside eternity there is just such an ordering of duration. There is first a duration which exists in such a way that nothing follows in it, and this is the duration of everlastingness. Next there is the duration in which something does follow, but without being continuous with what it follows, and they call this duration 'age'. And next there is the duration in which one thing precedes and also follows in accordance with the continuity of motion, and this is time.'

on this view there are three kinds of created duration or measure. One kind is stable and exists uniformly; in it nothing follows anything else. That is the duration of everlastingness. The second kind of duration is that in which one thing follows another without continuity. That is the duration of the age. The third kind is duration in which one thing follows another continuously. That is the duration of time.

123. But though that could be said very truly sometimes of spirits, as when a spirit suddenly changes into another existence and remains in it for a while, and then changes into a better existence, as obviously happens in the case of disembodied souls, nevertheless I do not see how this could be the case as regards the corporeal nature of those who are damned after Judgment. But if there will be change and motion there, then I say that the situation is the same as that of corporeal nature and its motion before the foundation of heaven.

124. Moreover, there is nothing between stable created existence and mutable created existence. What is the point, then, in positing an intermediate measure, since time measures, in respect of something of itself, every mutable existence, and everlastingness measures every stable existence, a point already dealt with [para.101].

125. Moreover, in the Psalm it is said of the damned: 'And their time will be in ages.'[84] Therefore there will be a time after Judgment which will measure the motion of the damned.

126. Moreover, if a man glorified after Judgment could move his body by his will suddenly or successively, how can time be a measure of such motion as it is now?

127. It should therefore be said that time limited and demarcated by fixed partial measures made by human skill did not exist before the heavens, nor will it exist after Judgment when the heavens will be at rest. But time which is unlimited and undemarcated though measurable by fixed measures if they already existed, did exist before the heavens and will exist after Judgment. It is therefore obvious that in one way time, in respect of inception and perpetual duration, is coeval with everlastingness.

⟨*Question Twenty: On the existence of the eternal God in time*⟩

128. The question now does not concern the relation between time and eternity in respect of their consonance and difference, but is about the existence of the eternal God in time. Anselm proves in the *Monologion* that God exists in all time,[85] and he writes that God is 'in every place and time,

---

84. *Ps.* 80, 16 [= 81, 15 in *NEB*]
85. Anselm, *Monolog.* 20, ed. Schmitt, pp.35–36

since he is absent from nothing.' Again: 'Whatever exists, if it is not to lapse into nothingness, is sustained by the divine essence which is present.'[86] Whatever exists at some time, is then present. Therefore God is present to it. Hence God is present in all time, since not even time itself could exist unless God who is present sustains it in existence.

129. On the other hand, Aristotle says: 'Those things which always exist do not exist in time, for they are not contained in time and neither is their existence measured by time.' [87]

130. Further on he says that 'things that neither move nor are at rest' are not in time.[88] And I say 'things at rest' which can by their nature move. Since, therefore, these descriptions seem to apply to God, it does not seem that God exists in all time.

131. Moreover, the unchanged existence of angels is not in time but in everlastingness. Therefore how much more so should this be said of God.

132. Anselm's reply in the *Monologion* is that there are two senses of 'being in time',[89] as will be clear later, God willing.

Question Twenty One: ⟨*How God is in all time*⟩

133. I say that God exists in all time. The question is how. For he exists in all time either simultaneously or distinctly. If you say 'distinctly' then, against that, he would exist like a man, yesterday, today, and tomorrow, whose age has distinct different existences. And in that case the divine age, which is God's eternity and his substance, would have distinct parts.[90] If you

---

86. *Ibid.* 22; p.41 (6–7)
87. *Physics* iv, 12 (221b3–5); *U* fol.53^v.
88. *Ibid.* (221b20–21); *U* fol.53^v.
89. Anselm, *Monolog.*, 22; ed.Schmitt, p.40 (26–33): 'For when the highest essence is said to be in space or time, although the language used regarding it, and regarding spatial and temporal natures, is the same because of the customary way of speaking, the understanding of the expressions is different because of differences in the things. For in the case of the spatial and temporal natures, the one expression has two significations. First, it signifies the presentness of the natures to the places and times in which they are said to exist; and secondly it signifies that those natures are contained in those places and times. In the case of the highest essence only one of those senses is involved, that is, the presentness of that essence, not the thought that the essence is contained in those places and times.'
90. *Ibid.* 21; p.37 (17–23): 'But how can something exist as a whole simultaneously at individual times if the times themselves are not simultaneous? If this being exists as a whole, separately and distinctly in those individual times, as a man might exist as a whole yesterday, today, and tomorrow, then it is said properly that it did, does, and will exist. Its age, therefore, which is just its eternity, is not a simultaneous whole. Instead it has parts corresponding to the parts of time.'

say 'simultaneously' then, against that, times are not simultaneous. Thus far we have Anselm's dilemma.

134. Moreover, if God exists simultaneously in all time, when he exists in the present he then exists in the past and in the future. But he does not exist in that which does not exist. Therefore the past and the future are in the present.

135. It seems from these arguments that God does not exist in all time, either simultaneously or distinctly.

136. On the other hand, it seems that God does exist in all time in both of these two ways. He exists distinctly in all time, for three times are fittingly applied distinctly to God; it is said that he is, will be, and was — simultaneously, too, for Anselm says: 'It is necessary that the divine essence be present as a simultaneous whole in each and every place and time.'[91] For that he is present to this or that place does not prevent him being present to some other place simultaneously and in the same way.

137. Reply to the question whether God exists distinctly in all time (para.133). It should be said that he does not exist distinctly in all time, where 'distinctly' qualifies his existence. But he does exist in parts of time which are distinct from each other in the order of succession.

138. As to the question how, that will become clear elsewhere.

139. Regarding the question whether God exists simultaneously in all time (para.133), a distinction should be made. For 'simultaneously' in that context qualifies either (i) the eternal existence of God, or (ii) times. If it is taken in the first way then this is true: 'God exists simultaneously in all time', and its sense is: his existence is a simultaneous whole in all time, so that his existence is not divided by partitions of time. The objection made, *viz.* that times are not simultaneous, is not contrary to this sense. If 'simultaneously' is taken in the second way, then a further distinction should be made. Either (iia) the word 'simultaneously' refers to times according as they exist in the providence or disposition of God, or (iib) according as they exist in their successive nature. If the word is taken in the first of these two ways, then it is true that God exists simultaneously in all time, since the sense of this is: 'Simultaneously in all time, (that is, in every difference of time, as times exist in his eternal disposition and providence simultaneously), God exists.' For in his eternal disposition and providence nothing is past, nothing is future, but the concepts and causes of all times exist there simultaneously. Nor is this to be wondered at, for it is in this way that a man has in his memory a whole action which was to unfold materially over a two-year or three-year period.

140. Regarding the aforesaid two senses, which amount almost to the same thing, Anselm observed that God exists simultaneously in all time, as

---

91. *Ibid.* 22; p.40 (15–19).

is obvious from his words (para.136). If he be understood in the second of the two senses (para.139, iib), it is false that God exists simultaneously in all time, for the sense is that all the differences of time exist simultaneously in God by their nature, and that God exists in those differences. And in that case, the first objection (para.133) goes through.

141. Reply to the second objection (para.134). If the argument is based on the aforesaid proposition taken in the sense according to which it is false, then something absurd follows from that proposition. If the argument is based on the proposition taken in the sense according to which it is true, then a distinction should be made regarding this conclusion: 'When he exists in the present, then he exists in the past and the future.' For 'when' can refer to the when of eternity and then the conclusion follows, but from that conclusion it does not further follow that the past and future thus actually exist simultaneously in his nature. Alternatively 'when' can refer to the when of time, and then the conclusion does not follow from the aforesaid proposition. But if 'when' is temporal and 'then' refers to eternity, so that a simple relation[92] exists between the 'when' and the 'then', the first inference can be conceded, but then it does not follow that the past and the future actually exist in God simultaneously.

Question Twenty Two: Are 'God always exists' and 'God exists in all time' the same?

142. Is 'God exists in all time' the same as 'God always exists'?

143. Reply. They are not entirely the same. But each has two senses, and the definition of what it is to exist in all time was given in the preceding question. But the definition of what it is to exist always is that when it is said of God it can mean either the whole of time in eternity, so that the sense is this: 'God is in all time or in the whole of time', or 'God exists eternally'. Augustine has the first sense in mind when he says that 'that which exists in all time is said without absurdity to exist always'.[93] Anselm is talking about the second sense when he says: '"Always", which seems to designate the whole of time, is understood much more correctly if it is said to signify eternity, which is never unlike itself, rather than to signify a changing of times, which is always unlike itself in some way.'[94]

---

92. *Cf.* para.110.
93. Aug. *De civitate Dei*, xii, 16; *CCSL* 48, 371 (31–33).
94. Anselm, *Monolog.*, 24; ed. Schmitt, p.42 (14–17).

ON TIME

Question Twenty Three: ⟨Why is there not a fourth thing which is measurable and a fourth measure?⟩

144. Since there are three measurable things and three measures of them, one measurable thing which lacks a beginning and an end, namely, what is eternal, a second which has a beginning and an end, namely, what is temporal (speaking here of time as demarcated), and a third which has a beginning and lacks an end, namely, what is perpetual, why is there not a fourth thing, namely, one which lacks a beginning and has an end?

145. And it seems that there ought to be, (i) first to make the universe complete,[95] (ii) secondly because from eternity, before the world existed, it was true that the world would be created, and when the world was made this ceased to be true.[96] (iii) If you should say that it did not cease to be true, because this truth passed from the future into the present, namely 'Before the world existed that truth was nothing but God', it therefore seems that when that truth passed from the future to the present, God passed from the future to the present, which is impossible.

146. Moreover, if the truth of 'The world will be created' is God, then the truth of 'The world has been created' is God, since it is the same truth as regards the thing, and it is different only in the mode of expression.

147. Reply. The fourth part is impossible since what lacks a beginning has in itself no non-existence, whether potentially or actually, and therefore it cannot be turned into non-existence. But what began to exist proceeded from non-existence, and therefore it is mixed with non-existence, namely with the potential not to exist, even though, by the will and the conserving act of the creator, it is maintained in existence and is perpetual.

148. Reply to the first objection (para.145 i). It should be said that perfection or completion of the universe does not require the existence of what cannot exist.

149. Reply to the second objection (para.145 ii). The truth of 'The world is to be created' was in God from eternity before the world, and there it was the same as God, and therefore that truth did not cease when the world was created.

150. Reply to the third objection (para.145 iii). It should be said that the truth of a created thing has one existence in the created thing and another existence in the creator, and according to the existence by which the truth

---

95. In which case it would contain all four kinds of measurable thing. The reply (para.148) is that the fourth cannot exist — from which it follows that it is not measurable.
96. Though this truth seems to have had an end though no beginning, the reply (para.149) will raise a question about the metaphysical status of that truth. As having existed in God, and therefore been identical with Him, it shares in God's eternity, hence is endless, and hence does not have the fourth kind of measurability.

exists in the creator, it is always the same and exists in the same way, and does not pass from the future to the present. But according to the existence by which it exists in the created thing, whether in the thing or in the intellect, or in speech, it passes from the future to the present and from non-existence to existence.

151. Reply to the further objection (para.146). It should be said likewise that in the way in which the truth of 'The world has been created' is in God, it is God, as is the truth of 'The world is to be created'. But in the way in which it is in the created thing it is not God. But the truth of the created thing, as it is in the created thing, is caused by the truth which is in God, and these two are not the same except with respect to the similarity of their beginning.

ON IMAGINATION

Index of Questions in *On Imagination*

Preliminary note (paras.1–4)

QUESTION ONE: Is the imaginative soul endowed from its origin with species or images of corporeal and sensible things, or does it acquire them later? (paras.5–27)

Reasons for saying that it acquires them later (paras.6–11)
Reasons for saying that it does not have them from its origin (12–16)
Arguments to the contrary (paras.17–22)
Reply (para.23)
Reply to arguments to the contrary (paras.24–27)

QUESTION TWO: In what way are species or images of corporeal and sensible things acquired by imagination? (paras.28–40)

Reasons for saying that they are acquired by sensing (paras.29–32)
Reasons for saying that they are acquired by intellectual acts (paras.33–35)
Reply (para.36)
Augustine seems to contradict himself on this matter (paras.37–40)

QUESTION THREE: How does imagination acquire images of corporeal and sensible things by means of sense? (paras.41–149)

From where does the sensory soul acquire them? (para.41)
From itself (para.42)
Not from intellect (paras.43–44)
Not from imagination (paras.45–46)
Not from the body (paras.47–50)
A quibble concerning Augustine's words (para.51)
Reply to the quibble, based on the passages cited (paras.52–54)
Reply to the quibble, based on reason (paras.55–56)
Possible reply: The sense organ does not act on the sensory soul. (para.57)
Arguments against that reply (paras.58–60)

Possible reply. The sensory soul is changed by the body (para.61)
Argument against that reply (para.62)
Conclusion in summary: The sensory soul forms in itself an image of a sensible thing (para.63)
Arguments in support of this conclusion (paras.64–68)
Arguments to the contrary i–ix (paras.69–80)
Doubts concerning Augustine's words (paras.81–92)
Arguments to the contrary — that images are made in the mind (paras.93–96)
Return to the principal question — the judgment of Aristotelians that sensible things produce images by means of impressions (para. 97)
Exposition of Augustine's judgment concerning sensing (paras.98–102)
Explanation of how a soul forms an image in itself (para.103–105)
Doubts about that explanation (paras.106–107)
Replies to the doubts (paras.108–109)
Another doubt and the reply (paras.110–111)
Replies to the arguments to the contrary i–iv (paras.112–115)
A doubt and the reply (paras.116–117)
Replies to the arguments to the contrary v–ix (paras.118–129)
A doubt concerning the material cause (paras.130–134)
Replies concerning Augustine's words (paras.135–142)
Conclusion (para.143)
The harmony amongst authoritative texts (paras.144–149)

Doubts concerning spiritual or imaginative seeing (paras.150–315)

I   How are likenesses or images of corporeal things supposed to be received by sense and retained by imagination? (para.150)
II   In what way do the likenesses reach, or how are they brought to, imagination, there to remain? (para.151)
Reasons for raising the doubts (paras.152–156)
Conclusion (para.157)
III Do the species remain in the body itself, in the organ, and there present themselves to be imagined when the mind directs itself to them? (para.158)
A reason for replying affirmatively (para.159)
A reason for replying negatively (para.160)
IV By means of what nature does the soul retain the species which have been received, and on account of what is it enabled to retain them in this way? (para.161)
V   (a) By what means does it retain such a multitude of species at the same time without bringing confusion to desire? (para.162)

ON IMAGINATION 69

(b) In what way could species move desire, given that nothing can move desire unless grasped by means of cognition? (para.163)
VI It does not seem that imagination can have a cognition, for every cognition is produced by means of a light and in the light. (para.164)
VII Since the imaginative soul turns itself toward something which is to be imagined, does it consider the images in themselves alone without any representation of them in a bodily organ, or do they also appear at the same time in a bodily organ? (para.165)

Reply to Doubt I (paras.166–167)
Reply to Doubt II (para.168)
First way to understand 'organ of sense' (paras.169–170)
Second way to understand 'organ of sense' (paras.171–173)
Digression: What kind of body is this spirit which is essentially and primarily an organ of mind? (paras.174–182).
Return to the principal topic — In what way do the species of sensible things get from the proper senses to the common sense? (para 183).
Explanations (paras.184–186)
Replies to arguments (paras.187–193)
Reply to Doubt III (para.194)
Incidental questions (paras.195–197)
Reply (para.198)
Replies to incidental questions (paras.199–201)
Other objections (paras.202–205)
Reply to Doubt IV (paras.206–208)
Reply to Doubt V (paras.209–211)
Reply to Doubt VI (paras.212–213)
Reply to Doubt VII (para.214)
Conclusion (paras.215–218)

QUESTION FOUR: What part of the body is the organ of common sense?(paras.219–315)

It seems that it is the brain. (paras.220–234)
A quibble — not the common sense but a proper sense (para.235)
Against the quibble (paras.236–238)
Arguments — the common sense especially must perform its acts in the brain. (paras.239–241)
Arguments for the contrary proposition, that the heart is the organ of common sense (paras.242–264)
A difference between Augustine, the doctors, and Aristotle (para.265)
Reply (paras.266–271)

Doubts (paras.272–273)
Replies to doubts (paras.274–287)
Reply to the principal question (para.288)
Concerning taste (paras.289–296)
Concerning touch (para.297)
Concerning hearing (para.298)
Conclusion (para.299)
Replies to arguments to the contrary (paras.300–306)
Another objection — concerning blood (paras.307–310)
Replies to the other objections to the contrary (paras.311–314)
Conclusion (para.315)

On Imagination

1. Since in the human mind above ⟨the faculty of⟩ sense the cognitive power has two parts, a superior and an inferior, of which the superior is the intellectual, and the inferior is the fantastic or imaginative, just as the mind, absolutely and without qualification, is called a soul, so sometimes each of these two parts separately is called a soul. For the human mind absolutely speaking is called a soul: 'Head bowed, he gave up his soul'[1] and 'Who knows whether the soul of Adam's sons goes upward?'[2] And the intellectual part of the mind is called a soul: 'Be renewed in the soul of your mind.'[3] For Augustine says that there the apostle did not wish that two things be understood, 'as if the mind is one thing and the mind's soul is another'.[4] 'Soul' is taken in the same way in Galatians: 'The flesh desires against the soul.'[5] The imaginative part of the mind also is called 'soul': 'If I should pray in such language, my soul prays, but my mind does not bear fruit.'[6] For Augustine says in his exposition of that verse, that what is there called 'soul' is that to which imaginings which are likenesses of bodies belong.[7] And he says that 'what is appropriately called a soul [*spiritus*] is a power of the mind [*anima*] which is inferior to the mind [*mens*], where likenesses of corporeal things are expressed'.[8] From these points it is obvious that 'soul' is sometimes used of the imaginative part of the mind, and sometimes of the intellectual.

2. Note next that though the aforementioned parts are essentially different, because by the one we surpass the irrational animals and by the other we have something in common with them, as Augustine teaches,[9] nevertheless the imaginative part and the sensory part are not essentially different but differ only in function or power and use. For what is a sensory part in the presence of something sensible, becomes a fantastic or imaginative part when, in the absence of any sensible thing, it considers the images of sensible things stored in itself and sensible things are imagined, in their absence, by means of those images. This is what Aristotle means when he says: 'Imagina-

1. *John* 19, 30
2. *Eccles.* 3, 21
3. *Eph.* 4, 23
4. *De Trin.*, xiv, 16; *CCSL* 50A, 452 (14–15)
5. *Gal.* 5, 17
6. 1 *Cor.* 14, 14
7. *De Trin.*, xiv, 16; *CCSL* 50A, 452 (19–20)
8. *De Gen. ad litt.*, xii, 9; *CSEL* 28, 3, 2, p.391 (9–11)
9. *De Trin.*, xii, 1–2; *CCSL* 50, 356 (1)–357 (2)

tion is motion made as a result of an actual sensing.'[10] And much later, speaking of that part of the inferior mind, the imagination, he says that in it 'avoidance and desire are not different either from each other or from the sensory part, but they are different as regards their existence.'[11] And elsewhere Aristotle says that the imaginative soul is identical to the sensible but the sensible and the imaginative differ as regards their existence.[12] From this it is obvious that we should not speak of the sensory soul and the imaginative as different in essence but only as different in mode and existence.

3. Note next that the sense organ consists of two parts, namely body and soul. Of these the body is like an instrument and the soul like a ruler and artificer. Hence the body does not know sensible things except through the soul, but the sense organ knows sensible things through itself and not primarily, and the sensory soul itself knows sensible things through itself and primarily.

4. Note finally that since nothing is known except through itself when present or through its likeness present to the knower, and since sensible things are not present through themselves to the senses or to the sensory soul, especially since a sensible thing placed above an ⟨organ of⟩ sense is not sensed,[13] the sensory soul which is in the act of knowing sensible things must have within itself likenesses of those sensible things, and these likenesses are called 'images', and 'species', and 'likenesses', or 'phantasms' by Augustine and Aristotle. These preliminary points have been made, without argumentation, as a guide to what follows.

⟨*Question One: Is the imagination endowed from its origin with species or images of corporeal and sensible things, or does it acquire them later?*⟩

5. In order therefore that it should be known how the imaginative, which is also the sensory, soul has images of sensible things, the first question is whether (i) the imagination is endowed, from its origin, with species or images of corporeal things and sensible things, or whether (ii) it acquires them later.

6. As regards the second part (para.5–ii), such reasons as these can be brought forward: Augustine, replying to Nebridius about this question, teaches that the imagination does not have images of corporeal things before the mind uses the senses.[14]

---

10. *De An.*, iii, 3 (429a1–2); ed. Stroick, p.175 (88)
11. *Ibid.*, 7 (431a11–13); p.211 (81–82)
12. *De Insomn.*, 1 (459a15–16); ed. Drossaart Lulofs, p.8 (4–6)
13. *Cf*, Aristotle *De An.*, ii, 7 (419a13–14, 23–29); ed. Stroick, p.118 (85–86)
14. Cf. Aug. *Ep.* 7, 3 (6); *CSEL* 34, 17

7. Moreover, if the imagination had from itself images of corporeal things, a man could correctly imagine corporeal things before he used his senses. But this is not true. For Augustine says: 'When those who have been blind from their earliest years are asked about light and colours they do not know what to reply. For they do not have any coloured images since they have not sensed any.'[15] But if this is true as regards the sense of sight, it is likewise true in the case of the other senses, and thus it is not possible correctly to imagine corporeal things before the use of the senses.

8. Moreover, Augustine says: 'The human mind, when asked, cannot speak about the arts which concern the senses of the body, such as many arts of medicine and everything about astrology, unless the mind has learned them.'[16] But the only obvious reason for this is that if it is to learn it has to use the senses. It seems therefore that, before it has learned and has used the senses, it would not have within itself images of sensible things.

9. Someone might say to this that he does not need the use of his senses for the acquisition of corporeal images, but for rousing them, so that he should notice what he has within himself. But this does not seem likely since neither Augustine nor Aristotle seems to agree with this.

10. Moreover, if the imagination had these images within itself and if, when aroused, it truly imagined them, then since something can be said about every sensible thing, one could be roused by an utterance to a correct imagining of all corporeal and all sensible things. If therefore someone speaks to you about Rome, which you have never seen, or speaks to you about Caesar or someone similar, then straightaway you would imagine, with its correct and true image, the thing he was speaking about. And that is not true.

11. Moreover, if the imagination had within itself images of corporeal things and nevertheless acquired them by sensing, for otherwise it could not be aroused by them, it follows that it would have duplicate images of these same things after the use of the senses, and this does not seem a satisfactory position. Why should one suppose this? For we have the same result with regard to the cognition of corporeal things, if we suppose that the only images we have are acquired by sensing, and if we suppose that at the same time there also exist other innate images.

12. Moreover, the following reason can be used to support the main contention: If images of corporeal things are naturally present in the imagination, then the reason for saying that some are is a reason for saying that all are. But this would seem to no purpose since in this life the mind would not succeed in imagining all corporeal things, and after this life the mind will not

---

15. *Ibid.*, (20–22)
16. *Retract.*, i, 7 (2); *CSEL* 36, 35 (13–15)

need such images naturally inherent in the imagination. The mind will be contemplating an eternal wisdom which contains all things.

13. Moreover, if the human imagination were naturally endowed with images of all corporeal things, then by the same token so also would the imagination of beasts. But there seems no reason to have things so.

14. Moreover, the potential intellect is at a worthier level of creation than the imaginative power. But Aristotle says that the former is like a bare tablet upon which nothing has been written before it acquires intelligible species.[17] How much more so, then, will this be the case as regards the imaginative power.

15. Moreover, Aristotle also says that the mind is in a way all things, that is, the intellect is all intelligible things and the sense is all sensible things.[18] And he explains how by saying that it is all these things potentially and not actually. Since therefore the sensory soul is all sensible things potentially only and not actually, it follows that it has images of sensible things potentially and not actually. But the sensory soul and the imaginative are the same in themselves as regards their substance even if they are not the same with respect to their mode. Therefore the imagination has the same images potentially and not actually.

16. You might say that so far as it is the imagination it has the images actually, and so far as it is the sensory soul it has them potentially, since the imagination is actually roused by the sense to contemplating images which it has within itself. But objections have recently been brought against this (paras.9–11). And that is enough for the time being.

17. Against the foregoing (para.6). A sign that the imagination has within itself by nature all images of corporeal things is that it can even imagine what a man has never seen, as well as what he has seen.

18. Moreover, if our intellect by its nature and within itself has intellectual objects which we learn, it seems by the same token that our imagination has by its nature and within itself images of corporeal things which we sense. That the antecedent is true can be seen from what Nebridius said to Augustine, with which, as it seems, Augustine agreed: 'The intellect, rather than receiving something, is reminded of its intellectual objects which are to be seen by sense.'[19]

19. The same point is also to be seen in Augustine's *Confessions* X where he says: 'Learning these things which do not reach our minds as images by means of the bodily senses, is a process of thinking by which we gather together and attend to things which the memory contained though they were

---

17. Cf *De An.*, iii, 4 (429b31–430a1); ed. Stroick, p.201 (85)
18. *Ibid.*, 8 (431b20, 26–27); p.223 (70–73)
19. *Ep.* 6, 2; *CSEL* 34, 12 (23–24)

scattered about and confused.'[20] It seems clear that he means that the intellectual things which we learn, and are not sensible things, are within us in the intellectual power.

20. Moreover Boethius seems to be of this opinion. He says:
> As when light strikes upon the eye
> Or voices clatter in the ear:
> The active power of the mind then roused
> Calls forth the species from within
> To motions of a similar kind;
> And fitting them to marks impressed
> From outside, mingles images
> Received with forms it hides within.[21]

21. Moreover, in the following chapter Boethius adds: '[When] in sentient bodies the qualities of an outward object affect the organs of sense, the passivity of the body precedes the vigour of the active mind, a passivity which provokes an act of mind in itself, and excites the inner forms which had meantime been at rest.'[22]

22. The same judgment is also to be found in *Consolation* III where he says that 'whatever the mind seeks outside (*sc.* by sensing) it possesses in its own treasure chests within'.[23] And shortly after that he adds:
> The seed of truth lies hidden deep within
> And teaching fans the spark to take new life.[24]

And a little thereafter:
> And if the muse of Plato speaks the truth,
> Man but recalls what once he knew and lost.[25]

Clearly Boethius seems to think that the species of all sensible things are within the mind, and that the mind is aroused by the passivity of sense to contemplating what it has within itself, and that a species coming by way of the senses from outside intermingles with those that are carried within, and thus it has in duplicate species of the same things, namely innate species and acquired ones.

23. Reply. Since Augustine and Aristotle clearly seem to agree with the earlier reasons (paras.6–16), it seems to me that that side of the argument is more correct. For I think that the imaginative part of the mind entirely lacks images of corporeal things until a man uses his senses.

---

20. Conf., x, 11 (8); *CCSL* 27, 164 (1–5)
21. *Phil.con.*, *metr.* 4; *CCSL* 94, 98 (33)–99 (40). My translation is taken from *The Consolation of Philosophy* (Penguin Classics) tr. V.E.Watts p.161.
22. *Ibid.*, *pros.*5; p.99 (1–5)
23. *Ibid.*, iii, *metr.* 11; p.59 (5–6)
24. *Ibid.*, (11–12). Translation from *Consolation* (Penguin Classics), p.109.
25. *Ibid.*, (15–16). Translation from *Consolation* (Penguin Classics), p.109.

24. In reply to the first argument (para.17), Augustine says that a power to diminish, increase, change, and compound is innate in the mind, and that, by means of that power, images of things which have not been seen are formed from images which sense has imported.[26] For since you have seen a man and have seen a horse, you will be able to form in your imagination an image of something which is human in front and a horse at the back, though you have never seen such an animal. Moreover, if you had never seen the sea, you could form an image of the sea from seeing a vessel or pond of water. Likewise in other cases it is possible to form images of things unseen by using that power to increase and diminish with which the mind is endowed. But this kind of image arises from images brought in by sense, in such a way that it copies those images in whole or in part. But if nothing similar was apprehended by the senses it cannot be imagined. Hence Augustine says:

> It is possible for the imagination, by subtracting from and adding to what the senses brought to it, to produce whole things which the imagination acquired from no sense. On the contrary, parts of these ⟨imagined objects⟩ are brought together from different things. Thus we, as children, had been able to imagine seas though we were born and brought up amongst inland people, for we saw water in small goblets. But before we had tasted strawberries and cornel-berries in Italy we would never have imagined their flavour. It is for this reason that those blind from their earliest years do not know how to reply when asked about light and colours. For those who have not sensed such things do not have any colour images.[27]

And elsewhere Augustine says: 'I think that if I had never seen human bodies I would not in any way be able, by thought, to make a form of them from a visible species.'[28]

25. Reply to the second objection (para.18). It should be said that intellect and imagination are not similar in the way suggested by the objection. For intelligible things, which are in the liberal disciplines, and are not apprehended by sense, reach the intellect in such a way that they are seen by an intellectual vision without the mediation of some other vision. But images of sensible and corporeal things do not reach the imagination in such a way as to be seen by an imaginative vision except by means of a corporeal vision. Moreover, suppose that the argument (para.18) was correct as regards the likeness ⟨between intellect and imagination⟩. It could then be inferred that just as intellectual things, which do not pertain to sense, are present to the intellect in themselves and not merely through their species, so also sensible and

---

26. Aug. *Ep.* 7, 3 (6); *CSEL* 34, 17
27. *Ibid.*, (13–22)
28. *De Musica*, vi, 11 (32); *PL* 32, 1180

corporeal things are present to the imagination in themselves and not through their images. And it is plain that this is not true and that there is no such similarity.

26. It should be noted, however, that there are two kinds of intelligible thing. One is infused or impressed from above. The other is acquired by means of a corporeal or spiritual vision. As regards an intelligible thing of the first kind, it is true that it reaches the intellectual soul without any other vision mediating, since that kind is elevated far above the senses. Both Augustine and Nebridius speak of that kind ⟨of intelligible thing⟩. As regards the second kind, this is not so. For that consists of sensible things, and hence such things reach the intellectual soul by means of a corporeal and imaginative vision, and by no other means in nature. And it is this sort of intelligible thing, and the way to grasp it intellectually, that Aristotle seems to be dealing with in *De Anima* III. For he says there: 'The mind does not think at all without an image',[29] and shortly thereafter: 'That which understands thinks the species in images.'[30] And he there says many similar things about which we shall perhaps learn more in the sequel.

27. Reply to the third objection (paras.20–22). It can reasonably be said that here Boethius disagrees with Augustine and Aristotle. Or it can be said, perhaps with more truth and subtlty, that Boethius is there speaking not about imagination but about intellect. And if you pay careful attention to what he says you will see that he clearly is talking about the intellect. For he says that the mind has species hidden within it,[31] and the seed of what is true lies hidden within, and is aroused when fanned by doctrine.[32] But such things concern not acts of imagining or the imagination but acts of understanding and the intellect. For that is what is meant by 'mind' and it is to the intellect that doctrine belongs. By God's grace this will be dealt with more fully hereafter.

⟨*Question Two: In what way are species or images of corporeal and sensible things acquired by imagination?*⟩

28. Granted that imagination does not have species or images of corporeal and sensible things except by acquiring them, we should see how they are acquired by it.

29. It seems that they are acquired by sensing. For Augustine says to

---

29. *De An.*, iii, 7 (431a16); ed. Stroick, p.211 (83)
30. *Ibid.*, (431b1–2); p.212 (80–81)
31. *Phil.cons.* v, *metr*.4; *CCSL* 94, 99 (35–40)
32. *Ibid.*, iii, *metr*. 11; p.59 (11–12)

Nebridius: 'Imagination is nothing but a blow struck by the senses.'[33] And later he says: 'It is possible for the imaginative soul, by subtracting from and adding to what the senses brought to it, to produce things which the imagination acquired from no sense.'[34] From these points it is obvious that the senses brought into the imagination the images of sensible things.

30. Moreover, speaking of geometry and its acquisition, Augustine says: 'On this matter I used the senses as a ship. For when they brought me to the place for which I was heading, where I dismissed them, as if placed alone I then began to turn them over by thought.'[35] He means by these words that he was transported by the senses as if by a ship from sensible things outside to the inner intellect where are the immutable things which the liberal arts are about. But this cannot be done unless images of sensible things are borne in by the senses and through those images an ascent is made to purely intelligible things.

31. Moreover, Augustine says: 'What is sensed by a bodily seeing is announced to a spiritual president, as it were. For when something is being discerned by the eyes, the image of it immediately arises in the soul, but the image made is not recognized except when, with our eyes withdrawn from the thing we were seeing with our eyes, we find in our soul the image of the thing.'[36] In that passage he calls 'soul' what philosophers call 'imagination' or 'fantasy'. But what we intended to show is obvious from these words.

32. Moreover, Aristotle teaches: 'Imagination is a movement made from actual sensing.'[37] And he teaches that it is of different kinds corresponding to the three kinds of sensible thing. The first kind of sensible thing is the proper sensible thing, the second is the common, and the third is the accidental. And truth and error occur in the imagination corresponding to truth and error in the senses. From this, according to him, it is obvious that, by sensing, imagination acquires images of sensible things, and since the matter is plain it is not necessary to say any more about it.

33. On the other hand, it seems that imagination acquires the images from intellect which is above, and by an act of thinking. For Augustine says that from the teachable things which are in the intellect 'some false colours and forms are poured as it were into the mirror of thought, and deceive enquirers, who often think that that is the whole thing which they know or which they enquire about.'[38]

34. He says the same thing in Letter 84, that is, that geometric figures and

---

33. Aug. *Ep.* 7, 2 (3); *CSEL* 34, 14 (26–27)
34. *Ibid.*, 3 (6); p.17 (13–15)
35. Aug. *Soliloq.*, i. 4 (9); *PL* 32, 874
36. *De Gen. ad litt.* xii, 11; *CSEL* 28, 3, 2, p.393 (10–14)
37. *De An.* iii, 3 (429a1–2); ed. Stroick, p.175 (88)
38. *Soliloq.*, ii, 20 (35); *PL* 32, 903

the rhythmic, musical, and infinite variety of numbers which are comprehended in the intellect, and are the true immutables which the liberal arts are about, nevertheless produce false images, which reason scarcely resists.[39]

35. Note also that Augustine says that this should be understood in the following way. In the highest position in the soul is pure intellect which is immediately bound to immutable things. Below that is the cognitive power which, like a mirror, is set up against the intellect, so that it should receive its splendour as it were from nearby. But the intelligible things which the liberal arts are about are, according to Augustine, in the intellect. And these are true intelligible things since they do not change. For there is there the circle on whose basis every circle large or small is judged, and likewise there is there the triangle and every figure which is entirely immutable and cannot be imagined to be augmented or diminished. There also is the point which has no part, and the line which is a length without breadth,[40] and the plane at a tangent to the sphere at a single point, and other such things, which neither are, nor can be, in sensible things, or in sense, or in imagination. For nothing is sensible except a quantum which has parts, and no other thing can be brought into the senses. Imagination is also an imitation of sense and therefore is like it. Therefore all these things and others like them which the liberal arts are about are, according to Augustine, in the intellect. And this is Plato's position. It is from these intelligible things therefore that certain imaginary lines and figures and imaginary points and tangents and such like pour down into the cognitive power which uses imagination, as into a mirror placed beneath. And these are called false images by Augustine, not because they are not images, but because they are imitations of the immutable things that teachable science is about and are not the immutable things themselves. And these images often deceive thinkers when they are believed to be the true things the sciences are about and in fact they are not. It is obvious from this that they are changed, augmented, and decreased at the will of those using their imagination, since the true things the sciences are about are immutable and exist in the same way always. I have added these words for the sake of a better understanding of Augustine's words (paras.33–34), by which he teaches that imagination receives images from intellect.

36. Reply. Imagination is intermediate between sense and intellect, just as the seeing by the imagination is intermediate between corporeal and intellectual seeing. And therefore perhaps it can be assimilated to the things existing on both sides, that is, (i) to intelligible things via the intellect which presides and can assimilate to itself what is subordinate; and (ii) to sensible things via

---

39. *Ep.* 7, 2 (4); *CSEL* 34, 16 (7–13)
40. Cf Euclid. *Elem.geom.*, i, def.1 & 2; *transl. Adelhardi* II, *cf.* Clagett, p.30: 'A point is that which has no part. A line is a length without breadth, whose extremities are two points.'

sense which is subordinate and has to serve the spiritual seeing in the acquisition of images of sensible things. And then it should be admitted that imagination acquires images of things from both sides. But strictly speaking it acquires images of sensible and corporeal things only by sense where there is a corporeal seeing. But it acquires images of intelligible and spiritual things via intellect where there is an intellectual seeing. Hence Augustine's arguments stated above can be conceded, since the earlier arguments (paras.29–31) only argue their way to the acquisition of images of sensible and corporeal things, and the later arguments (paras.33–34) only argue their way to the acquisition of images infused from above from spiritual and intelligible things. But for the present only images of the former kind are at issue. And therefore once the earlier arguments have been conceded it is not necessary to reply to the later ones, since they are not contrary to the earlier ones, as has already been said (para.35).

37. But from the foregoing Augustine might now seem to the less careful to be contradicting himself. For to judge from his words quoted above, he seems to be asserting that the imagination does not have images before the use of the senses (paras.6–8). But in this question (paras.33–34) he seems, from the words quoted, to mean that it could have the images without the use of the senses, by the refulgence of intelligible things upon the imagination, while the intellect assimilates to itself the subordinate imagination; and in this way the intellect can be imitated.

38. But it should be remembered that he did not say that without the use of the senses it was impossible for imagination to have any images, but that without their use it was impossible for it to have any images of corporeal and sensible things. But he said here that it is possible for imagination to have images of intelligible and spiritual things, while not settling whether it has them before the use of the senses, or after. So Augustine did not contradict himself.

39. Moreover, it can also be said that the mode of imagining infused by the intellect from above is of two kinds. One is a supernatural mode which was able to be directly in the mind of the saviour and will be able to be, and can be, in those who are glorified. The other mode is natural — the mode here touched upon by Augustine (paras.33–34). This sometimes befalls those who seek the truths in the teachable arts. The first of these does not need the prior use of the senses, in my opinion, and Augustine is not here speaking about that mode. The second mode does need the use of the senses, and it is of that mode that he here speaks.

40. For it is after he senses some material lines, figures, and points, and such like, which are not true lines, figures, or points according to the geometric definitions, that certain images of things which have just been sensed are conveyed to him. From there the mind tries to find out how a point is a

thing without quantity and parts, and how a line lacks breadth, for he sees no such thing with his eyes. And since these things are discovered only by reason and intellect, thought sometimes does not rise right up to them so that it gains an intellectual view of them. But striving to gain it, thought, though still imaginative, undergoes a sort of reflected light, and it imagines images of intellectual and immutable things which present themselves as true immutable and intellectual things, though they are not of such a kind. An imaginative act of such a kind comes about in this way: intellect assimilates imagination to itself in the way it can, while the mind strives to attain a pure intellect, without however divesting itself entirely of imagination. Therefore even if this way of imagining comes from above, from intellect and from intelligible things, it comes into a man after he has used his senses, not before. For it is aroused and prepared for him by the use of the senses, and by the way of imagining which is introduced by the use of the senses. It is therefore obvious that Augustine does not contradict himself.

⟨*Question Three: How does imagination acquire images of corporeal and sensible things by means of sense?*⟩

41. Granted that imagination acquires images of corporeal and sensible things from sense, the question is how. And since it would not acquire them from sense unless the sensory soul had already had them — for otherwise it would not sense — here one must first see from where the sensory soul, which is present in the organ of sensing, gets them.

42. The question therefore is by what efficient or impressing cause sense receives or begins to have those images. And it seems that it is by sense itself and not by any efficient or impressing cause other than sense. For there seems no other cause by which the images can be impressed upon sense than by (i) intellect or (ii) imagination or (iii) body — and I say 'body' whether it be the sensible object or the organ informed by the sensible object.

43. The first of these (para.42-i) does not seem right, because corporeal seeing provides species of visible things for the intellect by means of spiritual seeing, as Augustine teaches.[41] Therefore it is not the case that the intellect provides the species for the sentient soul.

44. Moreover, the mode of sensing does not seem equivocal in ourselves and beasts. But in beasts species of sensible things are not supplied ⟨*sc.* by the intellect⟩ to the sentient soul, since they do not have an intellect. Therefore neither in us are they supplied to the sentient soul ⟨by the intellect⟩.

45. The second of these (para.42-ii) does not seem right, because cor-

---

41. *De Gen.ad litt.*, xii, 11; *CSEL* 28, 3, 2, p.393 (10–14)

poreal seeing supplies species of corporeal and sensible things for spiritual seeing, according to Augustine.[42] Therefore the reverse does not happen.

46. Moreover, if the images were impressed upon sense by imagination, imagination would have those images before the sensory soul had them, and thus it would have them by a natural endowment. But we have already seen (question 1) that the contrary of that is true.

47. The third of these (para.42–iii) also does not seem right, from many things that Augustine said. For if by the action of a body images of bodies were impressed upon a sentient soul, a body would then act upon the soul, and the soul would be acted upon by a body as matter subject to a body. And that is contrary to what Augustine says:

> Neither is it sensible to think that a body can make something in a soul, for a soul does not stand in a matter-relation to a making body. For that which makes is in every way more excellent than the thing out of which it makes something. And body is not in any way more excellent than soul. Indeed soul is clearly more excellent than body. [43]

48. Further on he says: 'When a cause is from a body, so that such sights may be distinguished, the body does not produce those sights. For the body does not have the power to form something spiritual.'[44]

49. Moreover he says: 'Could we have subordinated the mind to the active body imposing measures upon it, so that the body is the doer, but the mind is matter from which, and in which, something measured is made? If we believe that, then we must believe that the mind is worse than the body. What could be more dreadful than that?'[45]

50. In the same place he says: 'I do not think that this body is animated by mind, except in the thought of the doer. Nor do I think that the mind is acted upon at all by the body. But I think that the mind, by divine influence, acts upon and with regard to the body as upon something subject to its power, though sometimes with ease and sometimes with difficulty.'[46] These and similar statements by Augustine clearly seem to mean that a body does not impress a sensible image upon a sentient soul.

51. Perhaps someone will quibble about this, and say that Augustine's words which have just been quoted (paras.47–50) are not about the sensory soul, but about imagination or intellect or both.

52. But that is wrong. For if imagination and the sensory soul are the same in substance though differing in their mode, as put forward above (para.2), it is just as absurd that the sensory soul should be acted upon by a

---

42. *Ibid.*
43. *Ibid.*, 16; p.402 (5–9)
44. *Ibid.*, 20; p.409 (3–4)
45. Aug. *De musica*, vi, 5 (8); *PL* 32, 1168
46. *Ibid.*, 5 (9); *PL* 32, 1168

body as that imagination should be. For in Augustine's view what is absurd is not that a soul as having such and such a function should be said to be acted upon by a body, but that a soul *qua* soul, and *qua* more excellent than the body by nature, should be said to be acted upon by a body.

53. Moreover, that Augustine's words apply as much to the sensory soul as to the other parts of the soul is shown by these words of his: 'Every soul is without doubt more elevated than every body, not in respect of position in space but in respect of the worth of its nature.'[47] And a little further on he says that the soul should therefore not be thought of as something that can be acted upon by a body because 'a soul is in every way more elevated than a body'.[48] Here Augustine does not except any soul from that judgment.

54. Moreover, where Augustine explains in what way a mind is not acted upon by a body but on the contrary acts upon it and with regard to it, though with greater or less difficulty (para.50),[49] he reveals what he has in mind especially in respect of sensing, teaching how the mind does not receive something from the body when it senses, but acts upon the body. Hence he says in the same place that to sense ⟨something⟩ in a body is not to be a passive recipient of something from a body, but to act more attentively with regard to its passivities.[50] And further on in the same chapter: 'I think that, when it senses, the mind displays acts of the body in its passivities, but not that it receives those same passivities.'[51] Shortly after he also clearly shows this in the case of the sense of hearing.[52] From all these points it is plain that Augustine means that when the sensory soul senses it does not receive images of sensible things from a body as a passive thing receives things from an agent.

55. One of Augustine's reasons for supporting this position is the following. It is more likely that any body could be acted upon by another body than that a soul could be acted upon by a body. But a circular body which bounds and contains straight bodies cannot be the passive recipient of something from them, but rather the action flows from it towards them. Therefore how much more so is it the case that a sentient soul which presides over the sense organ cannot be acted upon by it, but the soul's action flows towards the sense organ. And if the soul is not acted upon by the organ, then how much more so is it the case that the soul is not acted upon by a sensible body which is at a distance outside, for that distant body has no relation to the sensory soul except by way of the organ which is vivified by that soul.

---

47. *De gen.ad litt.*, xii, 16; *CSEL* 28, 3, 2, p.401 (23–25)
48. *Ibid.*, p.402 (5–9)
49. *De musica*, vi, 5 (9); *PL* 32, 1168
50. *Ibid.*
51. *Ibid.*, 5 (10); *PL* 32, 1169
52. *Ibid.*, 5 (11); *PL* 32, 1169

56. Moreover, since a man is a sort of world, it is probable that the kinds of different existence which are ranked some above and some below in man, are related to activity, passivity, governance, and influence, in the way in which they are related in the greater world. But in the greater world the situation is such that a nature that has a lower existence is entirely governed and acted upon by a nature that has a higher one, and does not act upon that higher existence. Therefore it will be like that in man. Here is a clarification of the minor premiss. In the greater world a created thing has a lower grade of existence than the creator, and the created thing is moved, governed, and acted upon by the creator, and the converse does not hold. Moreover, in the created order bodies have a lower existence than angels have, and bodies are moved, governed, and acted upon by angels, and the converse does not hold. Moreover, among bodies, straight ones are lower than circular ones, and the straight ones are moved and acted upon by the circular ones, and the converse does not hold. Moreover, among straight bodies matter has a lower existence than form has, and matter is acted upon, moved, and governed by form, and the converse does not hold. Likewise with spiritual creatures. The human mind in this life is in a certain respect lower than an angelic soul, and the human is moved and governed by that latter, and the converse does not hold. Therefore this is how it will be in man, where the body has a lower existence than the mind has, and the sense organ has a lower existence than has the soul which vivifies that organ. And since the sensible body which is external has the same grade of existence as the organ, for each can be acted on and each is composed of contraries, though the external body is more distant ⟨than the sense organ is⟩ from the sensory soul as regards the order of acting and being acted upon, the sensory soul is not acted upon by the external body, just as it is not acted upon by the sense organ.

57. Someone might reply here that the sense organ does not act upon the sensory soul, and neither does the sensible thing except accidentally. But by its nature the sense organ acts upon the species of the sensible thing, and the sense organ is affected by that species through the change in the sensible thing and in the medium.

58. But this reply does not block the foregoing arguments (paras.55–56), for since the sensible species in the organ which is sensing is nothing but an inflowing from the sensible thing, this inflowing will not be said to effect something which the sensible thing itself does not principally effect, since what pours into a power acts by means of it, and the power does not act except in so far as an action is performed by means of it.

59. Moreover, the purpose of a sense organ is that, by means of the in-forming received from the sensible thing, the organ should be the cause of sensory cognition. If therefore the organ in-formed by the species of the sensible thing, according as it is thus in-formed, has an effect on something,

then that body must have an effect on it. And the effect will not be accidental since, as I have said, it is essential to the organ that it receive a species and cause a sensory cognition by means of that species.

60. Moreover, even if we grant that that act and the efficient causality should be attributed to the species which is in the organ, and should not be attributed to the body except accidentally, as the reply assumes (para.57), it does not follow that absurdity is avoided. For the species is a thing of less excellent existence than is the body from which it is radiated or in which it is received. For the species either is an accident or has an accidental nature, and is not self-subsistent but instead is in something else and is from another thing which is immediately present. If therefore, on account of the fact that a spiritual nature has an excellence above that of a corporeal nature, it is absurd that a body should act upon something in a soul, then for the same reason how much more is it absurd that an image should by its nature act upon a soul.

61. Moreover, someone might reply to this by saying that, as Aristotle teaches,[53] there are two modes of change. For there is a change strictly speaking where a disposition which had previously been possessed is destroyed and another disposition, which had not previously been possessed, is brought in. And there is a change broadly speaking where a disposition is not destroyed but a new one is brought in which produces perfection and wholeness. The first kind of change is not in the act of sensing, but the second is, as Aristotle teaches. So someone says that it is absurd that the sensory soul be changed by a body by means of a change of the first sort, but not of the second sort.

62. But this does not undermine the conclusions drawn above (paras.42–50, 52–56). For in *De Anima* II, where Aristotle makes the foregoing distinction between kinds of change, he says that the second, broad kind is 'the well-being of that which is so potentially, ⟨produced⟩ by that which is so actually',[54] that is, because it produces a perfection. How therefore does what is less noble produce in the more noble, and the body produce in the soul, its well-being or perfection by means of efficient causality, so that the body or the corporeal thing is the efficient cause and the soul, as if it were matter, is subject to it? It is obvious therefore that these replies (paras.57, 61) do not block the conclusions already drawn.

63. Let us therefore bring together in this way the conclusions already drawn (paras.42–62): if, when the sensory soul senses, it begins to have impressed upon it an image or likeness of a sensible thing, it does not seem that the efficient causing of the impression can be done otherwise than by the

---

53. *De An.*, ii, 5 (417b2–7), iii, 7 (431a4–8); ed. Stroick, pp.98 (83–89), 210 (88–89)
54. *Ibid.* (417b3–7); p.98 (84–89)

intellect, the imagination, the body, or the sensory soul itself. It cannot be done by any of the first three. It seems that what is left is that it is done by the fourth. And thus the sensory soul forms in itself an image of a sensible thing.

64. Augustine seems in various places clearly to be saying the same thing. For in *On Genesis* he says: 'Although for the first time we see a body which previously we were not seeing, and from then its image begins to be in our soul so that in the absence of the body we will remember it, nevertheless it is not the body that produces its own image in the soul, but the soul which produces the image in itself with wondrous speed, a speed unutterably far removed from the slowness of body.'[55] And a little further on: 'In the case of hearing, unless the soul were immediately to form in itself an image of an utterance perceived in the ears, and unless the memory retained it, the soul would not know whether the second syllable was the second.'[56]

65. And further on: 'So how much more do I wonder at the great speed and ease with which the mind produces in itself images of bodies which it has seen with the aid of bodily eyes, than I wonder at the visions of sleepers in a state of extasy.'[57]

66. Augustine hints at the same thing in *On True Religion*: 'Phantasms are nothing but productions drawn by bodily sense from a species of a body.'[58] For if phantasms are drawn from a species of a body by bodily sense, then their existence in the imagination is attributable to the drawing power of sense. And certainly the drawing power of bodily sense can be attributed only to the sensory soul, since there does not seem to be ⟨in bodily sense⟩ any other moving and efficient principle. And hence the efficient causing of those phantasms in the soul is by the sensory soul itself. For it draws into itself that which should be placed in the imagination.

67. Augustine is clearly saying the same thing in *De Trinitate*: 'Since those are bodies outside which the mind desired through the bodily senses, and since it cannot by itself bring those bodies inside as into the realm of incorporeal nature, it collects and grasps their images made in itself and from itself.'[59]

68. From these and similar statements by Augustine it seems sufficiently clear that he means that the sentient soul itself forms within itself images of corporeal and sensible things. But as regards the last text quoted (para.67) there is some doubt about this, as will become clear hereafter (para.81).

69. There are, however, many expressions of the contrary position. First

---

55. *De gen.ad litt.*, xii, 16; *CSEL* 28, 3, 2, p.402 (10–15)
56. *Ibid.*, (17–19)
57. *Ibid.*, 18; p.407 (18–21)
58. *De vera relig.*, 10 (18); *CCSL* 32, 199 (10–12)
59. *De Trin.*, x, 5; *CCSL* 50, 321 (26–31)

there is Aristotle, for he says: 'Sense is receptive to sensible things without their matter, as wax receives the mark of the ring without the iron and gold.'[60] This is further expressed in *De Anima* III, where it is said that this reception and change comes about 'just as if the signet were pressed into the wax right up to the end'.[61] Since therefore the motivating terminus of the change which occurs when sensing occurs, is the sensible thing, and the end is the sensory soul, it seems that the change is extended continuously through the medium and the organ up to the sensory soul, so that the unmoved mover is the sensible thing or is that which draws the sensible thing into an act of producing change, and what is moved without being a mover is the sentient soul, and what the media are are moved movers. And so the sentient soul, according to Aristotle, seems to be informed by an image of a sensible thing by means of the action and influence of the sensible body, though this is done through a medium.

70. Moreover, surely the purpose of the sense organ is that it should impress a sensible species received from the medium upon a sensory power which we here call a 'sensory soul'. For this seems to be the teaching of the philosophers.

71. Moreover, in many places Augustine seems to have the same thing in mind. For in *De Musica* he says: 'The affecting of the ears when they are touched by a sound, cannot occur except when the cause of the sound is present.'[62] He seems here to mean that the corporeal sound affects the auditory sense when it hears, and this is to produce an image which is of the sound it senses.

72. The same point seems to be made more explicitly in Letter 84 where Augustine says: 'All images, which many call "phantasms", are most neatly divided into three kinds; those of the first kind are impressed by sensed things, those of the second by things thought about, and those of the third by things reached by calculation.'[63] Here he is saying that images are impressed by sensed things.

73. In *De Trinitate* he says the same thing: 'The informing of sense, which is called "seeing", is impressed just by the body which is seen, that is, by a visible thing.'[64]

74. Moreover, he says: 'In place of that species of a body which was sensed outwardly, there comes memory retaining that species which the mind took in by means of a bodily sense, and in place of the seeing which was outward, since the sense was informed by a sensible body, there comes a

---

60. *De an.*, ii, 12 (424a18–20); ed. Stroick, p.149 (65–66)
61. *Ibid.*, iii, 12 (435a9–10); p.245 (86)
62. *De musica*, vi, 2 (3); *PL* 32, 1164
63. *Ep.* 7, 2 (4); *CSEL* 34, 15 (6–9)
64. *De Trin.*, xi, 2; *CCSL* 50, 336 (60–62)

similar seeing within.'⁶⁵ Note what he says here: 'The mind took in the species by means of a bodily sense' and 'The sense is informed by a sensible body'. In these passages Augustine seems to mean that the sensible species is impressed by means of the body upon the sensory soul.

75. Moreover, it often happens that the mind is afflicted when it senses, as when fire is touched and gall is tasted, and so on. But in such cases the mind does not seem to be acted upon by itself. Therefore it is acted upon by the body and a painful affection or species is impressed upon the mind by the body. That the mind is not acted upon by itself is clear from the fact that nothing is more friendly to the mind and is more like the mind than itself. But what afflicts is the presence not of what is loved or is similar, but of what is hated and is contrary.

76. Moreover, our intellectual cognition is caused by sensible things outside. Therefore how much more is it the case that sensory cognition is also. For in the order of nature sensory cognition is closer to sensible things ⟨than is intellectual cognition⟩. However, for sensory cognition to be caused by sensible things seems to be the same thing as for the species of sensible things, by means of which the sensible things are sensed, to be conveyed into the senses by those sensible things. The first proposition is obvious from what Aristotle says in the *Posterior Analytics*, namely, that if the sense is defective then knowledge based on that sense is also defective.⁶⁶ And in *De Anima* Aristotle says that 'what is not sentient neither learns anything nor knows anything.'⁶⁷

77. Moreover, it is in virtue of this point that the distinction is made between divine knowledge and our knowledge, that divine knowledge is the cause of things, and our knowledge is caused by things.

78. From these points (paras.69–77) it seems that body impresses a sensible species upon a sensory soul. But that a mind, or a sensory power, or a soul which senses, does not form these images in itself, can be seen from this fact, that it would in that case be able to form them at will, even without the action of a sensible thing outside. And there could then be an act of imagination without a prior exercise of sense, though the opposite of this has already been established (q.2). Augustine agrees with this in *De Trinitate*. He says: 'We can only remember as many species of bodies as we have sensed, and species of the same size as we have sensed, and in the way we sensed them. For the mind takes species into the memory from a bodily sense.'⁶⁸

79. You might say that the sensory soul cannot form such images at will,

---

65. *Ibid.*, 3; p.340 (8–12)
66. *Anal.post.*, i, 18 (81a38–40); *AL* 4, 1–4, p.40 (4–5)
67. *De an.*, iii, 8 (432a6); ed. Stroick, p.223 (77–78)
68. *De Trin.*, xi, 8; *CCSL* 50, 350 (14–17)

but that it must have a model which can be imitated, and hence it is necessary that the sense organ should receive an image from the object, and then at last the sensory soul will form in itself an image which is an imitation of the object. But against this, (i) either the sensory soul forms in itself an image while sensing what it is making, or (ii) it does not. (i) If it forms in itself an image while sensing what it is making, it cannot sense before it has been assimilated to the sensed thing. Therefore it has the image which is to be formed, and has it before it forms it. For it does not sense what is distant and not touching it, but by nature it must be touched by the thing which is to be sensed and must be assimilated to it by a mental contact before it can sense it. (ii) If the sensory soul forms in itself an image while not sensing what it is making, then it acts blindly, and does not know its own deed. Therefore it is an accident if it forms an image correctly, and it seems more likely that very frequently it will not form the image correctly.

80. Moreover, if the sensory soul were to form in itself images of sensible things, then it would make them either from nothing or from something. Not from nothing, since it does not create. If from something, there is no suitable material except itself. For the matter of a mental image must itself be mental. But it is the soul, not the body, that is mental matter. And that the soul forms a mental image from itself seems to accord with Augustine's words quoted above, where he said that mind collects and grasps images of bodies, images made in itself from itself.[69] But if the soul makes an image from itself, then the matter in the thing coincides with the efficient cause, which men think absurd. For Aristotle says that the three causes other than matter coincide, and matter does not coincide with them.[70]

81. From these points (paras.78–80) it seems that the soul does not form within itself images of sensible things. But as regards the last objection (para.80) a reasonable doubt arises about words of Augustine quoted earlier (para.67) which were taken from *De Trinitate*. For he says that the mind makes images of bodies both in itself and from itself, which seem to contradict each other. For, according to Aristotle, accidents strictly speaking have matter in which they exist but not from which they are made, and substances have matter from which they are made but not in which they exist.[71] It seems therefore that if a soul makes images within itself, it does not make them from itself, and if it makes them from itself it does not make them in itself. Or if each of these is true, then those images are at the same time substances and accidents, which is impossible.

82. Moreover, if a mind or soul makes images in itself and from itself, then

---

69. *Ibid.*, x, 5; p.321 (30–31)
70. Cf. *Phys.*, ii, 7 (198a25–27); *U* fol.23ʳ: 'The three causes often coincide'.
71. Cf. *Praed.*, 2 (1a20–29); *AL* 1, 1–5, p.47 (19–25)

it is at the same time an efficient cause and a form and matter in the same deed or effect, which does not seem possible, because matter is not believed to be able to be the same thing as an efficient cause and as form.

83. Moreover, an efficient cause and a form can be specifically the same, according to Aristotle, but not numerically the same. For the form and the internal end can coincide in a thing which is numerically one, but the efficient cause of that thing coincides with them in that thing specifically, as Aristotle says.[72] Therefore either it will be false, as it seems to be, that a soul in itself and from itself makes images, or in it there are three numerically different substances; the first is that from which the image is made, the second is the image itself, and the third makes it into an image. And again that is not possible.

84. Moreover, in expounding how we should understand the claim that mind forms in and from itself images of bodies, Augustine says:
> Mind gives to the things which are to be formed something of its own substance. But it retains something so that it may freely judge about the species of such images. And this is mind in a higher degree, that is, a rational intellect which is retained in order that it may judge. For we think that we have in common with beasts those parts of the soul which are informed by likenesses of bodies.[73]

That is what Augustine says in the same place.

85. The foregoing points are subject to the following doubt. If the mind makes images in and from itself, then how is what he adds at the end true, namely, that 'those parts of the mind which are informed by likenesses of bodies are common to us and beasts'?[74] For in *De Trinitate* he himself says: 'If the soul alone thinks, something of it is in the mind as its head, or eye, or face. Therefore it is not the soul but that in the soul which excels, which is called mind.'[75] If therefore the mind is the highest part of the human soul where reason or intellect resides, and images of bodies are formed in the lower part which we have in common with beasts, how is it true that the mind forms images in and from itself? For without doubt that word refers to the mind about which Augustine spoke in the preceding quotations and about which he speaks here. This will be sufficiently clear to someone who looks carefully at what Augustine writes in *De Trinitate*.[76]

86. Moreover, surely the mind itself, which is the highest part of the soul, forms in itself these images. If not, how does it know them, since for the mind to know anything whatever it must have either the thing itself or its likeness

---

72. *Cf.* above, para.80
73. *De Trin.*, x, 5; *CCSL* 50, 321 (31–36)
74. *Ibid.* (34)
75. *Ibid.*, xv, 7; *CCSL* 50A, 475 (10–13)
76. *Ibid.*, x, 4; *CCSL* 50, 319–320

present to it? For the mind does not see those things which are conceived by sense or imagination unless it itself is assimilated to them. If so, why does he say that those parts of the mind which are informed by likenesses of bodies are common to ourselves and beasts?

87. Moreover, why does he say 'those parts of the soul, etc.' in the plural? For there are only two parts of the cognitive soul, the sensory and the intellectual, and of these two we have only one of them, namely, the sensory, in common with beasts.

88. Moreover, in the light of the aforementioned words of Augustine with which he indicates that the images we are speaking about are substances and accidents (para.81), I ask whether they are substances or accidents. He indicates that they are substances by asserting that they are made from mind or soul.

89. Moreover, he indicates it by the following, which he says in his *Commentary on Genesis*: 'The image of a body, which is in the soul, is more worthy than is the body in its own substance.'[77]

90. Moreover, in *De Trinitate*, he says: 'A thought of the body is greater than the body itself, which is known by that thought. For the thought is a sort of life in the reason of the knower, but a body is not a life. And any life is greater than any body, not in size but in power.'[78]

91. Moreover, in *De Trinitate*, he says that the species of a body existing in the memory, and the eye of the soul thus formed, and the intention of the soul which unites them, are 'a sort of unity of the three things not now distinct by a diversity of nature, but a unity of one and the same substance, since this whole is within and the whole is one soul'.[79]

92. Moreover, further on he says, regarding the same trinity, that 'although it has been brought into the soul from without, it is acted upon inside, and nothing of it is beyond the nature of the soul itself'.[80]

93. From these points (paras.88–92) it seems that these images are the substance and also the life and very nature of the soul in which they exist. But a contrary position seems to follow from Augustine's statement (para.67) that the images are made in the mind or soul, which is an attribute of accidents.

94. Moreover, ⟨the contrary position seems to follow⟩ from this, that they are likenesses or images of sensible things, and a likeness or image is in relation to something.

95. Moreover, it seems to follow from the fact that the thing is known

---

77. *De Gen.ad litt.*, xii; *CSEL* 28, 3, 2, p.402 (4–5)
78. *De Trin.*, ix, 14; *CCSL* 50, 297 (16–19)
79. *Ibid.*, xi, 4; pp.342 (39)–343 (51)
80. *Ibid.*, 7; p.348 (32–34)

from the images. Hence images existing in the mind seem to be knowledge dispositions, and knowledge is a quality.

96. Moreover, ⟨it seems to follow⟩ from what Aristotle says [81] that those things which exist by chance, and which are in the soul, are in a 'lesser genus of being'. But he has it in mind that the remaining things, such as substances and accidents which have determinate causes, are in the complete genus of being. For from this it seems that the likenesses of sensible things which exist in the soul, are of a lesser entity than are substances and even than accidents which have determinate causes. These then are questions which can reasonably be asked in the light of Augustine's words (para.81).

97. We should return now to the principal question (para.41). It could be said in reply that the sensory soul does not produce in itself images of sensible things, but rather the sensible things themselves change first the medium, then the sense organ, thirdly the soul itself or the sensory power. For it makes an impression of its likeness continuously right throught the media up to the soul itself. And in accordance with this view it would have to be said that the first mover which impresses and produces an effect is the sensible thing, but the immediate mover is the organ which is informed by the sensible thing. Assuming this, it should be said that it is not absurd that the mind or soul be moved by the organ or the sensible thing, because the sensory soul is in potency to the sensible species, and the organ and the soul have that species in act. And that act has a natural tendency to the fulfilment of that potency. Perhaps Aristotelians would say this, for to judge from those of his writings which have reached us he does not seem to have thought differently.

98. But since we know that Saint Augustine was much more sublimely enlightened than Aristotle, especially in spiritual matters, and since it is not easy, by this reply, to do justice to the arguments which they produce on behalf of Augustine, we therefore believe that the first side of the question, which is Augustine's judgment (paras.43–68), is true, and we shall adhere to that judgment hereafter.

99. In order to understand his judgment, note that because the sensory soul is a form it works and acts continuously by flowing into the body which is matter in relation to it, and holding together, uniting, and preserving the body, and organizing it in accordance with the power which was granted to it for this purpose. And since it is a form which is a sensory life, it is responsible for the inflowing of vital inspiration, of the power of growth, sensation, preservation, health, and the natural organization, so far as that is granted to it. And just as it acts continuously by flowing into the body, so it acts in different ways in respect of the different affections or passivities of the body. For just as the action of the mind and its in-flowing is necessary for

---

81. *Ibid.*, 7 (431a11–13); p.211 (81–82)

the health, conservation, and organization of the body, so also the continuity of the soul's action is necessary for the continuity of the health of the body, and a different mode of action of the soul is necessary for the different passivities and affections of the body. For these things correspond to it on the other side. Hence the soul acts in one way in a healthy body and another in a sick one, one way in a warm body and another in a cold one, and so on.

100. The next step: since the mind moves its body in different ways corresponding to the diversity of passivities in the body, the sensory soul will therefore move the sense organ in different ways corresponding to the different ways in which the organ is affected. For the sensory soul attends continually to the health and preservation of the sense organ, just as the whole soul attends to the preservation and health of the whole body. It is for this reason that the sensory soul works in one way in the eye of a sleeper and in another in the eye of a person who is awake. And it works in the eye of a person who is awake in one way when it is not struck by the light or colour from an object, and in another way when it is struck by these things. And when it is moved or struck by these things, this is in one way when it is moved by a dim light or colour, and in another when it is moved by an intense or bright one. And so on for the other senses.

101. But all this stems from the natural desire and attention of the soul by which it takes care of the well-being, safety, and preservation of the body. And this desire to see to the health of the body, and the attention or solicitude regarding the body, are endowments of the soul, because the body is destructible and can be injured, and because it is a pleasant and useful instrument of the soul for acquiring knowledge of many things, and for obtaining something suitable and pleasant from many things. For because of this, as if by a sort of natural foresight or prudence, the soul is continually solicitous about the body, so that the soul goes forward to meet passivities or affections, of whatever kind or however great, of the body whether they come from without or within, removing, if it can, or at any rate weakening the severity of, those that displease it, and accepting those that please it.

102. It is for this reason that when an organ of sense is acted upon by a sensible object, the sensory soul goes forward to meet this passivity by which the organ is affected, attentive to all the things that happen to the organ, and according as the affection of the body is greater or less, the attention of the soul which goes forward to meet the affection will be greater ot less. When, therefore, it is this more attentive act of the soul by which it goes forward to meet the passivity of the body, the passivity does not lie hidden from the soul; this is its sensing, according to Augustine. In this, as is already clear (para.54), the body is acted upon by another body and does not act upon the soul, but the active soul goes out towards the passivity of the body. Hence, in sensing, the body is acted upon and the soul or mind acts, but by nature

the passivity comes first and the action comes next. For this reason in *De Musica*, where Augustine had in mind the things we have just been clarifying, he says, among other things: 'Not to make a long story of it, it seems to me that when the mind senses in the body it is not acted on by the body, but acts more attentively upon the body's passivities, and these actions, whether easy on account of agreeableness or difficult on account of disagreeableness, do not lie hidden from the mind. And all this is what is termed "sensing"'.[82] He also says many things similar to these a little further on in the same chapter and in the two following chapters.[83]

103. From these points (paras.99–102) it is obvious what, according to Augustine, it is to sense, and how it is done, and in what way also Augustine's account is connected to Aristotle's. From the same points too it is now easy to see in what way the soul forms within itself the image of a sensible thing. For there are two things in sensing, namely, the more attentive action of the soul in the body which is acted upon, and the perception of this action. Therefore while the soul attends to the body which is acted upon so that it moves the body according to the requirement of its passivity, ⟨the soul⟩ assimilates itself to what is acted upon according as it is acted upon. But such assimilation is just the formation of the image of a sensible thing by which ⟨formation⟩ the sense organ finds in itself what has been affected, since the affecting of the organ by the sensible object is the being-acted-upon of which we speak. And this is just the impression, made in the organ itself, of a likeness of the object. But since the soul turns its eye upon itself when thus informed by the image, the more attentive action by means of which the spirit is informed is not concealed from the spirit. And that is to sense in itself the image which it has formed in itself by acting more attentively upon the body. This will be some kind of simile for understanding this: if you place a seal before wax so that it touches it, and you assume that the wax has a life by which it turns itself towards the seal and by striking against it comes to be like it, by turning its eye upon itself it sees in itself an image of the seal. For in this way the sensory soul, by turning itself more attentively to its sense organ which has been informed by a sensible species, makes itself like the species, and by turning its own eye upon itself it sees that it is like the species. And thus it senses the sensible object outside by means of the image which it has formed in itself. The image in the organ, or the organ informed by the image, is a necessary condition of the image coming to exist in the sentient soul. But it is not the efficient cause, for the action of the sensible thing or of its image does not rise beyond the limits of corporeal nature, but once it has reached the innermost part of the sense organ it stays there. On the other

---

82. *De musica*, vi, 5 (10); *PL* 32, 1169
83. *Ibid.*, (10–12); *PL* 32. 1169–1170

hand the sensory soul, which presides over the sense organ, and is directed towards its passivities while it flows more attentively into the organ which has been thus affected, penetrates it through and through, co-mingles with the mental image and assimilates itself to it.

104. At the same time that it sees itself thus assimilated, it also sees the image in the sense organ to which it has assimilated itself. But it does not distinguish one image from the other, that is, the image which the sensible thing made in the sense organ, and the image which the soul itself made when co-mingling with the image which is in the organ. However, since they are together and simultaneous, as I say, rolled together or conjoined, the one which is formed in the organ is seen or sensed by means of the one which is formed in the soul, though the two are sensed simultaneously; but the outer one by means of the inner one. For no cognitive power knows unless earlier, at any rate earlier in nature, it was assimilated to the thing which was to be known. And hence it should not be thought that the sensory soul senses the image which is outside ⟨it⟩ within the organ in such a way that it was not previously assimilated to it. For this does not seem possible to me. But because there are, in this way, two images, one in the bodily organ and the other in the soul which moves the organ, even though, in the act of sensing, these two are not distinguished, it is obvious from this that the image soon vanishes from the organ but remains in the soul. Hence reason acquires a diversity which the sensory power did not perceive.

105. On the basis of these points (paras.99–104) one can in some way gather what sensing is, according to Augustine, how it is done, how far the action of the sensible thing outside reaches, in what way and when the action of the sensory soul goes forward towards it, and why and in what way the soul forms in itself a likeness of the sensible thing and senses it.

106. Here someone might raise a doubt in the following way. If the explanation put forward is true, there seem to be not merely three seeings but four. For in the seeing which Augustine calls 'corporeal' there seem to be two, for in such seeing the soul which is informed by the sensible image is seen and so also is the sensible thing seen by means of its image in the sense organ.

107. Moreover, in corporeal seeing there will be not only one trinity for the purpose of discovering the traces of the uncreated Trinity but two. For there seems to be one when the eye of the soul is turned towards the soul itself, and a second one when what is seen is conjoined with the seeing. And on the two sides there is a single connecting intention of the mind. And in that case Augustine does not distinguish sufficiently the trinities of the outer man in which we find traces of the supreme Trinity. For he posits only one trinity in corporeal seeing, this consisting of the thing seen and the seeing and the intention of the mind which connects those two. And he calls 'seeing' the

sense informed by the thing which is sensed. And he also calls the sense the organ of sensing. These things are clear in *De Trinitate*.[84]

108. Reply to the first objection (para.106). It should be said that there are not two seeings there, since the two things are seen simultaneously and inseparably in the corporeal seeing. For as soon as the sensible thing outside ceases to be seen, the corporeal seeing ceases to exist and the imaginative seeing begins to exist.

109. The reply to the second objection (para.107) is now obvious. Augustine did not count two trinities there, for they cannot be separated, unless the second of them comes to exist inside the imagination when the sense ceases. And then there is an imaginative seeing and its trinity, which is what Augustine is concerned about in *De Trinitate* after the seeing which comes about with corporeal seeing.[85] Since therefore he does not posit different trinities unless they are manifestly mutually separable, and not distinguishable solely by the intellect, he did not posit two trinities in corporeal seeing, nor should he have done. But he included the sensory soul seeing itself under the heading 'seeing', for an organ of sense informed by a sensible thing is a living part, or under the heading 'intention of the mind conjoining seeing with thing seen', for the intention of the mind and the sentient soul and its eye are in reality the same thing, since they are the mind — and I mean the mind which is common to us and beasts.

110. But you will say to this: If the sentient soul first turns its eye upon itself and then upon its sense organ, why is it not said to sense both itself and the sense organ?

111. Reply. It is because it does not turn its eye upon these two things except in so far as they are informed by the sensible thing, and the eye of the soul does not stop at these things but passes on to the sensible thing. And neither the intention to sense nor the action itself terminates at these two things, but it is the sensible thing outside which is the end, and therefore that alone is rightly said to be sensed. I think that all the things that have now been said in the above explication (paras.103–105) have become sufficiently clear.

112. Once the arguments and texts introduced in connection with the first part of the question (paras.43–68) have been conceded, it is easy to reply to the first point made against the objection (para.69). For in sensing, two motions come together as if from opposite sides. For one proceeds from a sensible thing which is actually causing a change, and via the medium reaches the sense organ, coming right up to its innermost part where it is united with the sensory soul. The other proceeds from the sensory soul so as to meet the passivity which has been produced in the sense organ, and in the meeting of

---

84. *Cf.* Aug. *De Trin.*, xi, 2; *CCSL* 50, 334 (1)–336 (50)
85. *Ibid.*, 4; p.343 (45–51)

these motions, by the action of the sensory soul attending to its sense organ there is formed in the sensory soul an image of a sensible thing by means of which that sensible thing is sensed. Thus Aristotle's words: 'Sense receives sensible species without matter', are about the sense organ. For that organ is called 'sense', which is what Augustine calls it, as will soon be plain (para.118). This can be established by the fact that Aristotle speaks there (para.69) only of the change by which the medium and the organ are changed by the sensible object. For his investigation there does not proceed further or deeper. Moreover, in what he says, namely, that this change comes about 'just as if the signet were inserted into the wax right up to the end', 'end' should be understood to refer to the innermost limit of corporeal nature. For it is there that the end of action proceeding from a body is located. So the reply to the first objection is obvious.

113. Reply to the second objection (para.70). It should be said that strictly speaking the organ is a sense organ not because it impresses the received species upon the sensory power, but because by means of it, or with its support, the impression comes into existence. But it comes into existence by virtue of the sensory soul embracing, and co-mingling with, the species found in the organ. It is in this way that one should understand the physical doctrine concerning the way sensing occurs, and then Aristotle's doctrine will accord with Augustine's.

114. Reply to the third objection (para.71), where Augustine is invoked. It should be said that this is not contrary to the thesis. For a state of the ears is only a state of the body. But from that it does not follow that the state of the ears produces a state of the auditory soul, although it is one cause of that. And that is clear enough from things already set forth (paras.99–105).

115. Reply to the fourth objection (para.72) which is drawn from the Letter to Nebridius. It should be said that images, also called 'phantasms', are impressed by things which have been sensed, thought about, and calculated, that is, impressed by means of these things. But it does not follow that they are impressed by them as by their efficient causes. But images, by which sense organs are affected, are impressed by sensed things. And then, with the support of sensed things, images, called 'phantasms', are impressed upon the soul, but not by the sensed things as efficient causes.

116. But you might say that if an image in the sense organ is like a seal, and the sensory soul is like wax, as in the foregoing illustration (para.103), then just as it is conceded that the seal impresses a figure on the wax and is the efficient cause of the figure, so also it should be conceded here.

117. Reply. Something is an efficient cause (i) properly speaking and by its nature, or (ii) commonly and by accident. Taken in the first way, the seal is not the cause of the figure in the wax, but whoever impresses the seal in the wax is the efficient cause. For the person who impresses the seal is by his

nature the proper cause of the impression. Taken in the second way, the seal is the efficient cause of the figure because it is that by means of which the figure is effected. But the seal is effective only by being moved by the one who impresses it. Hence just as the instrument of an artificer is not the mover or the efficient cause of the artifact except accidentally and in an extended sense, so it is in the case of the foregoing example. We should understand the matter in the same way as regards the image, in the sense organ, of the sensible thing and the image made in the sensory soul. For the image in the sense organ is the efficient cause of the image in the sensory soul, taking 'efficient' commonly and accidentally, because it is effected by means of it. But the motivating sensory soul which applies to itself the image found in the sense organ, and co-mingles that image with itself, makes itself like that organ and makes in itself an image similar to the one in the organ. Thereafter the image in the sensory soul is called a 'phantasm'.

118. Reply to the fifth objection (para.74) which is drawn from *De Trinitate*. It should be said that the clause: 'the mind takes in the species through a bodily sense'[86] was said metaphorically. For just as a liquid is drunk through a straw so also the species is drawn in through the bodily organ, but with this difference, that in the former case numerically the same liquid which was in the straw is drawn within, but in the latter case what is within the soul is similar to, but not exactly the same as, what was in the bodily organ. And therefore Augustine says that the species was taken in through a bodily sense, that is, through a bodily organ, for that is a support and a sort of vessel from which the species is in some way drawn up. But that phrase, where he says that sense is formed from a sensible body, should be understood in such a way that 'sense' refers to the bodily organ and not to the sensory soul. Hence Augustine says in *De Trinitate* : 'The sense of the eyes is called a sense of the body for no other reason than that the eyes are themselves parts of the body. And although the body does not sense mindlessly, nevertheless the mind, mixed with the body by means of an organ, is called a 'sense', which is also extinguished by a passivity of the body when someone is blinded .' [87]

119. Moreover, in *De Musica* Augustine says: 'This sense, which nevertheless is inherent even while we are sensing nothing, is an organ of the body which, with that adjustment, is acted on by the mind in order that the sense, by its attentiveness, may be more ready to produce in the body passivities of the body.'[88] From these points (paras.118–119) it is obvious how Augustine understands 'sense', and the term should be taken in a similar way in Aristotle's *De Anima*, as we said above (para.112). And it is obvious from

---

86. *Ibid.*, xi, 3; *CCSL* 50, 340 (11–12)
87. *Ibid.*, 2; p.335 (36–41)
88. *De Musica*, vi, 5 (10); *PL* 32, 1169

these points that Augustine does not mean that the body forms in the soul an image of a corporeal and sensible thing.

120. Reply to the sixth objection (para.75). It should be said, according to Augustine, that the mind which suffers in sensing is not acted upon essentially by the body, neither is the species of something painful impressed upon the mind essentially by the body, but by the mind itself. For sometimes the mind goes out to meet the passivities of the body with an action which is easy on account of the agreeing ⟨of the passivities⟩, sometimes with an action which is difficult on account of the disagreeing ⟨of the passivities⟩. And this perceived or apprehended difficulty is called 'travail' and 'pain'. So the mind is not afflicted by an action of the body except so far as it is said that something that resists and is not obedient acts, but it is afflicted by its own action which is produced with difficulty. For, properly speaking, the soul is afflicted by something which produces a troublesome action and hence the soul is burdened by it. Thus Augustine says in *De Musica*: 'Whatever corporeal things are conveyed into our body or are thrown against it do something not in the mind but in the body itself, because it either opposes its work or fits in with it. For that reason when it resists something which opposes it and with difficulty strikes against the matter which is subject to it in its own ways of working, due to the difficulty it becomes more attentive to the action. This difficulty, by reason of the attentiveness (since it is not hidden from the mind), is called 'sensing', and it is called 'pain' and 'travail'.[89]

121. Moreover, in *De Musica* Augustine says: 'When the mind is acted upon by its own operations, it is acted upon by itself, not by the body.'[90] And you can readily understand this to be saying that the sense organ or the sensory body is hurt by the forceful prominence of a disproportionate sensible thing. But when injured it is less fitted to receive a motion of the mind and is less governable by it, and therefore the mind moves the sense organ by a more difficult action, and is troubled by this difficulty. Hence the troubled state of the mind is not due to the body as an efficient cause, but to disobedient and resistant matter. But the troubled state is from the mind's acting with difficulty, as from a moving and efficient cause. In such difficulties the body does not impress a species upon the mind, but the mind itself, penetrating and governing the body and co-mingling itself with the species found within it, impresses the species on itself by means of the species with which it co-mingles itself.

122. As to the argument (para.75) with which he wished to show that the mind cannot be acted upon by itself, it should be said that he commits the

---

89. *Ibid.*, v, 5 (9); *PL* 32, 1168
90. *Ibid.*, vi, 5 (12); *PL* 32, 1169-1170

fallacy of the accident.[91] For when he argues in this way: 'The mind is like and is friendly to itself, and nothing is acted upon by what is like and is friendly to itself; therefore the mind is not acted upon by itself', this is not valid unless this conclusion is drawn: 'therefore it is not acted upon by itself, like and friendly to itself, according as it is that kind'. If this conclusion is drawn then this does not follow: 'therefore the mind is not acted upon by itself', on account of the qualification. Therefore in so far as the mind seeks agreement and likeness, it is acted upon by itself with difficulty when acting on account of the disagreement and unlikeness.

123. Reply to the seventh objection (para.76). It should be said that cognition, whether intellectual or sensitive, is caused by sensible things as by a necessary condition, not as by a cause which principally and essentially is an efficient cause of cognition and informs the mind, but as by a necessary instrument or a necessary occasion. For the art of the artificer is essentially the cause of the statue, but the adze is the accidental cause as the necessary instrument by means of which the art is exercised. Likewise, the mind going out to meet the passivities of the body is essentially the cause of cognition; the sensible things and the sense organ are an accidental cause like an instrument or instruments used by the mind in order to become informed. Moreover, when an unskilled person considers the artificer at work and strives to imitate him in his work and thence acquires the art, the essential cause of the art in that man is his attentive consideration and studious imitation of the artificer. But the accidental cause, which is like a necessary occasion, is the example of the artificer who has been imitated. So it is in the case before us. The essential cause of the cognition is the operation of the mind in the body, going out to meet the passivities of the body. But the necessary occasion is the act of the sensible thing and the passivity of the body or of the sense organ.

124. Reply to the eighth objection (para.78). It should be said that though a human being generates a human being, he cannot do this whenever and wherever he wants, but a due opportunity must be present along with due accessories. Likewise though a writer write a letter, he cannot write without the use of accessories. Likewise with every efficient principle in nature as well

---

91. The fallacy occurs when: '...any attribute is claimed to belong in a like manner to a thing and to its accident. For since the same thing has many accidents, there is no necessity that all the same attributes should belong to all of a thing's predicates and to their subject as well', Aristotle *Sophistical Refutations* (166b23 ff). Aristotle immediately gives two examples, neither of which fits well his initial description of the fallacy: 'Thus, if Coriscus is different from a man, he is different from himself for he is a man; or if he is different from Socrates, and Socrates is a man then, they say, he has admitted that Coriscus is different from a man because it so happens that the person from whom he said that he (Coriscus) is different is a man.' See C.L.Hamblin *Fallacies* London 1970, 84-87; H.G.Gelber 'The fallacy of accident and the Dictum de Omni' *Vivarium* 25, 1987, 110-145.

as in art. And so it is in the case before us. For although the sensory soul forms in itself the image of a sensible thing it cannot do this without opportunity and due accessories, such as a sensible thing being present and changing both the medium and the sense organ. But the image of the sensible thing is not required in the sense organ as a model in imitation of which the soul forms an image in itself, for a model is properly placed before those acting by art and reason. But it is required as a necessary disposition of the organ in order to give an occasion to the soul, and as a natural prop for the soul, necessary if the spirit is to assimilate itself to the sensible thing outside.

125. Reply to the counter-argument which is proposed there (para.79), where it is asked whether the sensory soul forms within itself an image, whether sensing what it effects or not. The following distinction should be made: there are two things in sensing, as has already been said (para.103), namely, (i) the action of the mind which is attending to the body, in and by means of which action an image is formed in the mind, and (ii) the turning of the eye ⟨of the mind⟩ upon itself, in and by means of which ⟨turning⟩ the image is sensed. Therefore either these two things happen at the same time in the same instant, though one be prior, the other posterior, in nature, or they happen at different instants with an intervening mediate time, whether sensible or insensible.

126. If they happen in the first way, it should be said that the soul, sensing what it is making, forms in itself an image. That is, it forms the image at the time that it is sensing it. For the image is formed and sensed at the same instant. But what follows is not that before the soul forms the image it possesses the image which is to be formed, but that it has a formed image before it senses it. For the forming and the apprehending do not occur simultaneously in the order of nature, though they are simultaneous in time. For in the order of nature the forming occurs before the sensing, and in the order of time the forming and sensing are simultaneous. For that is how things are as regards the change in the medium and in the sense organ in the case of the sense of sight. They are changed simultaneously in the temporal order, but in the order of nature one is earlier and the other is later.

127. If they happen in the second way, it should be said that the soul forms in itself an image, but does not yet sense it since it has not yet turned its eye upon it. But it does not follow that it acts accidentally, like a blind thing, since it has acted naturally. For nature, acting without either art or its own cognition, is directed by higher cognitive principles as if they were principles of skill, in the way in which an instrument is directed by the artificer using his skill. For lower and particular nature acts, remembered by

higher causes, as Avicenna says.⁹² It is for this reason that nature, forming the parts of an animal's body, and leaves, flowers and fruits of trees and plants, and all such things, would do all these things as if by art and cognition. This is not because nature has the art and cognition within itself, but either because it is directed by certain souls which move, direct, and rule corporeal nature, whether or not those souls are the movers of heavenly bodies; or because it is directed by the spirit of God, who presides over all things, and moves, rules, and directs all things; or because directed by both, which is perhaps closer to the truth. For it is this third possibility that Augustine seems to have in mind in *De Musica*, where he teaches that temporal measures existing in silence precede spatial measures: 'Also a vital motion precedes and modifies them, serving the Lord of all things, not having separate temporal intervals of its own measures, but governing times with power. Above that power blessed rational souls transmit the very law of God, without which no leaf falls from a tree, and by which our hairs are counted without nature being interposed, coming as far as earthly and infernal laws.'⁹³

128. From these points (127) it is plain that the sensory soul, forming in itself an image of a sensible thing, even if it were to do this without sensing or apprehending the image up to this point, is not making the image accidentally but naturally and, as if directed by superior causes which have the cognition and the regulative art, is led by a natural instinct. And hence there is nothing accidental in its work except perhaps due to some accidental impediment, as often happens in the case of other works of nature.

129. Reply to the last objection (para.80), regarding Augustine's judgment that the soul in and from itself forms an image of a sensible thing. Though the argument is unsatisfactory, it does not seem to me that its unsatisfactoriness lies in this, that the same thing is the efficient cause of something and from itself also passes on to that same thing its matter. For it is in this way that a human generates a human being and a horse generates a horse. And in some way he who generates passes on from himself the matter to what is generated. And this seems commonly true in those things which generate by the separating of seed. But the argument from Aristotle is not in conflict with that. For in the same place Aristotle says that the three causes often coincide, but he does not deny that matter coincides with one of those three causes. It should be said therefore that just as something which generates by means of the separating of seed is an efficient cause in respect of something

---

92. Averroes (not Avicenna). See Averr. *In Metaph.*, xii, 3 (1070a28–30); ed. Venetiis, 1574, text.118, fol. 303ᵛˡ⁻ᴸ: 'Art does nothing in the body, except at the extremities only, whereas nature acts in the whole body. And this is not to be wondered at, even though nature does not understand such things. Nevertheless it does this by introducing a directedness [into the body]. This shows that something reminds it of nobler causes.'
93. *De musica*, vi, 17 (58); *PL* 32, 1192–1193

within itself and in relation to something else passes on matter, so also in the soul in respect of something of itself, whether a mode or a concept, it becomes an efficient cause, and in relation to something else it becomes the material for the image.

130. And if you ask why Aristotle does not mention matter when he says that the other three causes coincide since matter can coincide with those three causes or with one of them, it should be said that the reason for this may be that Aristotle is dealing there with the four causes so far as they are dealt with in the study of physics. But this study of physics concerns things in motion in so far as they are of that kind, namely, movers and movable things. Hence all things with physical power lead back to two pre-eminent genera, the active and the passive. But we now see that the three causes about which Aristotle speaks are contained within the genus 'mover'; matter however is not but is contained in the genus 'movable thing'. Since therefore Aristotle perhaps meant to say that the three causes fall under the genus 'mover', under which matter does not fall properly and essentially, he was therefore silent about matter.

131. Alternatively the explanation is that the three causes coincide in almost every act of natural generation, since that happens in all cases except in those where the generation is not univocal, as for example in the case of a celestial body, which is not a body in the sense in which generated bodies are bodies. But matter rarely coincides with the efficient cause. Therefore Aristotle says that the three often coincide, and he is silent about matter.

132. Alternatively, but in a way which fits sufficiently well what Aristotle says, it can be said that the three causes coincide, but that matter never coincides with any of the causes; so that Aristotle should be understood to be speaking only about things which can be generated naturally, which are subsistent, and about their causes; that is, he is speaking about substances of which there is generation without qualification, and which have strictly speaking a matter from which they are generated. And then the matter of the things which are generated by means of the separating of seed does not coincide with the efficient cause since what is separated is not the matter of such a thing except after the separation, that is, when there is actual seed. And then it does not coincide with the efficient generative cause, for it is not the same in genus, or species, or number. But the image formed in the soul is not that kind of generated thing. For strictly speaking it does not have a matter from which it came, and there is not an unqualified, but only a relative, generating of it, as will become clear later (para.138). Hence the words of Aristotle quoted above should not be understood to be about a generated thing of that kind or about its causes.

133. It should be said therefore, according to this form of reply, that there are two ways of understanding 'to have a matter from which a thing comes',

namely strictly and broadly. Taken in the first way, substances have a matter from which they come, and it is of these substances only that Aristotle's words, quoted above, should be understood. Taken in the second way, accidents also have a matter from which they come, and Aristotle should not be understood to be using the phrase in this sense. And among accidents there is an image in the soul, as will already be obvious (para.81), when the phrase is taken strictly and formally. It could also be said that Aristotle is speaking of those things which come into existence by a physical motion, strictly speaking, but an image does not come to exist in the soul in this way.

134. Moreover it could be said that when Augustine says (paras.67, 80): 'the soul or mind makes, in and from itself, likenesses of bodies', the preposition 'from' can denote natural power and not matter, so that the sense is this: 'from itself, that is, from its power and naturally', as if to say that it is from the strength and power of its own nature that it forms in itself images of corporeal things. And if it is understood in this way the whole objection concerning material cause is blocked.

135. On the basis of what has now been said (paras.97–134) let us try to give a satisfactory reply to the principal question. Accordingly a reply should be given to the questions raised concerning Augustine's words in *De Trinitate* (paras.81–96). Reply to the first objection (para.81). If the preposition 'from' is taken to denote strength or power, then the doubt vanishes. If it is taken to denote matter then it should be said that accidents can be considered in two ways, namely, (i) materially and in relation to a subject, and (ii) formally and essentially [= *per se*]. Taken in the first way images have matter from which they are made; taken in the second way they have matter in which they exist. For this white[94] has matter from which it is made and whiteness has matter in which it exists. Thus an image of Hercules, if that means a shape with matter, so that by the term 'image' something concrete is understood, has matter from which it is made. If 'image' means a shape as such, not a shape in relation to matter, it comes to exist in matter. The situation is the same as regards a board on which an image is painted, since sometimes the whole board with the painting is called an image, and sometimes the painting by itself. It is therefore in this way that ⟨the soul⟩ makes images of bodies in and from itself; in itself if the images are considered formally, and from itself if they are considered materially. And it is not absurd that in one of these ways they are placed in the genus of substance, and in the other way in the genus of accident, in accordance with these different aspects. For in virtue of their matter they are to be counted among substances; in virtue of their form they are counted among accidents.

136. Reply to the second objection (para.83). It should be said that there

---

94. 'this white' — a particular accident, not 'a white thing' or 'whiteness'.

are not three numerically different substances there but only one; but the one substance does have different powers or modes. For the sensory soul is active in the body towards the passivities of the body, and hence it conforms itself with those same passivities. Also it is conformable with those same passivities. In the first way it produces images in itself; in the second way it is the matter or subject of those images — matter if the images are considered materially, subject if they are considered formally.

137. As for the objection (para.82) that a material and an efficient cause ought not to coincide, enough has already been said (paras.130–132).

138. Reply to the objection (para.83) that form and efficient cause do not coincide in a thing which is one numerically, but rather one specifically. This is to be said of those things whose generation is simple, that is, substances where what generates and what is generated are numerically distinct and different, and also where the generative act is univocal; since sometimes what generates and what is generated are not specifically the same. For a donkey coupled with a mare generates a mule, which is an animal of another species. But the aforementioned proposition, so far as it contradicts this, is not true as regards the equivocal generation of substances, and nor should it be true as regards the generation of accidents, since white can be generated by non-white. This is especially the case as regards the generation of relations, which is mentioned in the passage under discussion. For someone can make himself a servant, and he is in fact the same person who makes the servant, and who becomes the servant or in whom servility comes to exist. Likewise someone puts himself on the right side of another, or makes himself a companion or friend of that other, and so on. Thus in the passage under discussion the soul makes itself like the sensible thing, and it is the same soul which makes like, and becomes like, and in which likeness comes to exist. But note this, that the efficient cause and the form do not coincide in what is in fact the same thing, if the image is considered formally, except as that which is in something, and that in which it is. If the image is considered materially they are the same in that way, since the one is the other.

139. Reply to the third objection (para.85). It should be said that 'mind' [= *mens*] is always taken to mean the rational and intellectual part. But this can be in two ways. In one way it involves, along with itself, the lower parts and powers of the mind; in the other it is itself alone and not involved with these other things. It is this second way that is at issue when the mind is spoken of in the text taken from *De Trinitate* 15. But it is the first way that is at issue in *De Trinitate* 10 (para.84). And the point is to be understood in this way, that the mind gives of its substance to the images in order to form them, so that the substance of the mind is understood to go along with the conjoining of the remaining parts and powers of the mind, since it gives to the images to be formed what we have in common with beasts, and it serves

to judge about those things, and in such judging we surpass them. And therefore the passage adds: 'that is more a mind, that is, a rational intellect', namely, that which judges, to indicate that 'mind' was not being used in its strictest sense when, in the passage, mind is conjoined with that which we have in common with beasts.

140. Reply to the fourth objection (para.86). So far as I can see, the mind not only gives over a lower part of the soul to receiving images of sensible things, but it also forms them in itself. But the mind is so simple and subtle by nature in relation to the lower [= *brutalis*] part of the soul, that it is assimilated to sensible things outside only by means of a mental image made earlier in that lower part, just as that same lower part, by virtue of its subtlety, is not naturally suited to be informed immediately by a sensible thing outside, unless the external thing first be elevated so that it have in some measure a spiritual existence in the sense organ by means of its image which was made in that organ. Therefore just as the sensory soul needs an organ and needs also an outside medium between itself and the sensible thing outside, so also the mind needs an imaginative and a sensory soul between itself and the sense organ. And that is because, in respect of spirituality and corporeality, there is so great a distance between the aforementioned extremes that the extremes are not naturally fitted to be united so as to produce and receive a cognition except via the media. In those media the species of the sensible thing is rendered subtle and is elevated so that it comes into harmony with a power which ought to know, so that by means of the species a cognition comes into existence. But although the mind is informed by these likenesses or images of corporeal things, nevertheless Augustine says that the mind gives over to the images which are to be formed the part of the soul which we have in common with beasts. For it is in that part that they are first formed, and via that part they rise right up to the mind itself.

141. Reply to the fifth objection (para.87). It should be said that the objection mentioned 'parts of the soul' in the plural, not because there are several cognitive parts which are essentially different and are common to ourselves and beasts, but because there are several powers, such as the fantasy or imaginative power, and a sensory power which is of more than one kind, the common and the particular, and the latter is itself divisible into various kinds.

142. Reply to the question which was then asked, and was occasioned by Augustine's words (para.88), namely, whether the image of a sensible thing in a soul is a substance or an accident. The question can now readily be answered on the basis of what has already been said (paras.135–136). For if the image is considered in respect of its matter it is a substance; if in respect of its form it is an accident. For just as a man, whether a friend, or on the right side, or a servant, is a substance whereas friendship, rightness, or

servility is an accident, so also an image, considered as a mind assimilated to a sensible thing, is a substance; whereas that image, considered as an assimilative act, which is nothing but a respect and a relation, is an accident. Taking 'image' in that first way, the arguments on the first side of the question (paras.88–92) should be conceded. Taking 'image' in the second way, the arguments on the second side (paras.93–96) should be conceded.

143. It remains now to see in what way the imagination acquires images of sensible things by means of the senses. This is now clear in the light of what has already been said. For since, in sensing, the sensory soul acquires those images, and then it retains them after the act of sensing has ceased, the imagination now has them from this retentive act. For the soul which is sensory on account of its turning towards the present sensible thing, is the very same in substance as the imaginative soul on account of its turning towards the image of that same sensible thing in the absence of the sensible thing outside. The images are acquired by the imagination in this way, namely, by the sentient soul acquiring the images and retaining them and, after the cessation of the act of sensing, passing them on into the imagination. And it should not be thought here that the image acquired by the sensory soul from itself begets the image in the imagination, but rather that that self-same image acquired in sensing produces a sensation in the presence of the sensible thing, and thereafter it produces an imaginative act in the absence of that same sensible thing.

144. Aristotle's definition in *De Anima* agrees with this. There he says: 'Imagination is motion made by sense in act.' [95] So also does Augustine's definition: 'Imagination is nothing but a blow struck by the senses'.[96]

145. Augustine has the same thing in mind in *De Vera Religione* : 'Mental images are nothing but figments, entrusted to the memory, which are drawn from the species of a body by a bodily sense.' [97]

146. Moreover, in the same book he says: 'Places present what we would love, times snatch away what we do love, and they leave in the mind throngs of images, by which desire would be stimulated to one thing and then another.' [98]

147. Moreover he says further on: 'Mental images, thrust forward, are pondered by the eyes of the mind.' [99]

148. Moreover in *De Trinitate* he says that 'from a bodily sense the mind takes into the memory species of sensible things'.[100]

---

95. *De an.*, iii, 3 (429a1–2); ed. Stroick, p.175 (88)
96. *Ep.* 7, 2 (3); *CSEL* 34, 14 (26–27)
97. *De vera relig.*, 10, (18); *CCSL* 32, 199 (10–12)
98. *Ibid.*, 35 (65); p.230 (8–11)
99. *Ibid.*, 39 (73); p.235 (31)
100. *De Trin.*, xi, 8; *CCSL* 50, 350 (16–17)

149. Moreover in *On Genesis* he says: 'When something is discerned by the eyes, an image of it immediately comes to exist in the soul. But the image which has been made is not known unless, with eyes removed from that thing which we were looking at with our eyes, we find an image of that thing in the mind.'[101] And a little further on: 'King Belshazzar saw the fingers of a hand writing on the wall, and the image of the thing made by means of something corporeal was immediately impressed, via the sense organ, upon his soul, and when the seeing was over and done the image remained in the thought.'[102] There are many such things which indicate clearly enough the aforesaid way of admitting species of sensible things into the imagination, or of impressing them on, or of their being acquired by, the imagination, to which imaginative seeing belongs.

⟨*Doubts about mental or imaginative seeing*⟩

150. But it is not inappropriate to seek something which would shed more light upon this way ⟨in which species are impressed upon the imagination⟩. First therefore I shall ask how it is supposed that likenesses or images of corporeal things are received by sense and retained by imagination, since it seems rather that it is certain motions of the mind towards passivities of the body that are stored in the imagination. For Augustine, speaking in *De Musica* about these things which are transmitted to the memory by means of sense, says this: 'Whatever things this memory retains from the motions of the mind which are directed to passivities of the body, are called 'fantasies' [= 'mental images'] in Greek.'[103] Since, therefore, sensing is nothing but a more attentive motion of the mind directed towards passivities of the body, a motion which is not concealed from it, as we learn earlier in the same book, the only things which seem to be transmitted to the memory from sense are motions or impulses of the mind which the mind produces in the direction of the passivities of the body when it senses. Aristotle also seems to mean this when he says that a fantasy is a motion made by sense when in act.[104]

151. A second doubt concerns the way in which these motions or likenesses reach or are brought to the imagination, there to remain. For since the imaginative soul and the sensory soul are in fact the same, as has already been said (para.2), this has to be understood to be true only, or especially, of the common sense, for imagination uses images of all sensible things and it is only the common sense that deals with, and knows, all sensible things. It is

---

101. *De Gen.ad litt.*, xii, 11; *CSEL* 28, 3, 2, p.393 (11–14)
102. *Ibid.*, 22 (25)
103. *De musica*, vi, 11 (32); *PL* 32, 1180
104. *De an.*, iii, 3 (429a1–2); ed. Stroick, p.175 (88)

for this reason that Aristotle teaches that dreaming is a passivity of the common sense in so far as it is the fantasy,[105] that is, the imagination, for dreaming especially involves acts of imagination. But the acquisition of the images of sensible things for the sensory power or soul comes about primarily and principally in the particular senses. For it is in the particular senses that the mind goes out to meet the passivities of the body. Regarding these images which have been acquired in the organs of the particular senses and which are to be placed in the fantasy or imagination which comes after the common sense, I therefore ask how they reach the common sense from the particular senses. For it is only by means of the intermediate common sense that they reach the imagination.

152. The reason for raising this doubt here is that the species of sensible things move only in a straight line, because they are mental lights that are produced from corporeal forms by radiation so that the forms may be revealed. But although the motion from the object up to the organs of the particular senses is straight, it is not thereafter straight from the particular senses to the common sense and its organ. For this organ, according to the authorities,[106] is in the front of the brain or in the heart or round about it. But it is not possible to draw straight lines from such an organ by way of the individual organs of the particular senses to the sensible object outside, and perhaps indeed they cannot be drawn by way of any of those organs.

153. Moreover, there is a second reason for raising this doubt, namely, that the species of individual sensible things proceed by moving via a necessary disposition in that which is changed and without which ⟨the medium⟩ would not be changed, as for example colour which changes something transparent and lit up, and sound which changes air or water which has been moved, and so on. But it does not seem possible to discover such inner dispositions from the organs of the proper senses to the organ of common sense. How, therefore, will likenesses of sensible things reach the organ of common sense from the organs of the proper senses?

154. You might say that it is not necessary for these likenesses to be borne beyond the organ of the proper senses, for the sensory soul is assimilated to the likenesses there, and after that assimilative act sense remains assimilated to them, and hence it is not necessary for the likenesses to be borne onward

---

105. *Cf.* Aristotle *De insomn.*, 1 (149a8–22); ed. Drossaart Lulofs. pp.6 (13)–8 (16)
106. *Cf.* Avicenna *Liber de anima*, i, 5; ed. Van Riet, 1, 87: 'The first of the vital, hidden, apprehensive powers is imagination which is the common sense. This is the power which is arranged in the first concavity of the brain, receiving by its own means all the forms which are impressed by the five senses and are led back to it.' See also Costa ben Luca *De differentia animae et spiritus*, 2: ed. Barach, p.126: 'Understanding, thinking, and practical reasoning are carried out by means of the soul which is in the ventricle shared by the two ventricles at the front of the brain.'

via bodily pathways, for the soul itself already informed by the likenesses presides, everywhere one and the same and not multiple in respect of its substance, in these pathways and in the whole body. But this does not seem true, for just as a proper sense must know the sensible thing appropriate to it, and each of the individual proper senses must know the individual sensible things appropriate to it, so also the common sense must at the same time know and distinguish all the individual sensible things. It is for this reason that just as a proper sensory soul cannot in any way do that except by means of the bodily organ, so also the common sensory soul cannot know and distinguish all the individual sensible things except by means of the organ of common sense. And so the species of all sensible things received in the organs of the proper senses must pass onward and inward from those organs to the organ of common sense.

155. Moreover, it is common to every sense, whether a proper or a common sense, to receive the species of sensible things and, in those species, to know the sensible things while still present. Therefore the species of sensible things must reach the common sense and its organ.

156. Moreover, if things were indeed as the foregoing reply supposes (para.154), why would the common sense need to have an organ? It does not seem that it would. But Aristotle plainly teaches otherwise. Thus he says: 'There is a common sense for all sensible things and there is its own organ of sensing.'[107] Since therefore the common sense has its own organ to which the organs of the proper senses are connected, and since Aristotle says towards the end of *De Anima* that a sense is moved by a sensible thing just as if a signet were pushed into wax to the end,[108] what does this mean but that the species of sensible things, received in the organs of the proper senses, carry on inward as far as the organ of common sense, where the end of the sensing and of the sensory soul is?

157. But given that species proceed from a proper sense to the common, and given the way in which they do so, questions can be raised as to (i) how a species passes from sense to imagination, and (ii) what the specific difference is between sense and imagination, and (iii) what the order of them is. For it will then be completely clear how images of sensible things are acquired by imagination via sense.

158. A third doubt. This concerns the permanence of the species received. For I ask whether or not the species remain in the body itself, in the organ, and there present themselves to be imagined when the mind directs itself to them.

159. For Aristotle seems to think that they do. He says: 'Sensible things

---

107. *De somno et vig.*, 2 (455a19–21); ed. Droissaart Lulofs, p.4*a (17–18).
108. *De an.*, iii, 12 (435a9–10); ed. Stroick, p.245 (86)

affect the sense in respect of an individual sense organ in us, and the passivity which is produced by the sensible things is present in the sense organs not only when the senses are active, but also when they are inactive.'[109] This is shown by experience of visible and audible things.

160. But Augustine seems to think the opposite. In *De Trinitate* he says: 'This informing of sense which is called "seeing" is impressed only by the body which is seen, that is, by something which is visible. When this thing is withdrawn then the form which was in the sense while what was seen was present does not remain, just as in water there is a trace of a body as long as the body which is impressed on the water is in it, and when the body is removed the trace will cease.'[110]

161. A fourth doubt. This concerns the permanence of species in the soul itself. The question is: By means of what nature does the soul retain the species which have been received, and on account of what is it enabled to retain them in this way?

162. Moreover, by what means does it retain such a multitude of species at the same time without bringing confusion to desire? For when many desirable things, or many things which should be avoided, or both, are grasped at the same time, desire seems to be confused since it does not know what to do.

163. Moreover, there is a doubt concerning the way in which species could move desire, given that nothing can move desire unless grasped by means of a cognition.

164. But it does not seem that imagination can have a cognition. For every cognition is produced by means of light and in the light, as when the bodily eye is illumined by the light of the sun or by a physical lantern so that it can see, and the mind's eye is illumined by the intelligible light which 'lights every man',[111] which is God, as Augustine teaches.[112] These two lights make for bodily and intellectual seeing, and, as it seems, there is not a third light, which makes for a mental seeing which is imaginative. Neither, so it seems, can it be said that one or other of these two lights is a servant of the [imaginative] soul's seeing, for bodily light does not transgress the bounds of bodily seeing. And the divine intellectual light does not transgress the bounds of intellectual seeing, for it cannot be received by a life below that of the intellect.

165. Moreover, if there is a light which illumines the soul in this seeing,

---

109. *De insomn.*, 2 (459a25–28); ed. Drossaart Lulofs, p.8 (12–15)
110. *De Trin.*, xi, 2; *CCSL* 50, 336 (60–66)
111. *John* 1, 9. A phrase central to Augustinianism, also quoted by Kilwardby near the start of his *De Ortu Scientiarum*, where he tells us that human reason has, above itself and also within, eternal *rationes* of the true light which lights every man who comes into this world (cap.1, 9, sect.1).
112. *Soliloq.*, i, 6 (12); *PL* 32, 875

I ask this: Since the imaginative soul turns itself toward something which is to be imagined, does it consider the images in itself alone without any representation of them in a bodily organ, or do they also appear at the same time in a bodily organ? For if the species which have been received remain in the soul and cease to exist in the bodily organ, then how can they appear to the imaginer except as just in the soul? And if they remain in both, and this is only on account of the imaginative act which is to be performed, then how could there be an act of imagination in souls separated from their body? In no way, seemingly. And then what was said in the Lord's parable about Dives and Lazarus will be false, which is not possible. These questions (paras.150–165) have been asked in order to clear up the topic of spiritual or imaginative seeing.

166. Reply to the first doubt (para.150). It should be said that according to Averroes 'motion' can be taken formally or materially. Taken formally it is nothing but the way to a terminus, without the particularization of that which is gradually acquired of a terminus, and it is in the genus of passivity. Taken materially it is the acquisition of one part after another until the motion is completed, so that in the concept of the motion and of the acquisition is included that which is acquired, and for this reason motion is in the same genus as is that which is acquired by the motion. It is in this way therefore that Averroes makes a distinction regarding natural motion.[113] But though in the act of mind by which it forms in itself the species of corporeal things there is not really motion and succession, there is nevertheless something like it there, and hence the foregoing distinction can be applied there. For when the mind goes forward by its act to meet a passivity of the body, the body moves and joins itself to, or intertwines itself with the image by which the body has been acted upon, and by such motion it acquires for itself a likeness of the sensible thing. If therefore we call 'motion of the mind' such a joining or intertwining, without that which is acquired of the likeness of the sensible thing, 'motion' is taken formally. But if it concerns the likeness which has been acquired, it is taken materially. And taken in this second way images of the mind acquired by motion are rightly called 'motions of the mind'.

167. It can also be said otherwise, and more easily, that it is customary in common speech to use 'motion' of that which is acquired by motion, as a carpenter says 'This is my work' of a bench, and as a clerk says 'This is my writing' of a letter, and as you say 'This is my desire' of something you like, and so on. It is in this way that Augustine and Aristotle sometimes use 'motion of the mind' to speak of likenesses of the mind acquired by its motion.

---

113. Cf Averroes *In Phys.*, iii, 1 (200b33–201a3), 2 (201b28–32); ed. Venetiis, 1574, text.4, 16, fols.87[rA-D], 91[vK]–92[rA]

168. Reply to the second doubt (paras.151–157). It should indeed be conceded that species of sensible things reach the common sense by way of the proper senses, and reach the organ of the former by way of those of the latter, and after the common sense the imagination comes next. But in order to explain the way in which it gets from a proper sense to the common, it is necessary to say something first about the organs of the senses. It should therefore be noted that according to the authorities who speak about these matters[114] an animal senses by means of certain nerves which contain a very subtle corporeal soul, which is the immediate organ of the mind. And this corporeal soul receives species of sensible things immediately up against the sensory mind, and from there the mind absorbs them. Therefore sometimes the whole conjunction of nerve and corporeal soul, and sometimes the soul itself, is called the 'organ' of sensing. For even if the whole conjunction is by its nature an organ of sensing, it is not so in a primary sense. But the soul itself is essentially and primarily that organ.

169. 'Organs of the senses' is taken in this first way in *On The difference between Soul and Mind*, where it is taught that in the front of the brain there are two ventricles in which the common sense and the imagination work. And many pairs of nerves lead from there, so that one pair leads to the eyes so that there should be a seeing in them, and another pair leads to the ears so that there should be a hearing in them, and so on.[115]

170. Augustine says the same thing in *On Genesis* : 'From the middle of the brain as from a sort of centre thin tubes lead not only to the eyes but also to the remaining senses',[116] and so on. And further on: 'The front part of the brain, from where all the senses are distributed, is placed at the forehead and the organs of sense themselves are in the face, except for the sense of touch, which is spread throughout the body, though it can be shown that it also starts from that same forward part of the brain.'[117]

171. In *De Musica* Augustine speaks about the organs of sense in the second way. He says: 'This sense, which is in us even when we are sensing

---

114. Cf Avicenna *Liber de anima*, iii, 8; ed. van Riet, 1, 269 (51–56, 61–64)–270 (1): 'Next is the soul leading back what is being seen, without apprehending it again; otherwise apprehension would again be divided on account of the division of the nerves. And this leading back is part of the substance of seeing, and it penetrates the soul placed in the first ventricle of the brain, and the visual form is again impressed within that soul which bears the power of the common sense, and the common sense receives that form. ..Next this power which is of the common sense leads the form back to another part of the soul which is continuous with the part of the soul which has that power, and it impresses upon it that very form, and places the form there in that formal power which is the imaginative power...which receives the form and conserves it.'
115. *Cf.* Costa ben Luca *De diff. animae et spiritus*, 2; ed. Barach, pp..124, 126f, 130
116. *De Gen.ad litt.*, vii, 13; *CSEL* 28, 3, 2, p.212 (15–17)
117. *Ibid.*, 17; p.214 (15–19)

nothing, is an organ of the body, an organ which is acted upon by the mind by this adjustment, so that the mind may be more prepared for the passivities of the body which are to be acted upon attentively in that organ, in order that it connect like with like, and repulse what is hurtful. In my opinion it makes, in addition, something luminous, the clearest of airs, in the eyes, and something most mobile in the ears, something misty in the nostrils, something humid in the mouth, and something earthy and as it were muddy in the sense of touch.'[118]

172. He has the same thing in mind in *On Genesis*, where he says: 'Bodily sense, which is distributed through five channels as it were, relates to seen corporeal things, when light, which is the most subtle thing in the body and on that account closer than the rest are to the mind, is first diffused alone through the eyes, and leaps out in ocular rays to the visible things which are to be surveyed, and then in a certain mixture, first with pure air, then with misty and foggy air, thirdly with a thick fluid, fourthly with an earthy thickness, it produces the five senses.'[119]

173. It is obvious from these points that 'organ of sense' can be taken in two ways. However, what it is essentially and primarily is a subtle body by means of which the mind vitalizes and moves the body and produces acts of sensing; it is called 'soul' in *On The Difference between Soul and Mind*.[120] It is also obvious that the organs of the proper senses are connected with the organ of common sense, and they arise from it and proceed from it. And the common sense is the one which operates in that common source without a root, and proper sense is sense which operates essentially and distinctly in each of the streams.

174. If someone enquires here about the kind of body that this soul is which is essentially and primarily the organ of the mind, it should be said that it is a body composed of the four elements in their most subtle parts and most finely strained so that this soul is essentially not a visible body; and its composition is such that in due order the earthiness is penetrated by a watery humidity, and that humidity by humid air, and that air by a fiery light which is the loftiest and most inward thing in that with which the mind is immediately conjoined, and the mind is conjoined with the other things by means of that fiery light, and it is by means of such a body that the mind acts and controls the gross and heavy body. Hence Augustine's statement (para.172) that light is first diffused alone through the eyes so that seeing can occur, should be understood as saying that the soul itself, on account of being light, is diffused through the eyes and is thus a visual organ, and not otherwise.

---

118. *De musica*, vi, 5 (10); *PL* 32, 1169
119. *De Gen.ad litt.*, xii, 16; *CSEL* 28, 3, 2, p.401 (10–19)
120. Costa ben Luca *De diff. animae et spiritus*, 1; ed. Barach, p.121

Hence though soul, which is a composite body, is there essentially an organ, nevertheless light alone is essentially and primarily an organ.

175. What he says next (para.172), that the light is mixed with pure air, is due to the fact that, for the production of hearing, the soul itself, in which pure air is the principal thing, is the primary organ of hearing. But light is said to be mixed with the air because the light is that with which the mind is immediately united and in whose absence that corporeal soul ceases. And the same sort of thing happens in the case of smell, taste, and touch, of which Augustine speaks thereafter.

176. Moreover, some writings speak of this soul as if it were composed only of fire and air, as in *On Soul and Mind* where this is said: 'A certain fiery power, warmed[121] by air, rises from the heart to the brain as if to the heaven of our body, and purified and gathered together there, it proceeds outwards through the eyes, ears, nostrils, and other organs of sense, and formed by the touch of external things, it produces the five senses of the body.'[122]

177. Moreover, in *On Genesis* Augustine says as follows: 'Since mind is an incorporeal thing, a body which is next to the incorporeal, such as fire, or rather light and air, acts first, and through these the remaining things, which have a grosser body, such as moisture and earth, act.'[123]

178. Moreover, he adds later: 'By means of light and air — which are the most excellent bodies in the world and have a pre-eminence at acting rather than having the bodily capacity for being acted upon, as have moisture and earth — by means of these things which are more like soul, the mind controls the body.' [124]

179. In these passages and in all such writings it should be understood that fire and air are referred to only on account of their primacy, for a gross body is only moved, and mind only produces motion, but corporeal soul, which is intermediate, produces motion and is also moved, and hence in the same soul fire and air are moved and produce motion. But water and earth are only moved and do not produce motion. Hence, though the mind essentially acts on, and controls, gross body by means of the corporeal soul, nevertheless it controls it essentially and primarily by means of the fire and air which are in that same soul, and even more principally by fire than by air. But on account of its subtlety and heat air is highly mobile and productive of motion, and on account of its humidity it tempers the fire. For that reason

---

121. 'warmed', literally 'tempered', though this implies 'cooled' whereas in the present context the fiery power is heated up.
122. Ps.-Aug. (Alcher. Clareval.) *De spir.et anima*, 33; *PL* 40, 802
123. Aug. *De Gen.ad litt.*, vii, 15; *CSEL* 28, 3, 2, p.213 (22–25)
124. *Ibid.*, 19; pp.215 (24)-216 (1)

authorities[125] attribute control of the body to fire mixed with air, and not to fire alone.

180. Note that on account of the primacy of such fire '⟨corporeal⟩ soul' is defined in *On Soul and Mind* in this way: 'What I call 'corporeal soul' is air, or rather fire which on account of its subtlety cannot be seen, and it vitalizes bodies within by causing them to grow.'[126]

181. These points (paras.174–180) have been made, by way of a digression and incidentally, about corporeal soul which is intermediate between mind and the rest of the body, because it is the organ of sensing essentially and primarily.

182. From these points it is obvious that there are two souls in an animal. There is a corporeal soul which is moved and is vitalized, and there is another, incorporeal soul which causes motion and vitalizes. It is necessary now to speak about the first of these along with the second. In the foregoing questions (qq.1–3) the second was spoken about without the first.

183. Let us return therefore to the principal topic and, assuming that the primary and essential organ of sense is the corporeal soul by means of which the mind gives sense to a gross sensible body, let us see in what way the species of sensible things pass from the proper senses to the common sense.

184. But this can be understood in two ways. One way is as follows. Sense organs are like vessels prepared by nature so that they should receive species of sensible things poured into those organs, species which are to be displayed to the mind. Therefore just as liquid poured into a vessel expands at once to the full length and breadth of the vessel, so also the image of a sensible thing, impressed upon the corporeal soul which is a sense organ, acts at once throughout it right up to the common sense. But there is a difference between the two examples. The liquid poured into the vessel expands lengthways and sideways so that part of the liquid is contained in a part of the space and the liquid as a whole is in the whole space. But the image does not act in this way through the whole organ of the proper sense right up to the organ of common sense so that one part of the image is in one place and another part is in another. On the contrary, the whole image is everywhere and the whole as a whole is at each point in the organ. For just as the whole species of a colour or of a sound is in the whole medium outside and the whole species is in every part of the medium, and is not less in one part than in the whole, (even though it has a different existence in different parts of the medium), so it is also, as regards one and the same species which has been received in an organ of sense, that the whole species is at the outermost part of the proper sense

---

125. *Cf*.Ps.-Aug. (Alcher. Clareval.) *De spir.et anima*, 33; *PL* 40, 802: 'A fiery power warmed [= *temperata*] by air rises from the heart to the brain...'
126. *Ibid.*, *PL* 40, 803

where it looks out upon the medium outside, and the whole species is immediately in the common sense, and the whole species is in the intermediate path connecting the common sense to the proper sense. And in this respect it is like the mind itself or a sensory power. But the cause of this is the spiritual nature of the image, for Aristotle says that sense, universally, is the receptivity of the species without matter.[127] And so just as the likeness of a sensible thing suddenly or in a short time comes to exist throughout the medium outside, so also either suddenly or in an insensible time the likeness comes to be throughout the whole sense organ right up to its depths where the common sense resides.

185. The same thing can be understood in a second way as follows. When the vitalized corporeal soul is first touched by a sensible species transmitted to it at the extreme of the soul which faces outward, then at that very same instant the vitalizing sensory soul co-mingles with a passivity of the body and forms in itself a similar species. And since that vitalizing soul is a simultaneous whole the same both in the organ of common sense and everywhere throughout the whole medium, through itself as thus informed and existing everywhere, soon the sensible species is everywhere in the organ of sense right up to its innermost extreme. An example of this concerns many lines going from one base and terminating at a common point. For if to the many lines terminating at that point there is added another, as soon as it terminates at that point, it is in contact with all the other lines which terminated at that point. For every part of the vitalized corporeal soul which has extension and dimension is just like that line. But the vitalizing soul which is a simultaneous whole in every part of that vitalized soul, is like the terminal point of the many lines which terminate at the one base. Hence as soon as the vitalizing soul is formed by the image of the sensible thing, all the parts of the vitalized soul are informed, through and from the vitalizing soul, by that same image.

186. This way of understanding the matter (para.185), therefore, or the one before (para.184), or perhaps both, make it sufficiently clear how the species of a sensible thing passes from the extreme of a proper sense right up to the innermost part of the common sense.

187. Reply to the first reason for raising the doubt (para.152). It can reasonably be said that the motion of sensible things in moving is not properly in a straight line but in a circle or after the fashion of a spherical figure — so far as that is possible for them. For a sound is heard in every part, and a colour is seen in every part, as far as is possible, for it is seen in every part after the fashion of a hemisphere almost. Likewise with the other kinds of sensible thing.

188. Moreover, if it should be said that this motion is unceasingly

---

127. *De an.*, ii, 12 (424a18–20); ed. Stroick, p.149 (65–66)

straight, then it seems that this should be conceded not universally but only in the case of an object of sight, for colour is not seen directly unless the colour be directly opposite the sense of sight in a straight line. For light and colour radiate, strictly speaking, and rays are always straight. For they can be reflected and broken, but not bent. But this does not seem to be the case as regards the other kinds of sensible thing. For one can smell something directly though it is not opposite the olfactory sense, since often something is smelled though it is to the side or rear. Likewise also as regards something which can be sounded, which is an object of hearing.

189. Moreover, let it be granted that in these three things which are sensed through an external medium the change takes place in an unceasing straight line, since if it were so the doubt would be particularly relevant. It should be said that this ought to be understood as regards the motion by which they move the external medium right up to the sense organ, and not as regards the motion by which they move the organ within. For that motion in the organ is like the motion of liquid in a vessel, not like the motion into a vessel, or like the motion of a sensory power by which it moves the whole organ, carrying to its innermost part what was impressed upon its outermost part, in the way clarified above (para.184).

190. But as regards the second reply (para.188) someone might ask why the colour is not seen directly if it is not placed opposite the eyes, given that the situation is otherwise as regards the senses of smell and hearing. This seems to me to be because it is not possible for a sense to be informed by its sensible object unless they go to meet each other, and in their own way make mutual contact by means of a certain mutual resistance. For in every sense there is a certain contact and resistance; otherwise there would be neither motion nor passivity there. But when a visible thing is to the side or rear, visual intention and visible species do not meet. But they travel in the same direction and each of them is so spiritual that neither resists the other. And although the viewer is looking into the medium in which the species of the visible thing exists, nevertheless that species, as regards its displayed face, is not turned towards the viewer, but its rear part, as it were, in which nothing of the visible thing is displayed, is turned towards the viewer. But if the light of the medium, or the sight of the viewer, or something else could turn the species which is in the medium towards the sense of sight, so that the intention of the viewer and the displayed face of the species of the object in the line of sight met and touched each other in a suitable manner, then what would be beside one or to the rear would be seen directly. Now, that is not how things are, and so nothing is seen in that way. But the situation is different in the cases of smell and hearing. For something is smelled by inhalation, and the intention of sense and a sensible species drawn in along with the air, meet each other directly and make mutual contact with a due

resistance, and the species, thus drawn in, meets the sense with face displayed. It is the same with hearing and sound, for sound is carried along by the motion of airwaves; the sound is driven upon the air and collides, as I would say, with the organ of the sense of hearing, and there the intention of the hearer and the sound, with face displayed to the hearer, meet each other and make mutual contact with a due resistance. And the cause of these things is that sound and smell are material to the extent that they are moved by the attraction and repulsion of the air; but a species of colour is spiritual to the extent that it is not moved in this way by the air.

191. Reply to the second reason for raising the doubt in the foregoing question (para.153). It can be said that such dispositions are required in the medium, illumination in the case of sight, the wave motion in the case of hearing, and so on, and that these dispositions are not needed in the sense organs. For in the sense organs other dispositions are appropriate. Alternatively it can be said that the kinds of dispositions that are necessary for the medium outside are also necessary inside, that is, dispositions which imitate the ones outside. And the organ of sight is very bright inside, for light itself, or the corporeal spirit by means of light (as was clear from what Augustine said (paras.171–172)), is the primary, essential, and immediate organ of seeing. And hence, just as the medium outside is prepared, by a light poured into it, to receive a species of colour, so also the organ of seeing is prepared by a light which is innate to it. But according to Augustine the chief thing in the organ of hearing is the pure air, as has already been said (paras.171–172). Aristotle also agrees with this. He says: 'We say that the organ of the sense of hearing is of air'.[128] And so it is obvious that it receives the disposition to take in sound, as does the air outside, whether this is by a certain wave motion which is achieved by a push, or in some other way. In the organ of smell also, according to Augustine (paras.171–172), a misty or foggy air abounds, in which it is obviously possible for the organ to have or receive the same disposition which the air outside has to receive a smell. And likewise with the other organs. On the basis of these points one should try to ascertain how the species of sensed corporeal things pass from the outermost part of the proper senses right up to the common sense.

192. Reply to what was next asked (para.157) concerning how a species passes from sense to imagination. It should be said that the sense acts when the sensible thing is present, and the imagination when the thing is absent. Hence, when something has been grasped by sense and thereafter, in the absence of that thing outside, when the mind directs itself inward to imagining what had previously been sensed, by means of the image which had been left behind in it, then the imagination is being exercised. So the species passes

---

128. *De part. animalium*, ii, 10 (656b16); *R* fol.197vb, *H* fol.37vb

from sense to imagination, as from that which precedes in the order of nature to that which follows in that same order, and as from a cause to its effect. From these points it is obvious what the sought after passage ⟨of the species⟩ is, and what the difference is between sense and imagination, and what the relation is ⟨between them⟩ (para.157).

193. And this is what Aristotle has in mind when he says in *De Anima* that 'fantasy, or imagination, is a motion actually made from sense'. [129] And it is what Augustine has in mind when he says that 'imagination is a blow struck by means of the senses'.[130] The same doctrine is in *On Soul and Mind* where this is said: 'A fiery power tempered by air, (that is, the corporeal soul of which we have spoken (para.180)), which, formed outside, is called "sense", is led inwards to the chamber of the imagination through the organs of the senses, and it is in this way that an act of imagination is produced.' [131] This should be understood to be saying not that the organs of the proper senses are left empty by the soul, but rather that the vitalizing soul which moves and animates the corporeal soul is first directed outwards, and by itself it turns round the motion of the corporeal soul in order that it may be informed by things outside, and as such the corporeal soul is sense. Then it is directed to that which has been left inside by sense, and by itself it turns the motion of the corporeal soul so that it reviews what is inside, and as such it is imagination. And it is, as it were, a certain turning and re-turning of the corporeal soul. Hence, a little later in the same work 'imaginative act' is defined as follows: 'It is a likeness of a body, received from the outside via the bodily senses, through contact with bodies, and brought inwards through those same senses to a purer part of the corporeal soul, and impressed on it, in the highest part of that soul.'[132] It is on the basis of the foregoing points (paras.168–193) that one should try to deal satisfactorily with the second question (para.151).

194. Reply to the third question (para.158). Both alternatives can reasonably be doubted, a position touched upon when the question was raised (paras.159–160). But it seems to me more likely that images received by means of the corporeal soul would not remain permanently in the same place, though they would remain for some time. For, as already indicated, Aristotle says: 'During the day, (that is, during a period of wakefulness,) the images are driven out; and when the senses and intellect are active, they are destroyed.' [133] And a little further on he says, of those who are asleep, that when

---

129. *De an.*, iii, 3 (429a1–2); ed. Stroick, p.175 (88)
130. *Ep.*7, 2 (3); *CSEL* 34, 14 (26–27)
131. Ps.-Aug. (Alcher. Clareval.) *De spir.et anima*, 33; *PL* 40, 802
132. *Ibid.*, *PL* 40, 802–803
133. *De insomn.*, 3 (460b31–461a1); ed. Drossaart Lulofs, p.20 (2–4)

an overly vigorous motion is produced in them by food or something of that sort, the images are totally destroyed.[134]

195. But then you might ask how it is that the images appear during sleep if the ones received during a wakeful period do not remain. And how is it that they appear during a period of wakefulness after sleep if they are destroyed in sleep due to a vigorous inner motion?

196. Moreover, the following is said in *Anatomy* : 'The brain is harder in its rear part both on account of the nerves which produce motion and which arise there, (for those nerves have to be harder than the nerves which can sense), and also on account of the part in which the store of memory and the repository of forms are situated.'[135] Why, then, is there a repository of forms in that part if it is not because images are conserved in the corporeal soul by means of which they are received?

197. Moreover, why posit a memory chamber and mind to return to for the purpose of remembering if not because images of things previously sensed had been placed in it?

198. Reply. I do not think that the corporeal soul is so well limited by its own surface that it retains for a long time images impressed upon it by virtue of its nature. For in the presence of the impresser it retains those images just as does water or air, and it does not retain them by means of its own surface. It can therefore be said that though the images are promptly erased from the corporeal soul and destroyed, they nevertheless remain in the incorporeal soul. And since the images have appeared inside, with the senses outside closed down, whether in a period of wakefulness or of sleep, they appear in the incorporeal, not in the corporeal, soul. And though this way of speaking seems to be at odds with Aristotle, it seems all the same to be in accord with Augustine in *On Genesis* (para.149). If however one has to say that after the senses have ceased to be used these images appear within the corporeal soul, then I think that beforehand the mind, by means of the corporeal soul which produces motion, assimilates to itself the images which it has received and has retained in itself, and the mind makes in that soul images which are like those which it received from things outside. And in this way images which were destroyed during a period of wakefulness return in sleep, and images destroyed and erased in sleep return during a period of wakefulness. For I do not think that the vitalizing soul has less power to assimilate to itself the soul which has been vitalized and over which it presides, than to assimilate the

---

134. *Ibid.*, (461a20); p.22 (2–3)
135. Ps.-Galen *Anatomia vivorum*, 41; ed. von Töply (under the name of Ricardus Anglicus), p.28. Cf. C.H.Talbot and E.A.Hammond, *The Medical Practitioners in Medieval England: A Biographical Register* (London, 1965), pp.270–272, 'Ricardus Anglicus'

sensible body outside, but rather very much more. From this the reply to the first objection (para.195) is obvious.

199. Reply to the second objection (para.196). It should be said that the memory chamber is said to have a store of memory and a repository of forms, not because images received from outside remain in that chamber shut up in the corporeal soul, but because the mind, about to seek species which a while earlier it had committed to the care of memory, directs itself there and, as it were, shuts itself up there until it finds those species. However, what the mind finds is not something formed in the corporeal soul outside the mind; on the contrary, the mind finds in itself what perhaps thereafter it impresses upon the soul. And a chamber of that kind was made into an aid to memory. For when the mind, about to seek within itself what it deposited in itself, that is, in memory, which is a sort of bodily enclosure, restrains itself from running around and from aimless wandering, something in some way present to it is produced, and what is sought is more easily found. Since therefore an intention of the mind which is about to remember something leads the mind, as it were, to such a chamber so that it should search the mind there and find in it what is sought, rather than find what is sought in the corporeal soul itself which is surrounded by that chamber, the chamber is therefore said to be a memory store and a repository of forms. For the mind, shut up in there, finds in itself the forms which are sought after, as if the forms were shut up in the same place. For it is as if the images seem to be found there in the enclosed corporeal soul when in fact they are found in the memory of the mind which is shut up there after its own fashion.

200. Reply to the third objection (para.197). It is now obvious that it is sufficiently correct to posit the memory chamber as well as the mind's recourse to that chamber for the purpose of remembering, although images of things previously sensed are not shut up there in the corporeal soul; for the chamber was made into an aid to the recollective power so that what is sought may be found more promptly, as has already been said (para.199).

201. It should be added that every one of our thoughts of what is sensed is a thought of things which are present or are past. Since therefore present things are, as it were, right before us, God has rightly arranged the chamber of common sense with its imagination in the fore part of the brain, since sensible grasp of present things is in the fore part. And perhaps for that reason two chambers are placed in the fore part of the brain, one to serve common sense, the other to serve imagination. And since past things have, as it were, been sent to the back, God rightly arranged that the chamber to which the intention to remember would make its way should be in the rear part of the brain. For that intention, as it were, makes its way to things put behind one, when it recollects past things. And since the rational mind reasons about, and judges, both present things and past ones, and also

considers both sorts of thing, God rightly arranged the chamber called the 'rational chamber' in the middle of the brain as an aid to thought and to rational consideration. For this should draw from each of the extremes and should adjudicate about all the things which each extreme contains. That the brain is divided in this way into chambers is taught in *On the Difference between Soul and Mind*[136] and in *On Soul and Mind*.[137] We seem already to have said here why there are just that number of chambers and why they are arranged in just that order. It is thus obvious that it is not pointless to posit a memory chamber and to posit the recourse of the recollective mind to that chamber, even though images of sensed things are not shut up in that chamber.

202. If someone should object to this on the grounds that Aristotle shows, by means of sensible experiences, that a passivity inflicted upon the senses is present in the sense organs not only while the senses are active but also after that,[138] it should be said that he shows only that it remains for a very short time, but not that it does not disappear quickly. For his demonstration is based on the following examples, as will be clear if you look at his book: 'If sight is turned from the sun to darkness, it does ⟨not⟩ see nothing, because of the continuing motion in the eyes, which is from the light. And if we should look at a colour for a long time, whatsoever we turn our sight to will seem to be of that same colour.'[139] All the experiences there adduced are of the same kind; all indicate that the passivities last just for the moment. Augustine teaches the same thing in *De Trinitate*, as has already been said (para.160).

203. But if someone is not satisfied with this sort of reply, and instead insists in every way that the species of sensible things remain whole for a long time in the corporeal soul, and that, as if by the hand of the mind, they are placed and arranged in the memory chamber so that memory can revert to them when the occasion demands, and there contemplate or withdraw them, whether this be in sleep or in a state of wakefulness, then I do not see how this could be said with as much reasonableness as the doctrine which we have presented (paras.198–202). But it can be said that just as there are many lights and many rays simultaneously, and that nevertheless it is possible for just one light or one ray to be apparent to the senses on account of the pre-eminence it has which absorbs the presentness of the others, so also the species of many sensed things may exist simultaneously in one corporeal soul, though of them all only those to which an intention of the mind is on some occasion directed are apparent.

---

136. Costa ben Luca *De diff. anim. et spir.*, 2; ed. Barach, pp.124–127
137. Ps.-Aug. (Alcher. Clareval.) *De Spir. et anima*, 22; *PL* 40, 795
138. *Cf. De insomn.*, 2 (459a25–28); ed. Drossaart Lulofs, p.8 (12–15)
139. *Ibid.*, (459b9–13); p.10 (10–13)

204. Thereafter other more vigorous motions occurring inside, whether during sleep or a period of wakefulness, do not erase or entirely eradicate those species of sensible things from the inner corporeal soul, but eradicate only their presentness.

205. And then Augustine's words (para.160): 'When the visible thing outside has been withdrawn, the form, which was in the sense while what was being seen was present, does not remain in the sense' should be understood as referring to the more material passivity produced in the organs of the proper senses rather than to the more spiritual passivity within, left behind in the corporeal soul, ministering to the common sense, imagination, and memory.

206. Reply to the fourth doubt (para.161). It should be said that the vitalizing sensory soul was so made in order that by its nature (i) it should be assimilable to sensible things, (ii) it should preserve this assimilation and (iii) it should show the assimilation to itself while contemplating itself. And this power which it has, which is of such a kind, is memory. For that power of the sensory soul by which it assimilates itself to sensible things outside, when it has brought back from outside and retained a sensible image which is to be shown to its own eye at another time in the absence of the sensible thing outside — that power is rightly called 'memory'. Therefore the nature by means of which the sensitive power retains the species it has received is memory. It is like a natural pocket which retains species that have been received, and at a suitable time can produce them for display.

207. But the reason why such a power has been given to the sensory soul seems to be as Aristotle says in *De Anima* III: For the sake of its health the mind needs to pursue things agreeable to it, or to seek them out when they are not present and to flee from harmful and hostile things even before they are present.[140] But this is possible only by a progressive motion. Such a motion only proceeds from desire. There is, however, no desire without imagination of what is desirable or of what is best avoided. But there can be no imagination without memory, since imagination is the contemplation of the image of an absent sensible thing which is represented within by the memory.

208. From these points (paras.206–207) it is obvious not only what memory and imagination are, but also how memory is related to imagination, and how it is related to contemplation, which is done by an act of imagining.

209. Reply to the fifth doubt. It should be said that for the motion of desire the mere presence of the species of a desirable thing in memory is not enough. There must be a perception of the present species itself in an actual imaginative act. For it is when the animal actually imagines the desirable thing that the animal moves in search of it. Moreover, it does not move

---

140. *Cf. De.an.*, iii, 9–11 (432a15–434a22); ed. Stroick, pp.228 (57)-238 (85)

progressively towards the desirable thing immediately on desiring it unless it also imagines there to be an opportunity to get what is desired. Therefore although memory contains at one and the same time the species of many desirable things and of many things best avoided, desire is not confused as if ignorant of what it desires. For desire is moved only by an actual and determinate imaginative act, and there is no such act without a determinate and actual act of contemplation. And, if I may speak of what commonly happens, an animal does not at one and the same time imagine, or contemplate by an act of imagination, many desirable things or things best avoided. Instead it imagines such things separately and distinctly, first one thing and then another. And it therefore desires separately and distinctly first one thing and then another. But if it should so happen that the animal imagines many of those things at one and the same time then the desire is divided so that something of it tends towards one desirable thing and another part of it tends to another desirable thing, and desire is still not confused.

210. Moreover, after the desire is in motion within, the animal does not at once move forward unless perhaps it imagines there to be an opportunity to get what is desired. And therefore the motive power is not confused as if the animal were ignorant of what it was doing. I say 'commonly' because it does not commonly happen that an animal imagines many desirable things simultaneously, and simultaneously imagines the opportunity for getting them. What it imagines, distinctly and separately, is an opportunity for getting one of the desired things now, and another opportunity for getting another of them at another time. And therefore the animal now moves forward towards one of the desired things and, distinctly and separately, it moves forward towards another at a different time. If at some time it should happen that the opportunities for simultaneously getting several desirable things should simultaneously occur to the imaginer, then in men the situation is that the motivating power is in some way confused for a time, with its not knowing what it should do until by means of a deliberate act it overcomes desires for another thing — if, I say, the desires are equal. And it is clear how often a man has conceived of two things each of which he desires to carry out, though until he has deliberated he does not know to which he would rather turn. Perhaps the same sort of thing happens in the case of beasts, though that is something hidden from us. That is, if an animal imagines two desirable things simultaneously along with the opportunity for getting them at the same time, then either the motion of the greater desire is followed, while the other desire disappears, or, if the motions of the appetites are equal, neither is followed in effect until one of them weakens or disappears.

211. Moreover, just as in one and the same matter many original forms of things lie hidden, which however appear distinct and separate and without confusion in an act, and appear also in an orderly way, because no form

appears except at suitable opportunities suitably grasped, and no form appears except by way of opportunities appropriate to itself, so also in one and the same memory there are many species of desirable things or of things best avoided, which however do not move desire, nor prompt any forward motion, unless suitable opportunities are grasped. And hence those species do not produce motion in a confused way since motivating opportunities are grasped distinctly, and are also grasped separately, singly, and in appropriate ways.

212. Reply to the sixth doubt (paras.163–164). A necessary condition of any single thing being seen is that it is in the light. Thus just as bodily seeing occurs in an outer bodily light and intellectual seeing occurs in an inner intellectual light, so also spiritual seeing occurs in an inner spiritual light which is needed for such seeing. But so far as I can see, this light is the product of two cooperating elements. For the vitalizing soul is itself a sort of light, and the vitalized soul is itself luminous, since it has that light in rich measure, and its perfection, by which it is joined to the mind, is light. For by that light it shares a sort of homogeneity[141] with the vitalizing soul so that it is united to it, and so that something which is naturally one should be made out of those two things. It is for this reason that Aristotle says: 'Not only does sight undergo something from the air, but it moves the air and makes the air undergo something, just as shining things do. For sight is one of the shining things.' I think, however, that this light, which is a product of two dissimilar things, is enough for spiritual seeing. And the homogeneity[142] of the two lights allows them to have such an effect at the same time. For the essential light of the vitalizing soul allows an image it possesses to be seen. And the essential light of the vitalized soul allows the image to be seen in that soul.

213. If someone were also to claim that species would remain in the corporeal soul without being erased, despite the presence there of a vigorous inner motion, it could be said that they themselves are lights of sorts bestowing ⟨light⟩ in the seeing of its own species. There would thus be a three-fold light. Therefore, just as nature, which does not fall short in respect of necessities, endowed light upon a cat's eye to illumine the medium in the dark and did not bestow such a thing on other creatures, for much of a cat's work, *viz.* hunting mice, is conducted in the dark, so also nature bestowed upon the imaginative soul the inner light due to it and which is sufficient for its work which is conducted within, for that soul is at a distance from the other lights which help the other sorts of seeing, as has already been said (para.212).

214. Reply to the seventh doubt (para.165). As it seems to me, there is no doubt but that a man's imaginative soul, when separated from his body,

---

141. 'homogeneity', or 'common origin'.
142. 'homogeneity', or 'common origin'.

could by itself and without the corporeal soul perform imaginative acts. For the Lord's parable about Dives and Lazarus[143] seems to show this and to show also that after this life minds are punished, as is believed, by a spiritual seeing of things which are here loved illicitly. Augustine, also, clearly thinks this, as is obvious from *On Genesis*.[144]

215. As regards the spiritual seeing by the soul which yet vitalizes the body, Augustine seems to speak as if the vitalizing soul itself would see within itself the images of things by means of an impression made in the corporeal soul and would do so whether during a period of sleep or of wakefulness. Whoever looks carefully at *On Genesis* [145] will judge that Augustine does indeed hold this. Nevertheless so long as the vitalizing soul can (i) produce from the storehouse of its memory species hidden there, and (ii) contemplate them, and (iii) assimilate to itself the corporeal soul by means of which it controls the body, I cannot reject this.

216. But whether the spiritual seeing of a man living here is always so made that the image appears in each soul, that is, in the corporeal and the incorporeal, or so that it always appears in the incorporeal soul only, or so that it appears sometimes in both and sometimes in one only, I cannot determine. I think, however, that Aristotle, who claims that such activities or passivities of the mind exist together, would say that the images always appear and are seen together, and so are seen in both the incorporeal and the corporeal soul.

217. It seems, however, that there is a probable argument for this. It is as follows. If the eye of the mind turns toward memory, and memory produces the species which is to be contemplated, not in any way with regard to the body which is to be controlled, nor with regard to some concern or duty to act upon that body, then there is no need for an impression to be made upon the corporeal soul, nor a need for the appearance or seeing of the image, except in the incorporeal soul. But if this comes about with respect to the body which is to be helped or in some way moved it seems reasonable that the corporeal soul should be assimilated here to the incorporeal by an intention of the incorporeal soul flowing down into the body itself. For memory, so far as I can see, is the lowest part of the incorporeal soul, and it is by the memory that the incorporeal soul is conjoined with the corporeal, and it is that lowest part that first receives such passivities from the corporeal soul and makes them appear to the eye turned upon itself. Hence, when an intention, which arises from the conjunction of the eye ⟨of the mind⟩ and memory or which conjoins them, does not have regard to lower things, it is

---

143. *Luke* 16, 19–31
144. *De Gen.ad litt.*, xii, 34–35; *CSEL* 28, 3, 2, pp.431–433
145. *Ibid.*, 16; p.402 (10–15, 17–19)

not necessary for such an impression from these lower things to be left behind in the eye ⟨of the mind⟩ or memory, as it seems to me. But if it does have regard to them, it is reasonable that such an impression should indeed be left behind in them.

218. It is on the basis of these considerations (paras.166–217) that we should try to meet the questions raised with regard to the evidentness of mental or imaginative seeing (paras.150–165).

⟨*Question Four: What part of the body is the organ of common sense?*⟩

219. It is appropriate to add here a discussion of a secondary topic, the organ of common sense. For that will contribute a great deal to the evidentness of things which have already been settled, and especially to the evidentness regarding the second of the seven questions recently asked (para.151), concerning the way in which images of sensible things pass from the proper senses to the common sense and the imagination. Since therefore in reply to this question (paras.168–169, 173, 183–186, 191) there was a brief discussion concerning the organ of common sense, a topic on which the authoritative texts seem in conflict, let us digress a little and ask which part of the body is the organ of common sense.

220. It seems that the organ is the brain, either some part of it or something in it, according to the two texts quoted earlier where reference was made to the two ways of speaking about 'the organ of sensing' (paras.169–170). One of the texts is from *On The Difference between Soul and Mind* and the other is from *On Genesis*.

221. *On Soul and Mind* is to the same effect: 'Power in animals is in the brain, and it is from there that the five senses are enlivened. It also orders voices to utter, and limbs to move. For there are three ventricles of the brain, one at the front, from which every sense comes, a second at the back, from which every motion comes, and a third in the middle, which is the rational ventricle.' [146]

222. Moreover, the following is said in *Anatomy* : 'Galen says that the liver is the principle of nutrition, and the brain is the principle of sense and motion.' [147]

223. Moreover, in *Anatomy* ch.40, which is about the brain, this is said: 'The brain is cold so that it should not be heated up by the motion of the sensible nerves, or by sensible, imaginative, and cognitive acts.' And a little further on: 'The front part of the brain is softer and damper because of the

---

146. Ps.-Aug. (Alcher. Clareval.) *De spiritu et anima*, 22; *PL* 40, 795
147. Ps.-Galen *Anatomia vivorum*, 20; ed. von Töply, p.7

sensible nerves which arise there, and which have to be softer than the nerves which produce motion.'[148]

224. It is clearly implied here that the brain, either some of it or the brain in itself, is the organ of the first sense, and of imagination, and of thought.

225. Moreover, Aristotle's words seem in agreement with this. For he says: 'Song and every sound reach the cavity of the ear, and from there they go on to the brain. One blood vessel goes from the brain to the right ear and another to the left.'[149]

226. Moreover, he also says: 'We should know that there are two passages extending from the brain. They have been made sinewy and strong, and they extend to the roots of the eyes.'[150]

227. From these points it seems that Aristotle means that in the brain there is a sense which is common to sight and hearing. And this can only be what we call 'common sense'.

228. Moreover, Aristotle says: 'If the part surrounding the brain were very fleshy, the operation of the brain would be the very opposite of the natural operation for which the brain was created. For then it could not keep ⟨the rest of the body⟩ cool, because the brain itself would be very hot. Neither could sense exist in it; the brain would, instead, be like one of the residues.'[151]

229. These words imply that sensing is a natural operation of the brain. But certainly not sensing by means of a proper sense; therefore by means of the common sense.

230. Moreover, a little later Aristotle says that from these things it is manifest that 'because of the sense in the brain there is no flesh on the head.'[152] By 'flesh' he means a great weight of flesh.

231. Moreover, he adds further on: 'Every animal which has a brain has it in the front part of the head, for it is the organ of sense by means of which sensing occurs in the front part.'[153]

232. From these considerations (paras.225–231) it seems that since the brain has sense and is the organ of sense, and since this cannot be made out as true of any of the proper senses, it must be understood of common sense.

233. Moreover, Aristotle says: 'The stomach could not be placed above the heart where the primary power is, nor above the divine organ, which is highly active. Also the operation of the divine organ is only an operation of sense and understanding. And no other organ could be placed above the

---

148. *Ibid.*, 41; pp.27, 28
149. *Hist.animalium*, i, 11 (492a18–21); *R* fol.152rb
150. *Ibid.*, iv, 8 (533a13–15); *R* fol.164ra
151. *De part.animalium*, ii, 10 (656a19–23); *R* fol.197vb
152. *Ibid.*, (656b11–13); *R* fol.197vb
153. *Ibid.*, (656b22–23); *R* fols.197vb–198ra

divine organ on account of its weight, since weight hinders the motion of the understanding, and affects the common sense, and especially if the body were very heavy.'[154]

234. It seems from these words that Aristotle means that the brain is, or has within itself, the organ of common sense, for it seems that the part which he calls 'divine' is not the heart but the brain. This follows from his statement that the stomach cannot be either above the heart or above the divine part, and from his statement that 'the nature of the brain is an eternal nature'.[155]

235. In reply to these passages (paras.225–234) someone might offer the quibble that it is true that there is a sense in the brain, but that it is not the common sense; instead it is a proper sense, namely touch, since it is not possible to allot to any other of the proper senses a primary place in the brain.

236. But as against this quibble there are Aristotle's words: 'The brain does not have the sense of touch at all, any more than do the blood or animal residues.'[156]

237. Moreover, he says: 'Taste and touch are connected to the heart.'[157]

238. From these considerations (paras.236–237) it is obvious that according to Aristotle touch is not primarily in the brain. So there is no obstacle to the conclusion drawn from the foregoing passages (paras.220–234), that the common sense is in the brain.

239. Reason as well ⟨as authority⟩ is in favour of this position. The power of a spiritual operation needs a spiritual organ where it can perform its acts, and the power of a subtle operation needs a tranquil part and a part where the spirituality and subtlety of the corporeal soul flourish. But the power of the most spiritual and most subtle operation in the whole animal is the common sense, which is also the imaginative soul and serves both the operation of the cogitative power and also memory. And the spiritual organ is the brain rather than the heart, since the brain is whiter, clearer, and brighter, and is also the part which is more tranquil. For the heart is in continual motion because of the breathing and the pulse and because of the continual generation of the corporeal soul and the blood, none of which occurs in the brain. Also the corporeal soul is more subtle and more spiritual in the brain than in the heart, because, according to doctors, vital soul is produced in the heart, but animal soul in the brain, and vital soul is material in relation to animal soul. Hence animal soul is purer, more subtle, and brighter than vital soul. It seems therefore that common sense especially must

---

154. *Ibid.*, iv, 10 (686a14–15, 27–32); *H* fol.45rb
155. *De part.animalium*, ii, 7 (652b5); *R* fol.196rb
156. *Ibid.*, (652b5); *R* fol.196rb
157. *Ibid.*, 10 (656a30); *R* fol.197vb

performs its acts in the brain, and I include in 'common sense' whatever is below reason and above any proper sense.

240. Sacred Scripture also seems in agreement with these positions (paras.220–239). Thus we find in the *Book of Daniel* that the dreams of Nebuchadnezzar are called his 'visions of his head'.[158] For if dreams are visions, and yet not a proper sensing which is exercised by means of the eyes, it is common sense that is left. And if the dreams are rightly called 'visions of the head', then common sense and its organ seem to be in the head.

241. From these points (paras.220–240) and similar ones it seems that the organ of common sense is the brain, whether some feature of the brain or something in the brain.

242. However, many things Aristotle says seem to point to a contrary position. For he teaches: 'All animals which have blood have a heart, and it is here that the source of motion and of the proper sense is to be found.'[159] But if the source of the proper sense is in the heart, and that by which the source of the proper sense exists is the organ of common sense, it follows according to Aristotle that the heart is the organ of common sense.

243. We find Aristotle writing the same thing elsewhere regarding the heart: 'Since it receives everything which has been sensed it should be one of the simple parts. And since it is a cause of motion and a source of desire it should have the nature of an organ. And this organ in bloodless animals is that which is analogous to the heart.'[160] Note that he says here that the heart receives everything which has been sensed, a description which can apply only to the common sense and its organ.

244. And in the same work he says the following: 'We say that the source of animal sense is in the heart.'[161]

245. Moreover, he says this: 'I say that the heart is the source of life, and every motion and every sense is in it.'[162] And a little further on: 'The heart is the motive source of agreeable and of disagreeable things, and universally the motions of every sense begin from the heart and return to it.'[163]

246. Moreover, Aristotle says this: 'It is in the heart that the source of the senses and all the animal virtues must exist, and for this reason the heart is created first.'[164]

247. Moreover, he says: 'The pathway of the organs of all the senses is

---

158. *Dan.* 4, 2
159. *De somno et vig.*, 2 (456a4–6); ed. Drossaart Lulofs, pp.5*a (41)–6*a (2)
160. *De part.animal.* ii, 1 (647a28–31); *R* fol.194rb
161. *Ibid.*, 10 (656a28); *R* fol.197vb
162. *Ibid.*, iii, 3 (664b11–12); *R* fol.200vb
163. *Ibid.*, 4 (666a11–13); *H* fol.40ra, cf. *R* fol.201ra
164. *De gen.animal.* ii, 6 (743b25–26); *R* fol.220vb

extended to the heart or to a part which links up with the heart.'[165] But that part to which the organs of the senses are extended seems to be just the organ of common sense.

248. Moreover, if the organ of common sense is that, and that alone, with which all the organs of the proper senses are conjoined, and if that, as Aristotle says, is just the heart, it follows that the heart alone is the sole organ of common sense. But that not all the organs of proper sense are conjoined with the heart, as Aristotle says, seems to follow from his words. For he says: 'The organs of taste and touch are close to the heart.'[166]

249. He provides a reminder of this same point: 'We said in *De Sensu* that there are two senses which are conjoined with the heart, namely those of touch and taste, and this is plain to see.'[167]

250. He adds: 'The organ of hearing is at the back of the head';[168] and shortly thereafter: 'Pathways go out from the auricles and are conjoined with the back of the head.'[169] Moreover, a while later he says: 'The brain is the organ of sense by means of which something is sensed in front.'[170] This seems to apply only to sight and smell, which are in the face.

251. On the basis of these points (paras.248-250) I argue as follows. If taste and touch have their organs around the heart, and hearing has its at the back of the head, but sight and smell have theirs at the front, so that they are all at a distance from one another, then according to Aristotle the organs of the proper senses do not all seem to come together in the brain. So they must do so in the heart alone. And so the heart will be the sole organ of common sense.

252. This position receives further support from something else that Aristotle says: 'The brain is not conjoined with any of the sensing organs. And this', as he says, 'is plain to see'.[171] For the proper sense organs should, so it seems, be conjoined with the organ of common sense.

253. Moreover, if an animal consists of many powers and many organs, it is reasonable that the primary power should perform its acts in the primary organ. But the primary organ in an animal is the heart. Hence Aristotle says: 'The heart appears first in actuality among all the other parts, and this is plain to see.'[172] And a little further on: 'All animals have this principle within. For this reason the heart is the first thing to appear as something distinct in all

---

165. *Ibid.*, v, 2 (781a20-23); *R* fol.233va
166. *De sensu et sensato*, 2 (439a1); MS Oxford, Corpus Christi Coll.114, fol.170rb
167. *De part.animalium*, ii, 10 (656a29); *R* fol.197vb
168. *Ibid.*, (656b14-15); *R* fol.197vb
169. *Ibid.*, (656b18-19); *R* fol.197vb
170. *Ibid.*, (656b22-23); *R* fol.198ra
171. *Ibid.*, 7 (652b2-3); *R* fol.196rb
172. *De gen.animal.*, ii, 4 (740a3-4); *R* fol.219rb

blooded animals.'¹⁷³ And then: 'The heart is the first part in blooded animals. But in other animals the first part is the counterpart to the heart, as we have often said.'¹⁷⁴ He proves this as follows: 'That the heart is first is plain to see. And not only from this, but also from the end ⟨of the creature's life⟩, for the spiritual power remains at the last in the heart. And death overcomes all other parts before it overcomes the heart. For nature proceeds in circular fashion, since there will be no generation except from non-being to being.'¹⁷⁵

254. Moreover, the primary power in the animal, in virtue of which it is an animal, is the common sense. For sense is the perfection of the animal in so far as it is an animal, as Aristotle says.¹⁷⁶ And of the senses the first is the common sense. Hence he says: 'Sleep is an interference with the primary organ of sensing with the result that it cannot act.'¹⁷⁷

255. From these considerations (paras.242-254) it seems that common sense performs its acts in the heart. And this is supported by the passage quoted above (para.233) where it is said that the stomach could not be placed above the heart, where the primary power is.

256. Moreover, Aristotle says: 'Pure blood is warmer and of greater sensitivity.'¹⁷⁸ Such blood seems most suitable for the primary sense, which has the most subtle act, and that sense is the common sense. But such blood is especially the blood of the heart. For blood seems to be purer at its source than elsewhere and the heart is the source of blood. For this reason Aristotle says: 'The primary power creating blood is in the heart.'¹⁷⁹ The blood of the heart is also warmer, since the heart is the warmest part of the whole animal.

257. Moreover I assume that the apprehensive power and the desiderative power corresponding to it are not essentially different. If therefore the primary animal desiderative power is in the heart, it follows that the apprehensive power corresponding to it is in the same place. But the apprehensive power corresponding to the primary animal desiderative power is the imagination, as is obvious from *De Anima* 3, where the question at issue is the forward motion of animals.¹⁸⁰ I am taking 'apprehensive' in general to mean the same as 'cognitive'. It is for that reason that I said that the imaginative power is apprehensive. It seems therefore that the imaginative power of animals is in the heart, where their desiderative power is. Since therefore the imaginative power and the common sensory power are not essentially dif-

---

173. *Ibid.*, (740a16-18); *R* fol.219ʳᵇ
174. *Ibid.*, 5 (741b15-17); *R* fol.219ᵛᵇ
175. *Ibid.*, (741b17-23); *H* fol.54ʳᵃ
176. *Cf. De an.* ii, 2 (413b1-2); ed. Stroick, p.73 (79-81)
177. *De somno et vig.*, 3 (458a28-29); ed. Drossaart Lulofs, p.10*a (15-17)
178. *De part.animal.*, ii, 2 (648a3-4); *R* fol.194ᵛᵃ
179. *Ibid.*, 1 (647b5-6); *R* fol.194ʳᵇ
180. *De an.*, iii, 10 (433a9-10); ed. Stroick, p.231 (90-91)

ferent, the common sensory power will be in the same place. But that the motivating or desiderative principle of animals is in the heart, and also that the sensory principle is in the same place at the same time, is maintained by Aristotle: 'Since the heart receives everything that is sensed, it must be one of the simple ⟨parts⟩, and since it is a mover and a desiderative principle it must have the nature of an organ. And this organ in bloodless animals is that which is analogous to the heart.'[181]

258. Moreover, further on he says: 'The heart is the source of agreeable and disagreeable things, and universally the motions of every sense begin from the heart and return to the heart.'[182]

259. Moreover, that the brain is not the organ of common sense, and consequently that the heart is the organ, can be seen from the composition of the brain, for, as Aristotle says: 'The brain is composed of earth and water',[183] and these are elements which are especially distant from the spiritual operations of the mind. Hence he says in the same place: 'The brain is very cold, colder than all the ⟨other⟩ organs.'[184] But a bit further on he says: 'Heat in bodies serves activities of the mind, since sense and motion are among the activities of the mind, and a necessary condition of these activities is the power of heat.'[185] It seems therefore that it is incompatible with the natural composition of the brain that it should be an organ of either sense or motion.

260. Moreover, further on in the same work Aristotle says: 'No part has sense unless it has blood. Not that blood is the organ of sense; rather, something made out of blood is. For this reason nothing which has sense in a blooded animal lacks blood.'[186]

261. But elsewhere Aristotle says: 'The brain is entirely bloodless in every animal. And hence there is no blood vessel there, whether large or small.'[187] From these considerations (paras.256–261) the same points follow as before, as can be seen.

262. Moreover, in the same work he says: 'There are no nerves in the head.'[188] It seems to follow *a fortiori* that there are none in the brain either, since there seems no need for them. But in *On the Difference between Soul and Mind* it is taught that by means of the corporeal soul the mind produces 'life and pulse in the blood vessels, and sense and motion in the nerves'.[189] It seems

---

181. *De part.animal*.ii, 1 (647a28–31); *R* fol.194rb
182. *Ibid*., iii, 4 (666a11–13); *H* fol.40ra
183. *Ibid*., ii, 7 (653a21); *R* fol.196va
184. *Ibid*., (652a28); *R* fol.196rb
185. *Ibid*., (652b10–13); *R* fol.196rb
186. *Ibid*., 10 (656b20–22); *H* fol.37vb
187. *Hist.animal*., iii, 3 (514a18–19); *R* fol.158vb
188. *Ibid*., 5 (515b13); *R* fol.159rb
189. Costa ben Luca *De diff.animae et spir*., i; ed. Barach, p.121

from this that unless there are nerves in the brain there will be nothing there by means of which sensing can occur.

263. From all these points (paras.242–262) it seems that neither the brain itself, nor anything in it, could be posited as the organ of common sense. Hence the organ in question must be the heart.

264. All this is supported by Aristotle's words: 'The residue of the stomach does not have sense, neither does the brain or the medulla.'[190] And from this claim, if it be compared with earlier ones, it seems that Aristotle is contradicting himself. For in this last claim he says that the brain does not have sense, whereas according to earlier claims of his the brain does have sense (paras.225–233).

265. How different are the views about common sense and its organ! For theologians, following Augustine, and doctors also, clearly mean that the brain, whether a feature of it or something in it, is the organ of common sense. But Aristotle seems to mean that in blooded animals the organ of common sense is the heart, and in bloodless animals it is something corresponding to the heart. What, then, should be maintained?

266. Reply. Either it should be said that the opinions of Aristotle and of the others are incompatible, and that they have therefore set out different positions; or, as would perhaps be better, it should be said that Aristotle's opinion is not incompatible with that of the others, but complementary, and a corrective to theirs, for what was missing from their account of this matter Aristotle filled in. For from the fact that in the preceding claims (paras.225–233) Aristotle said that the brain has sense, and is an organ of sense, and is a divine organ of a great activity, that is, intellection, sensing, and so on, he does not seem to have disagreed with those who claimed, or claim, that the common sense and its organ are in the brain. But, as it seems, he attributed the sense and its act to the heart. For with those preceding words where he spoke of the heart (paras.242–245), he said that the heart is the source of sense, that it receives everything which is sensed, that sense is in the heart, that the motions of the senses start from the heart and return to it, and so on. It seems from this that he attributed sense both to the brain and the heart, but more to the brain as its organ than as its source; and more to the heart as its source than as its organ. Each, however, can be called a source. For the heart is the primary and remote source of the proper senses, and the brain is the secondary and proximate source, so that the heart is the source of the primary in-pouring on the proper senses, and the brain is the source of the secondary in-pouring. And again, each can be called the organ of common sense. For the brain is the organ which primarily receives and judges sensible things, and the heart is the organ which does these things secondarily. Thus

---

190. *Hist.animal.*, iii, 19 (520b15–17); *R* fol.160[va]

the motions of the proper senses start from the heart as from the first thing, which pours in soul, heat, and life, and those motions return to the heart as to the last thing which comprehends and judges.

267. The words of Aristotle which were quoted earlier, *viz.* 'The brain is the organ of sense by means of which sensing occurs in front' (para.250) agree with the foregoing position. And in the same place he adds: 'This sense must come from the heart.'[191] Moreover, there are his words quoted earlier (para.233), where he said that the primary power is in the heart, and yet the brain is the organ of the divine activity where there is both intellect and sense. Likewise there are his words, also touched on above (para.245), where he says that the motions of the senses start from the heart and return to it, and so on.

268. This, then, seems to be Aristotle's judgment. For he lays it down that the heart is the first organ and also the source of heat, blood, bodily soul, sense, and motion, and it is by means of this organ that the bodily soul, along with heat and blood, rises to a place around the brain. He also seems to mean by this that he attributes sense to the brain, because that bodily soul proceeds from the brain to the organs of the proper senses as from the place and organ of common sense, and the soul, duly formed by its contact with outer sensible things, carries back, or transmits, the species of the outer sensible things to the brain so that the brain should make a judgment about them. And he seems to mean that even if this motion perhaps always proceeds onwards to the heart, this fact is nevertheless not apparent during a period of wakefulness when the senses and intellect are active. The reason for this might be the great attention paid to other things, whether outer or inner, and the repeated transference of attention from one thing to another. But it is plain that in sleep they are borne onward to the heart, first by the return of the [bodily] soul to the heart, because the outer senses are closed; then because it is pushed downward from the brain to the heart by the motion of the gross humours which become cold around the brain and then descend; and then by means of the vitalizing soul which is in control and is essentially the same everywhere in the sensory pathways. And so, because the vitalizing soul has an image of a sensible thing, the image can exist everywhere in the pathways of sense and can rush about or move in accordance with the sense of sight and with the direction of attention of that same vitalizing soul. But the appearance of these things is manifestly due to the fact that sense and intellect cease to perform other acts. And in this motion of images in sleep there sometimes appear images which are shaken about or distorted, monstrous or improvised, on account of the great and contrary motion which is produced within, for heat, blood, and vapours rise from below, from the heart, as a result of

---

191. *De part.animal.*, ii, 10 (656b24); *R* fol.198[ra]

food and such like. And likewise other things descend on account of the causes just mentioned. But sometimes whole images appear in due order and correctly. This happens after the completion of the digestive process, and after the sedation of the motions just mentioned, and the separation of impure blood from pure.

269. Aristotle seems to teach all these things when he says: 'The motions of images occur not only during periods of wakefulness but also in sleep, and then they are more apparent. For in the daytime, when the senses and intellect are active, that is, during periods of wakefulness, the images are destroyed, like a small fire near a big one and like small pains and pleasures near big ones. But at night, on account of the withdrawal of the senses and the inability to do anything, (which is because the heat flows from the outer parts to the inner), the motions of images are borne back to the source of the sensing part',[192] which according to Aristotle is the heart, as is obvious from the *De Somno* and the *De Partibus Animalium*.[193] He adds: 'Images become plain when turbulence stops.'[194] He also adds: 'It must also be judged that these motions are like small whirlpools which are carried along in rivers.'[195] And shortly after: 'In this way sometimes in water if it be moved vigorously no reflection appears, and sometimes it does appear but is distorted, so that something seems to be otherwise than it is. And when the water becomes still an accurate and clear image appears. So likewise in sleep sometimes images, and the other motions which are produced by images, are entirely destroyed when there is a more vigorous motion due to food and other inner corporeal things, and sometimes disturbed and monstrous visions arise and bad dreams. But when, in blooded animals, the blood has become still and separated out, the motion of the images produced by each of the senses survives and makes for healthy (that is, accurate and sound) dreams.'[196] These are Aristotle's words in the *De Somno* and there is little doubt that they represent his view. It seems to me that there is contained clearly enough in those words the judgment which I put forward about the motion of images toward the heart being apparent during sleep and not apparent during periods of wakefulness.

270. It should also be added here that since doctors divide the corporeal soul into the vital and the animal, of which, according to them, the vital is produced in the heart and as such is incapable of producing in the body either sensation or motion which follows from sensation, whereas the animal corporeal soul is produced in the brain from the vital soul and from then the

---

192. *De insomn.*, 3 (460b29–461a7); ed. Drossaart Lulofs, pp.18 (18–19), 20 (2–10)
193. *De somno et vig.*, 2 (456a4–6); ed. Drossaart Lulofs, pp.5*a (41)-6*a (2)
194. *De insomn.*, 3 (461a7–8); ed. Drossaart Lulofs, p.20 (10–11)
195. *Ibid.*, (461a8–9); p.20 (11–12)
196. *Ibid.*, (461a14–27); pp.20 (17–21), 22 (1–5, 7–10)

soul activates sense and motion,[197] this also can be accommodated to the foregoing judgment of Aristotle's. For he can readily be understood as saying that since the heart is the source and as it were the mine of the corporeal soul, on account of the grossness and excessive heat of the corporeal soul it is not immediately suitable for sensing, though it is however further purified in the brain by a more complete digestion and is rendered more subtle and more clear and its heat is moderated. It thus becomes fit to receive the species of sensible things and to transfer them not only to the brain but also to the heart, which is the source of sensing, in the way stated above (para.266).

271. Granted these things, it is obvious that there are two organs corresponding to the common sense to which images of sensible things come, and there are two sources of sensing from which the proper senses originate. The organs of the proper senses are joined to ⟨both heart and brain⟩, though joined to one of them by way of the other. But there is essentially only one sensory power, distinguished only in respect of existence in those organs.

272. But there is reason to doubt this. For if nature does nothing in vain, why has it provided two organs for only one power, the power of common sense? For since it apprehends and judges all sensible things sufficiently well by means of one of the organs, the other seems superfluous.

273. Moreover, if neither is superfluous, what is the difference between apprehending and judging sensible things by means of one of the organs and by means of the other?

274. Reply. Regarding the first question (para.272) it should be said that nature did not establish the two organs, the heart and the brain, essentially and primarily, in order that the operation of common sense should be by means of the two organs; they perform this operation incidentally. For nature established them for the sake of the well being of the animal and because of the need for regular activity, and as a concomitant of this the work of common sense is done by and in the two organs. The point can be made clear in the following way. The mind does not produce acts of sense and motion in the body except by means of heat. But in blooded animals a great deal of heat is needed for this task, and so in such animals there had to be a very hot part, the heart. But since that hot part needed to be regulated lest perhaps the continual heating consume the body and shorten the animal's life, there had to be a cold part, the brain, in an area above the heart. So these two organs

---

197. *Cf.* Costa ben Luca *De diff. animae et spiritus*, 1–2; ed. Barach, pp.123–124: 'It is now obvious therefore that the soul which is in the ventricle of the heart is the cause of life, of breathing, and of pulse, and this is what must be known about the vital soul which emanates from the heart. (2) But the soul which goes from the brain and passes to the other parts of the body, is called 'animal soul'; its nutriment or sustenance is the soul which is in the ventricle of the heart...'

were established for the sake of the animal's well being and because it needed them.

275. And that is what Aristotle says in *De Partibus Animalium* : 'Since heat in bodies serves the activities of the mind, for sense and motion are among such activities, and these activities only occur by the power of heat, it is plain that an animal must have some heat in it, (that is, a hot organ, the heart). And since all things need a counterbalance to control them, so that there should not be an imbalance, the brain was made cold. And to counterbalance it there is the heat of the animal's heart, since there cannot be an organ of one construction without there being another of essentially the opposite construction. Hence nature devised the placing of the brain in opposition to the heart. For this reason nature made the brain out of a combination of earth and water. Hence every blooded animal has a brain.'[198]

276. There is a further reason for this. Just as food, at the first stage of digestion, is not immediately suitable for nourishing the parts of the body, but needs to be further digested and to be made much more subtle, so also since, according to Aristotle, an animal's heart is where blood and soul are first generated, they are then very hot, thick, and turbulent, and less suited to regular use of sense and motion until they are further dissolved, rendered more subtle, and purified. The brain, therefore, was established for this purpose, placed above and opposite the heart, so that blood and soul should rise to it, and be moderated by its coolness, and by this moderating be purified and made more subtle, so that by means of them the heart should become regular and suitable for being of use to sense and motion.

277. Aristotle hints at this argument when he says: 'The brain improves the blend of heat and boiling in the heart so that the heart should have a moderate heat in two blood vessels, the great blood vessel and the aorta. And these great blood vessels reach the brain at the membrane surrounding the brain. And in order that harm should not befall the brain from the heat from those vessels, the blood vessels which surround the brain are densely packed and thin in place of the two great blood vessels, for the two great ones branch into the thin ones, and so the blood surrounding the brain is pure and thin in place of the thick and disturbed blood.'[199]

278. Aristotle also says: 'The head was made just for the sake of the brain, since blooded animals have to have a brain, and the brain has to be opposite the heart. And nature placed some senses in the head because the blend in the brain is temperate and appropriate for the blend in the senses on account of the tranquility and subtlety of the senses.'[200]

---

198. *De part.animal.*, ii, 7 (652b10–24); *R* fol.196rb
199. *Ibid.*, (652b26–33); *R* fol.196^{rb-va}
200. *Ibid.*, iv, 10 (686a5–11); *H* fol.45rb

279. It is therefore obvious that the need for well being as well as for regular activity meant that there had to be a brain and a heart in blooded animals.

280. Along with this is joined the fact that the work of the common sense is accomplished by means of this organ, that is, the reception of all sensible things and the judgment concerning what is received. For this reason common sense has two 'residences', as I shall call them, which are apart and facing each other. Between the two run blood and the corporeal soul which is under the direct control of the common sense. By means of the corporeal soul coursing to and fro, and under the unifying control of the sensory power which is everywhere essentially the same, in the two 'residences' and also in the entire intermediate pathway through which the ⟨corporeal⟩ soul descends from brain to heart or returns to the brain, the species of the sensible thing passes not just from the proper sense but goes from there right to the heart. And in both the brain and heart the common sense and the imaginative power recognize and judge, being, as they are, in their own residence. But the two organs were not made essentially for this purpose; they fulfil it only incidentally, as has already been made clear (para.274). Neither is one of the two organs redundant; on the contrary each has a proper use.

281. Reply to the second objection (para.273). It should be said that the acts of common sense and imagination are primarily in the brain, and secondarily in the heart, because the heart is further from the proper senses.

282. Moreover, they are principally in the brain, which is the more spiritual organ and the organ which was made principally for this, and secondarily in the heart which was made principally for another purpose, as will now be obvious.

283. Moreover, the act ⟨of common sense⟩ is performed more evidently, more tranquilly, and more fully in the brain than in the heart. For perhaps the turbulence in the heart would not allow there to be evident and full cognition and judgment there of all sensible things if there were not another organ where these acts would be performed. But now, since they are adequately performed in the brain, the motion in the heart is no obstacle to the same acts being performed in the heart. For what is sufficiently well known by one organ and is discerned by another does not need as much tranquility in that other in the repetition of the same cognition and discernment, as it would need if it were not known elsewhere and discerned by other things. And it should be noted here that it is a matter of earlier and later only in nature, for at one and the same time, in the same instant, there is in both brain and heart an apprehension and a judgment about sensible species. But these acts occur principally, evidently, and fully in the brain, and secondarily in the heart, less evidently and less fully. If someone should contend that the

acts do not occur in the brain and the heart at the same instant, that does not trouble me just now, for the time gap will not then be a sensible one.

284. Moreover, there is a further point to be made on this matter. The same power which first senses and imagines, thereafter desires in one way or another, and produces an impulse to move, and also produces motion according as it is affected by its desiring. Since, therefore, common sense and imagination, which are cognitive powers, need a clear, spiritual, and tranquil organ, the brain, which satisfies these conditions, was made for this purpose. And since the desiderative power needs the power to produce an impulse and to move an animal, which cannot be managed without great heat and a strong ⟨corporeal⟩ soul, the heart, which satisfies these conditions, was made for this purpose. But I am not saying that motion does not proceed from the brain and that the heart lacks sense and imagination. For since the impulse to move proceeds from the imagination, as Aristotle says in *De Anima*,[201] it is rightly said that imagination is in the heart, from where the impulse to move comes. But the impulse to move proceeds principally, especially, and primarily from the heart, and imagination proceeds secondarily, less especially, and not primarily from the heart.

285. Moreover, since it is cognition or full imagination that directs motion and follows it through in a regular way, the controlling of motion and the regular following through of that control proceed from the brain, the principal seat of that cognition. This therefore is the order, as it seems to me: (i) common sense and imagination, which are one power as regards their substance and which preside simultaneously in the brain and the heart, produce the act of imagination completely in the brain; (ii) this act reaches the heart, and from there the desiderative power, which is not essentially different from sense and imagination, produces an impulse to move the animal; (iii) and the desiderative power follows that same impulse, made in the heart, through into a regular motion which started in the rear part of the brain, as *On the Difference between Soul and Mind* teaches.[202] And hence the source of those cognitive and imaginative acts is in the brain. But the end is in the heart. However, the source of motion is in the heart and it is followed up through the brain. This whole act is performed by a single mind simultaneously moving both brain and heart, but principally moving sense and imagination in the one, and principally beginning motion in the other.

286. The clear sign of this is that as regards people whose imaginations are working hard their heads are affected and are acted upon, and especially

---

201. *Cf. De an.*, iii, 10 (433a20-21)
202. *Cf.* Costa ben Luca *De diff.animae et spiritus*, 2; ed. Barach, p.128: 'Flesh mixed with blood vessels, by means of which ⟨flesh⟩ there comes to be motion in the parts, also proceeds from the rear part of the brain...'

the front part where the chamber of common sense and imagination is situated. And as regards those who are beginning to be moved by desire, their hearts are affected and are acted upon, and this can clearly be seen in the change of pulse throughout the body.

287. On the basis of this reply we can deal satisfactorily with the two questions asked above (paras.272–273). For it is obvious in what different ways the mind uses these two organs in sensing or imagining and in moving, and how each organ was needed and neither was superfluous.

288. Once these things (paras.274–287) are understood it is obvious what should be said in reply to the principal question (q.4, para.219). I grant all the points brought to bear in respect of the first part (paras.220–241), since they show only that the brain is an organ of common sense. Likewise I grant the points brought to bear in respect of the second part, up to the argument which tries to show that only the heart is the organ of common sense on the grounds that not all the organs of the proper senses seem to be connected with the brain (paras.242–247). Since therefore Aristotle's words do not contradict the words of the doctors and the theologians, it can be held, as is taught in *On the Difference between Soul and Mind* and as the doctors teach, that the organs of the proper senses converge on the front part of the brain, where the chamber of common sense and of imagination is situated.[203]

289. As regards the sense of taste it can be said that the nerves descend from that front part of the brain to a position adjacent to the heart, where the acts of the sense of taste occur.

290. This point however can be criticized on the grounds that in *On the Difference between Soul and Mind* the following is written: 'A pair of nerves goes from a ventricle in the front part of the brain and is joined to the tongue. The sense of taste arises from this.'[204]

291. Moreover, as against each of these opposed claims (paras.289–290) there is Augustine's judgment: 'Thin tubes lead from the middle of the brain, at just about the centre, to the eyes, ears, nose, and palate, so that seeing, hearing, smelling, and tasting can occur.'[205]

292. So we see three different judgments (paras.289–291) regarding the organ of taste. According to one it is around the heart, according to the second it is in the tongue, and according to the third it is in the palate.

293. But why does Augustine say that the tubes go from the middle of the

---

203. *Ibid.*, pp.124, 126: 'The brain is divided into two parts, the larger one being at the front, and the other at the back. In the front part are two ventricles which enter into a common area in the middle of the brain... (126) Understanding, thinking, foreseeing, and knowing are done by means of the soul which is in the ventricle shared by the two other ventricles which are in the front of the brain.'
204. *Ibid.*, p.127
205. *De Gen.ad litt.*, vii, 13; *CSEL* 28, 3, 2, p.212 (15–19)

brain (para.291) when a little later in the same book he says, as do the doctors, that they go from the front of the brain?

294. As regards the first of these difficulties (para.292), one has to say either that these are three different and mutually incompatible views or that they can be squared with each other in the following way. Since food is the object of taste and is of two kinds, namely food in its first form and not digested and food in its final form and already digested, the first being coarse food taken into the mouth, and the second being blood — since Aristotle says: 'Blood is the final form of food in blooded animals, and something corresponding to blood ⟨is the final form of food⟩ in other ⟨bloodless animals⟩'[206] — it is possible that nature has arranged things so that gustatory nerves should go from the brain to the mouth as well as to a position next to the heart; and that they should go to the mouth for the sake of the taste of the food which is still coarse and not yet digested, and to a position next to the heart on account of the taste of the food in its final form, for, according to Aristotle (para.256), blood is produced in the heart. And both *On the Difference between Soul and Mind* and Augustine (paras.290–291) are speaking about the first of these two sorts of taste, and Aristotle is speaking about the second (paras.248–249). It is possible, then, that *On the Difference between Soul and Mind* (para.290) and Augustine (para.291) are both correct, the former in saying that the gustatory nerves go to the tongue (para.290), and the latter in saying that they go to the palate (para.291). For perhaps tasting is done neither solely by the tongue nor solely by the palate, but by the two together. Perhaps, therefore, as regards the nerves which go to the mouth for the sake of the sense of taste, some go to the tongue and some to the palate, and so perhaps all three of the foregoing views are true together. But no one of them contains the whole truth. However the truth about the organ of taste is established on the basis of the three taken together.

295. Alternatively it could be said that the gustatory nerves descend first from the brain right down to an area next to the heart so that they should be strengthened there by the heat of the heart, for a great deal of watery liquid is in the organ of taste. And from the heart the nerves rise again, to the tongue and palate where the act of tasting occurs. It is in this way that *On the Difference Between Soul and Mind* speaks about the organ of taste. It says that a pair of nerves descends from the brain 'to the entrails, exhibiting the sense to them, and some of those nerves go back to the uvula moving it so that it should be contracted upwards'.[207] According to this way of speaking about the organ of taste it is obvious that Aristotle speaks about the organ in terms of the place

---

206. *De gen.animal.*, i, 19 (726b1–2); *R* fol.215[ra]
207. Costa ben Luca *De diff. animae et spiritus*, 2; ed. Barach, p.127

where it is strengthened so that it should produce an act of tasting, but others speak about it in terms of the place where the act of tasting occurs.

296. As regards the second of the difficulties (para.293) it should be said that when Augustine speaks about the middle he means not what is equidistant from every part at the extremities of the brain, but what is within these extremities, since whatever is between one terminus and another is in the middle of those termini. But he says 'centre' not in relation to the brain, but in relation to the proper senses, whose organs go from the front part of the brain right to the extremities of the body so that sensing should occur by means of them, just as lines go from the centre of a circle to the circumference.

297. The same sort of thing that has just been said about taste can be said about touch, that is, that tactual nerves go from the front of the brain downwards to the neighbourhood of the heart, so that they should be strengthened there by the heat of the heart, since the organ of touch contains within itself a good deal of earthy coldness, and from there the tactual nerves are diverted to all sensitive parts of a body. And then Aristotle's words (para.248) will not be at odds with the position of the doctors when they say (para.288) that the tactual nerves arise in the brain as do the nerves of the other senses. Neither will Aristotle be at odds with Augustine when the latter says: 'The organ of touch is spread throughout the body, but it can be shown that it makes its way from the front part of the brain.'[208]

298. As regards the sense of hearing, it can be said that just as there are two nerves of the eyes where they are connected with the eyes, and are then conjoined, and are again divided before they reach the brain, as the author of *Perspective* teaches,[209] so also perhaps, as Aristotle teaches, the same holds as regards the organ of hearing, namely that the pathways of hearing which go from the auricles are connected with the back of the head, and nevertheless reach the front part of the brain, where the sensory nerves arise. And when he says that the organ of hearing is 'at the back of the head' (para.250), 'back of the head' can perhaps be taken to mean whatever is behind the face. Alternatively if it be taken to mean the lower part of the head, it can be said that 'organ of hearing' refers to the convergence of the two pathways going from the auricles, which are connected with the back of the head, just as

---

208. *De Gen.ad litt.*, vii, 17; *CSEL* 28, 3, 2, p.214 (17–19)
209. Cf. Alhazen, *Optica*, i, 4; ed. Basileae, 1572, p.3: 'Two similar optic nerves grow out of the front part ⟨of the brain⟩, and they begin to proceed from two places in the two parts of the front of the brain; and it is said that each of these has two membranes and that they grow out of two webs in the brain, and reach the middle of the outer part of the brain and of the front of the brain, where they converge and produce an optic nerve. Then this nerve divides, and two equivalent and similar optic nerves are produced. Next these two nerves are extended until they reach the two cavities of the two hollow bones of the eyes containing the two eyes.'

'organ of sight' refers to the convergence of nerves going to the eyes within the brow. But this does not stop the organ of common sense being where the auditory pathways are connected in the front part of the brain.

299. Thus it is obvious that it is reasonable to say that the organs of the proper senses are connected with each other in the brain, and yet that they are connected further on with the heart, since the organ of common sense extends from the brain to the heart, so that the brain and the heart as well as that intermediate pathway constitute the place where the common sense operates, in the way already described (paras.266–267). And so the brain as well as the heart are involved in the organs of the proper senses, as their source, though the brain is involved more immediately than is the heart.

300. As regards the subsequent objection (para.252) that according to Aristotle the brain is not connected with any of the organs of the proper senses, it can be said that 'brain' can be taken in two ways. Taken in the first way, it is just that soft substance which is composed predominantly of water and earth, and ⟨taken in this way⟩ it is not connected with the other things. Taken in the second way, it is the same as the ⟨vascular⟩ net (para.301), with which it is involved, and the same as the soft sensory nerves which arise from there and are contiguous with the ⟨vascular⟩ net. And so the brain is connected with the organs of the proper senses. Aristotle should be taken to be using 'brain' in the first of these senses, and Augustine and the doctors in the second of them.

301. In *On the Difference Between Soul and Mind* it is, therefore, taught that large blood vessels, rising from heart to brain, branch when they reach the brain, and the fine, branched vessels intertwine like a net, and this net encloses the brain, with one part of the net extended from the lower part of the brain to the front; and the net brings the vital soul to that front part. It is from that same front part of the brain that the sensory nerves which go to the various parts of the body arise, in order that the proper senses should operate in those various parts. Hence the vital soul, taken from the ⟨vascular⟩ net round the brain, is digested, purified, refined, and clarified in the ventricles of the front of the brain, and thus it becomes the animal soul, which is then transmitted by way of the sensory nerves in order to activate the ⟨power of⟩ sense in the body, and it is transmitted by way of the motivating nerves in order to produce motion. This is the judgment passed on in *On the Difference between Soul and Mind,* and the teaching of *Anatomy* is in agreement with it.

302. I have said these things (paras.300–301) in order to make known what is meant by 'brain' in so far as it is said to be the organ of common sense, both what the brain is in so far as it is not connected with the sensory organs, and what it is in so far as it is connected with them. For it must be laid down that the organs of the proper senses are connected with the organ

of the common sense. Therefore either the ventricle of the brain which contains the source of the sensory nerves arising from a single root, or the original root itself of those nerves, or the animal soul in them, should be called the 'organ of the common sense', or each of these should be, though in different ways. And just as the organs of the proper senses are connected with that organ of the common sense, so also a pathway or pathways are extended from that organ right to the heart, whether by means of the blood vessels of the ⟨vascular⟩ net round the brain, or by means of the sensory and motivating nerves, or more likely by means of both.

303. The further objection (paras.253–255) can be conceded, since its conclusion is merely that the common sensory power performs its acts in the heart; and from this it does not follow that the power performs those acts especially, or primarily, or principally in the heart. But just as the heart is the first organ, working outward from within, so also it is the last in which the act of sensing occurs, for such an act works inward from without, and hence it eventually reaches the first organ.

304. Regarding the next objection (para.256) it can be said that it is the thin and subtle blood that is there said to be pure. For Aristotle appears to mean that such blood is warmer and more conducive to sensation than thick blood, while in other conditions thin blood and thick are equal. For Aristotle says there: 'Thick blood contains more food for the body, and is less conducive to sensation. But pure blood is warmer and more conducive to sensation.'[210] It should be conceded therefore that pure blood is suitable for the operation of the common sense. But it will not follow from this that the blood in the heart is especially suitable for the operation of the common sense. For blood in the heart is still thick and cloudy and thereafter is refined in the blood vessels.

305. And as to your statement (para.256) that it is purer and therefore more subtle at its source than elsewhere, it seems that this should be not be conceded. For water in soft earth bubbling in a spring is cloudy and thick, and thereafter it becomes clear and thin in streams, and that might also be how things are in the case of the production of blood.

306. Moreover, if it were conceded that blood at its source was purer, then it seems that this should be conceded only in the sense that in the heart the blood is not mixed up with bad humours, and not in the sense that the blood is thinner and more subtle in the heart. For when it is first produced the blood is thick and cloudy, and thereafter becomes thin and subtle, as already stated (paras.304–305).

307. But perhaps you will now offer the following objection. If pure, that is, thin and subtle, blood is warmer and more conducive to sensation, as Aristotle says (para.304), and if such is the blood in the blood vessels rather

---

210. *De part.animal.*, ii, 2 (648a2–4); *R* fol.194[rb–va]

than the blood in the heart, as you say, then the blood in the blood vessels is warmer and more conducive to sensation than is the blood in the heart. And it does not seem reasonable to say that there should be blood outside the heart that is warmer than the blood in the heart.

308. It seems to me that the reply is that blood is accidentally warmer in the heart than elsewhere, warmer in virtue of the place it is in, but elsewhere it is essentially warmer. For while the blood in the heart is very watery and earthy on account of its thickness and turbulence, it is essentially less warm. When it is purged of these things it becomes warmer ⟨which is what it is⟩ essentially.

309. Moreover, there was the objection (para.256) that if warmer blood is more conducive to sensation, it is more suitable for an act of the common sense, and in that case the blood in the heart, which is the warmest blood, is more suitable for such an act. It should be said that it is to the extent that it is warmer by virtue of an essential, not an accidental, warmth that it is more suitable for an act of the common sense. But to the extent that it is warmer by virtue of an accidental warmth, it is less suitable for such an act. But, as has already been said (para.308), the great warmth of the blood in the heart is accidental, either wholly or in large measure. For this reason, lest it be thought that accidental warmth is suitable, Aristotle adds a little later: 'And some blooded animals have colder and more subtle blood, and are wiser than animals that have blood of the opposite sort.'[211] But lest it be thought that an essential coldness is suitable he immediately adds: 'Better animals have blood which is warm, subtle, and pure since such animals stand better in respect of wisdom, courage, and such like.'[212] In the first of these two texts, therefore, he dismisses warmth which is accidentally greater, and in the second he notes the usefulness of essential warmth.

310. An indication of this is the fact that in delirious people the blood is much warmer than it ought to be, on account of the abundance of accidental heat, and in such people the blood is not suitable for use by the common sense or the imagination. But when their heat has been moderated so that the accidental heat does not have greater power than the essential heat, the blood begins to be suitable for the regular operations of the common sense and of imagination.

311. The following objections (paras.257–258), where it is argued that the common sense and the imagination use the heart since the desiderative power is there also, should be conceded.

312. Regarding all the objections which follow (paras.259–261), the reply is obvious, given the distinction made above (para.300) concerning the meaning of 'brain'. For if 'brain' is taken for that damp, white, softer mass

---

211. *Ibid.*, (648a7–8); *H* fol.35[va]; *cf. R* fol.194[va]
212. *Ibid.*, (648a9–11); *H* fol.35[va]

which is surrounded by the skull, a membrane, the ⟨vascular⟩ net, and the nerves, with other things enclosed, it is somewhat colder than is needed for the operation of the mind as such. And thus it lacks blood, nerves, and sense. But if it is taken for that mass in so far as it is wrapped in the membrane and the ⟨vascular⟩ net, and in so far as it is the source of the nerves and purifies and helps the corporeal soul, so that by the word 'brain' we understand the entire aggregate, it has enough soul and warmth to perform the operations of the mind. In this way, by means of the animal soul, it also has blood, nerves, and sense in those same parts. Thus all the objections are refuted.

313. But it should be noted that when Aristotle says (para.262) that there is no nerve in the head, this should be understood as a reference to the harder nerves in the body, nerves of a kind ordained by nature for the sake of the strong impulse that has to be produced for pushing, pulling, jumping, and so on. But there are also softer nerves there, the sensory and motivating ones, which, because of their softness, he does not there call 'nerves'.

314. Note also that Aristotle seems there to be speaking about the nerves by which bones are joined to each other, and not about other nerves. And hence he says that there are no nerves in the head, as it seems, since the bones in the head are not joined to each other by nerves but by sutures. For he says in the same place: 'There is no nerve in the head, and the bones in the head are joined only by zig-zag sutures.'[213]

315. We have therefore discussed these points (paras.219–314) about the organ of the common sense, by displaying, without any rash assertions, the agreement which obtains between things said by Aristotle and by others. At the same time, reader, note that we have squared the words of Aristotle with those of the others, because it is unlikely that all the ancient doctors and their modern imitators have made a mistake in claiming that the organs of the proper senses arise in the brain and converge in the same place in the one organ of the common sense. And Aristotle does not seem to contradict them when he says that the brain is the organ of sense. However, we dare not casually assert that things are not otherwise than they have claimed they are, for Aristotle does not say explicitly that the organs of all the proper senses converge in some place other than the heart. For he says (para.278) that nature placed some senses in the head next to the brain. It seems sufficiently clear from this that he means that the brain is an organ common to the three senses of sight, smell, and hearing. But as regards taste and touch he does not appear to make such a claim. But whatever be the truth about this question (q.4, para.219), it is certain that the teachings of Aristotle probably accord with those of the others. These points are for the present a sufficient reply to this secondary question.

---

213. *Hist.animal.*, iii, 5 (515b13–14); *R* fol.159[rb]

APPENDIX

Questions concerning time, from the *Commentary on the Sentences of Peter Lombard*, by Robert Kilwardby

Index of Questions in Appendix

QUESTION FOUR: Is there an order between existence and non-existence in creation? (paras.1–13)

Distinction 2: On the measure of the existence of angels, which is said to be everlastingness (para.14)

QUESTION TEN: How does everlastingness measure things? Is it a measure intermediate between eternity and time? (paras.15–26)

QUESTION ELEVEN: Of what things is everlastingness the measure? (paras.27–49) As regards pure spirits, such as angels, demons, and separated spirits, are their acts entirely in everlastingness or are they partly in everlastingness and partly in time? (paras.37–49)

QUESTION TWELVE: In what way are things in everlastingness? (paras.50–62)

QUESTION THIRTEEN: What is everlastingness? (paras.63–66)

The difference between an instant and everlastingness (para.64)

What is it of which everlastingness is essentially the measure? (para.65)

Question Four: Is there an order between existence and non-existence in creation?

1. The fourth question concerns the order in which this existence of the created world stands to its preceding non-existence: Does the order exist, and what kind of order is it? That there is an order is obvious, since in every relation of earlier and later, the two have some order to each other. That is the situation here. Since there was non-existence earlier, and existence thereafter, non-existence and existence are in some order. But what sort of order? In the *Confessions* Augustine distinguishes between four kinds of 'earlier', namely, (i) earlier in eternity, for example, God is earlier than all things; (ii) earlier in origin, for example, the sound is earlier than the song; (iii) earlier in time, for example, the blossom is earlier than the fruit; and (iv) earlier in choice, for example, the fruit is earlier than the blossom.[1] It is obvious from this that the order of non-existence and existence is like the order of eternity and time, for non-existence was in eternity but existence is in time.

2. But it seems that no order exists between them, for the following reason. A relation is of something to something. An order is a relation. Therefore it is to something. But the order of this existence is to non-existence. Non-existence, however, is not something. Hence there is no order between the two. Furthermore, an ordered existence presupposes an earlier existence. But non-existence is not at all an existence.

3. Moreover, if then at the first instant it was true to say 'The world exists' or it was true to say 'It does not exist', then either both these propositions were true in the same instant as the first now, or they were not. If they were, then at the same time the world both did and did not exist, and hence no order existed between existence and non-existence. But if they were true in different instants and not in the same one, then some intermediate time falls between them. There will therefore be a time before the first instant of time.

4. Moreover, the first instant is indivisible. Also non-existence is indivisible, since there is no earlier and later within it. Therefore those two things are two indivisible things, and they belong to the same order since one is earlier and the other is later. Therefore either there is something intermediate between them or there is not. Suppose there is. But any two indivisible things of the same order which have something between them are at a distance from each other on account of the divisible intermediary. In that case there will be a time before the first instant. Alternatively there is no intermediary between them, in which case they are touching. For all indivisible things between which there is no intermediary are wholly in mutual contact, since they are

---

1. See *Conf.*, xii, 29, 40; *CCSL* 27, 239 (10–12). Priority in choice is priority in goodness or worth. Assuming that our aim is nourishment, we should prefer the fruit to the blossom.

indivisible and do not have separate parts. Hence there is no order between them. Or if there is an order, it is an order of time, a temporal earlier and later.

5. It should be said that there is an order between them. In reply to the first objection to the contrary (para.2), therefore, it should be said that that non-existence is a non-existence without qualification, since it exists neither in matter nor in a thing. But in a way it is existence, for it exists potentially or in the foreknowledge of the good pleasure of the agent. It is in this way that it exists in eternity, and it is in this way that there is a relation and an order between them.

6. Reply to the second objection (para.3). It should be said that it is in different instants that it is true to say 'The world exists' and 'The world does not exist'. And when it is said that between any two instants there falls an intermediate instant, this is true as regards those instants which are of the same sort of measure, as for example, time is intermediate between two instants in time. But when they are not of the same sort of measure, as when one is in time and the other in eternity, it is not necessary ⟨that there should be an intermediate time⟩. So it is in the case under discussion. For non-existence was in eternity, but existence was in time.

7. Reply to the third objection (para.4). It should be said that between these two indivisible things there is no intermediary. But it does not follow from this that they occur at the same time, because indivisible things which belong to the same order, and which are also of the same kind of measure, are simultaneous if there is no intermediary between them, as is the case with two instants, and two points. But if they are not of the same kind of measure, then even granted that they belong to the same order, they are not necessarily simultaneous. This is the situation in the case under discussion, as is obvious from the preceding reply (para.6).

8. But since it is argued (para.4) that they must be simultaneous since they touch each other, or as it were touch each other, it should be said that this is not so. For indivisible things of the same measure touch each other and exist simultaneously when they do not have an intermediary, since they are on a path of the same nature, and, as I shall put it, they are directly present at the same limit. But indivisible things of different measures are not related in this way. For they are present at different limits which are placed next to each other, or one below and one above the other. And hence they never meet. This is obviously the case as regards an instant of time and an instant of eternity. Nor is there properly an intermediary in that case, but there is as it were a connection or a true connection between the one indivisible thing and the other, for, as Aristotle says: 'An intermediary is what a changing thing, changing continually in accordance with its nature, is naturally fitted

to reach before it reaches that into which it changes last.'[2] But there is no such thing between an instant of eternity and an instant of time.

9. But there is the following objection. Non-existence existed along with eternity, and eternity existed along with the first instant of time. Therefore non-existence existed along with the first instant of time.

10. This does not follow. It commits the fallacy of the accident or of the consequent, as here: 'A head exists along with the sense of touch. And touch exists along with a foot. Therefore there is a head with a foot.' For on account of its greater capacity, eternity exists along with non-existence and also along with the first instant of time, just as touch exists along with both a head and a foot, but non-existence and the first instant of time do not necessarily exist simultaneously.

11. Moreover, an instant of time exists along with an instant of eternity, and non-existence exists in that same instant of eternity. Therefore the instant of time and non-existence exist together, since they are simple things.

12. Reply. It does not follow, since existence and non-existence exist in different ways in eternity. For existence is in eternity as in a container; non-existence is in eternity as in its measure. And therefore it does not follow that that simple and indivisible instant of eternity can contain more than the whole of time. For although it is indivisible it is nevertheless in it as in a stable permanency as if it exists along with both existence and non-existence. That non-existence is in eternity, therefore, as in its proper measure. But the instant of time is in time as in its proper measure, and either the instant of time does not exist in eternity as in its measure but exists under it or along with it, or it does exist in eternity but as in a common measure.

13. Likewise the following argument is not valid: 'That you are seated is true in eternity since it is true in time. Likewise, that you are not seated will now be true in eternity for the same reason. Therefore you are both seated and are not seated at the same time, in the same instant. Therefore that you are seated and that you are not seated, are true at the same time'. This is because they are not true under the same aspect, but are true in accordance with different relations to time. And universally it is not valid when a first thing with which something is taken has a greater extent and a wider power than, and a different nature to, the second, and ⟨the argument⟩ means to present the two as being the same. And that is the situation here.

---

2. *Phys.*, v, 3 (226b23–25); *U* fol.59^r

On the angelic nature, etc. 'Distinction Two: ⟨On the measure of the existence of angels, which is said to be everlastingness'⟩[3]

14. Next there is a question especially about the creation of angels with respect to their when. And since the first question of Master ⟨Peter Lombard⟩ in this second Distinction is 'When were they created?', let us ask first about everlastingness, which is what the measure of their existence is called. Regarding this matter let us ask the following questions: (i) Does everlastingness exist in the way posited, namely, as a measure intermediate between eternity and time? (ii) What are the things that it measures? (iii) How does it measures them? (iv) What is it? (v) How is it related to an instant of time or of eternity?

Question Ten: How does everlastingness measure things? Is it a measure intermediate between eternity and time?

15. First, it seems that everlastingness is a sort of measure intermediate between eternity and time. For everlastingness is a measure, and it is neither time nor eternity. It is not time, for according to Augustine it differs from time in that time is mutable and everlastingness is stable.[4] And it is not eternity, since according to Augustine God is before everlastingness but He is not before eternity, for His eternity is the same as He. It will therefore be an intermediate measure.

16. Moreover, there is a kind of existence that is immutable without qualification, for example, the existence of God, whose measure is eternity; and there is a kind that is mutable — that can change, that is, from existing to not existing — but not from form to form. There are two kinds of mutability. Some things, for example, angels, are mutable by nature, but by grace they are not changed; and some things, for example, bodily things, are both mutable and are also changed. If therefore something, namely eternity, is a measure of the first kind of existence, and something, time, is a measure of the third kind, there will be another measure, everlastingness, which is a measure of the intermediate kind of existence.

17. Against this, it seems that eternity is the measure ⟨of the third kind of existence⟩. Isidore says: 'Everlastingness is perpetual age, of which neither its beginning nor its end is known.'[5] But only eternity is of such a nature. Therefore ⟨eternity is the measure of the third kind of existence⟩.

3. Peter Lombard *Sent.*, ii, 2, 1; ed. Grottaferrata, 1971, 1, 2, p.336 (12)
4. *De div.quaest.*, 83, q.72; *CCSL* 44A, 208 (8–10): 'Between everlastingness and time there is this difference, that everlastingness is stable and time is mutable.'
5. Isid.*Etymol.*, v, 38, 4; ed. Lindsay, 1

18. Moreover, Plato says that the archetypal world exists in everlastingness, but the sensible world exists in time.[6] Either this archetypal world is God or it is a model in accordance with which He made the world. But God exists only in eternity. Therefore everlastingness is the same as eternity.

19. Against this, it seems that everlastingness is time. Aristotle says that a measure is that by means of which a quantity is known.[7] But everlastingness is a measure. Therefore a quantity is known by means of it. Not a discrete quantity, since everlastingness is not a number and not a verbal expression either — for everlastingness is a measure which is not interrupted, whereas number and a verbal expression are interrupted — nor is a permanent continuous quantity, such as a line, surface, body, or place, known by means of everlastingness, since what can be subsumed under everlastingness cannot be subsumed under a measure appropriate to a line or a surface. Therefore everlastingness is a successive, continuous measure. But that is what time is. Therefore ⟨everlastingness is time⟩.

20. Moreover, the same thing is a discrete measure of all equal created things, whether corporeal or spiritual; for example, it is the same number ten that is the number of ten horses and of ten men, according to Aristotle.[8] Therefore, by the same token, the same thing will be a continuous measure of all things, corporeal as well as spiritual. And that measure is time.

21. It should be said that everlastingness exists, but that neither saints nor philosophers have said anything about it explicitly. The reason for this is perhaps that for a long time there has been an opinion that every spirit except the highest Spirit was conjoined to a body. But it should be noted that 'everlastingness' can be taken in several ways. For sometimes 'eternity' is used instead of 'everlastingness', as in *The Book of Causes*, proposition two: 'Every existence is either above eternity or in eternity, etc'.[9] And it says that God is above eternity, that is, above everlastingness, for certainly He is not above His true eternity. Sometimes 'everlastingness' is used instead of 'eternity', for example, by Isidore and Plato in the passages referred to earlier (paras.17–18). Sometimes 'everlastingness' is taken broadly to mean time, and vice versa; for example, everlastingness is said to be the age of one man. Sometimes it is said to be a whole generation. It is clear that this distinction

---

6. *Tim.*, 38B–C; ed.Waszink, p.30 (16–19)
7. *Metaph.*, x, 1 (1052b20); ed. Venetiis, 1574, fol.251^{rC}
8. Cf. *Phys.*, iv, 12 (220b10–12); *U* fol.52^v: 'It is one and the same number which is the number of a hundred horses and a hundred men.'
9. *Lib. de causis*, prop.2, 19; ed. Pattin, p.138 (71–73): 'Every higher existence is either above eternity and before it, or is along with eternity, or is after eternity and above time.'

is brought under the heading 'age' [= *saeculum*] by John of Damascus.[10] But everlastingness is, properly, the measure of the stable existence of perpetual things, for perpetual things are things that begin to exist and do not cease.

22. On this basis the reply to the words of Isidore and Plato (paras.17–18) is obvious, for they are speaking of everlastingness broadly and not strictly.

23. Hence, as regards the first argument (para.19), it should be said that it forces us to place everlastingness in a genus of entities. But according to Augustine at the start of *On the Quantity of Mind*, a distinction should be made. There are two kinds of quantity, quantity of mass and quantity of power.[11] But Aristotle (para.19) should be understood as speaking only about the quantity of mass. But by means of a measure, it is sometimes a quantity of mass that is known, and sometimes a quantity of power. The objection goes through if Aristotle is understood to be speaking about quantity of mass, but not if he is understood to be speaking about quantity of power, for everlastingness is a measure of the quantity of a power, not of a mass. But the power of what? It should be said that a stable permanence which exists in perpetual things is caused by a great power flowing into them, or endowed upon them at their creation. This power is what is measured by everlastingness. If this is true, it is obvious in what genus of entities everlastingness is to be found, for it is in the genus of quality, not of quantity. For this stable permanence is a quality of those things which are permanent in this way, and, as it seems to me, it has to be reduced to the second genus of quality, namely, to natural power, just like the stability and rigidity of body, and so on.

24. It is not to be wondered at that a quality should be a measure. For Aristotle says that knowledge is a measure of knowable things,[12] and yet knowledge is certainly a quality. But it is called 'a measure of knowable things' because things become known by means of knowledge.

25. Suppose it is asked why time more falls under the heading of 'quantity' than does everlastingness, since each of them is a measure of existence. It should be replied that what makes something a quantum is that it has a part next to, or outside, a part, as is obvious in the case of motion, magnitude, and number. In time, therefore, a part exists outside a part, and each part differs from the other in respect of existence, but the parts are connected to each

---

10. *De fide orthodoxa*, 15, 2; ed. Buytaert, p.66 (6–10): 'It should be noted that the noun "age" [= *saeculum*] has several significations. For it is used of each lifespan. "Age" is also used of a thousand year timespan. Furthermore it is used of the present life. And it is used of the future life which will be infinite after the resurrection.'
11. Aug.*De quant.animae*, 3, 4; *PL* 32, 1037: '...for we are accustomed to ask how big [= *quantus*] Hercules was...and likewise how great [= *quantus*] a man was, that is, of how great a power and strength.'
12. *Metaph.*, x, 1 (1053a31–32); ed. Venetiis, 1574, fol.254^{rF}: 'We also say that knowledge and sense are, for the same reason, a measure of things.'

other in an order of succession. And thus there is in time an extensiveness of parts which makes for ⟨the kind of⟩ existence which comes under the heading of 'quantity'. But in everlastingness there is not one existence and another, but an unchangeable duration of the same existence. Hence everlastingness and time are not alike.

26. Reply to the second argument (para.20). It should be said that number commonly follows upon a principle which exists in bodies and spirits, and so the same thing can be the number of bodies and the number of spirits. But time follows upon the existence of bodies, and hence, unlike everlastingness, it cannot be a measure of spirits. For there are different kinds of existence. Existence of one kind is both changeable and changed, and in that case time is its measure. Existence of another kind is unchangeable, and everlastingness is its measure.

Question Eleven: Of what things is everlastingness the measure?

27. Secondly there is a question concerning what things are measured by everlastingness. It seems from what Augustine says that angels are measured by it. No variation of time is in good angels, since 'they feel no change in themselves',[13] and hence they are not in time. And further on he says that 'all these things show that the holy angels are created by the holy Trinity',[14] and therefore do not exist in eternity, and hence exist in everlastingness.

28. The same thing seems to be true of the whole of rational creation.[15] For an intermediate measure is a measure of what has an intermediate nature. But rational creation is intermediate between a corporeal creation, which stays in time, and God, who is in eternity. Rational creation will therefore be in everlastingness, which is an intermediate measure between the other two measures.

29. Moreover, it seems, from what Augustine says, that prime matter exists in everlastingness: 'Where there is no species and no order nothing comes and nothing passes away, and where these things do not occur, there are no days or change of temporal periods.'[16] ⟨Prime⟩ matter, therefore, is above time. And it is certainly below eternity. Therefore it is in everlastingness.

30. The same thing seems true of the sky. For the sky is in potency with

---

13. Ps.Aug. (Fulgent. Rusp.) *De fide ad Petrum*, 30; *CCSL* 91A, 730
14. *Ibid.*
15. I have chosen the translation 'the whole of rational creation' rather than 'a wholly rational creature' because in para.27 Kilwardby dealt with angels who are wholly rational spirits. In para.28 he extends his argument to include other creatures who are also, though not wholly, rational.
16. *Conf.*, xii, 9, 9; *CCSL* 27, 221 (10–12)

respect to motion and posture,[17] but not with respect to its substance, and hence with respect to its substance it is not in time. Therefore with respect to its substance it will be in everlastingness.

31. The same point can also be extended to cover all the elements. For when they have ceased with respect to motion and have remained with respect to substance, it is obvious that with respect to substance they will be in everlastingness.

32. Moreover, since nothing is made into nothing, as Dionysius and the philosophers say,[18] but things change into spiritual forms, it seems that those spiritual forms remain, and thus the essence of everything remains always. And it will not remain in time, therefore in everlastingness.

33. Against this, it seems, from what Augustine says, that our minds are not in everlastingness: 'Even if there is no local motion in rational spirits which have been placed in earthy and mortal bodies, nevertheless the variety of thoughts reveals a diversity of temporal motion and change in rational souls. While they know something, there is something that they do not know; now they do not desire, now they do, now they consider,[19] now they do not.'[20] It is obvious that this is true also of contemplative souls,[21] who sometimes are more directed towards, and influenced by, God, and sometimes less. But such change can only be in time. Therefore it is not in everlastingness.

34. From what Augustine says, the same seems true of every rational nature: 'A creative spirit moves itself without time and place, but it moves a created spirit in time but not with regard to place. But it moves a body with regard to both time and place.'[22] Therefore every such nature falls under time.

35. The same also seems true of corporeal nature. In the Timaeus Plato says that the archetypal world is in everlastingness, but the sensible world is in time (para.18).[23] Therefore the parts of the sensible world, that is, heaven and all the elements, will be in time, not in everlastingness.

36. The solution to all the foregoing problems (paras.27–35) is obvious from the following distinction. All those things can be considered under two different aspects, either in respect of their substantial existence, in which case they are in everlastingness, or in respect of their active existence, in which case they are in time. For essences are not subject to time, but actions are. Hence

17. 'posture', that is, the heavenly sphere does not move in the sense of successively occupying different parts of space, but it does move in relation to the poles.
18. *Cf.* Ps.-Dionys.*De cael. hier.*, 7; ed.Chevallier, 2, 1413-1414: '...others think, unreasonably, that it recedes into non-existence.'
19. 'consider' (= *sapiunt*), that is, 'savour', as in 'savour an idea'.
20. Ps.-Aug.(Fulgent. Rusp.) *De fide ad Petrum*, 29; *CCSL* 91A, 730
21. or 'contemplatives', that is, people who have reached the level of contemplation (which is a technical term for a state of prayer).
22. *De Gen.ad litt.*, viii, 20; *CSEL* 28, 3, 2, p.259 (22-25)
23. *Tim.*38B–C

the second last proposition in *The Book of Causes* is: 'Between a thing whose substance and action are in a moment of eternity and a thing whose substance and action are in a moment of time, there are intermediate things whose substance is in a moment of eternity and whose action is in a moment of time.'[24] Likewise Dionysius says that there are some things intermediate between eternal things and temporal ones, which share in everlastingness on one side, and share in time on the other.[25] Hence it follows that some bodies, and also our spirits while in bodies, are in everlastingness in one respect, and are in time in another.

37. But as regards pure spirits, such as angels, demons, and separated souls, there is a question concerning whether their acts are entirely in everlastingness, or are partly in everlastingness and partly in time. It seems, from Augustine's words, that they are entirely in everlastingness, at least as regards the good angels. He says that a 'rational creature' who clings 'to God with a chaste love does not become subject to the fluctuation and vicissitude of time'.[26] From this it is obvious, so it seems, that their act will be in everlastingness.

38. Against this are the words of Anselm: 'Is it also in this way that you surpass even all eternal things, since your whole eternity and theirs is wholly present to you?' But they do not have that part of their blessedness which is future, 'just as they do not have that which is past'.[27] Therefore since their blessedness is not a simultaneous whole it will be in time, and hence at least one of their acts will be in time.

39. Moreover, it is believed that in purgatory the souls of the just are changed successively from sorrow to joy, and also from one grade of joy to another. So it seems that in them something passes away and something remains, and thus ⟨their act is⟩ in time.

40. The same seems true of full blessedness. For at the resurrection the joy of the good will be increased. There is therefore a change in them, since a level they possessed passed away and a different one replaced it.

41. The same thing is true of the damned: 'The pride of those who hate you always rises',[28] 'pride', that is, 'their inordinate passion'.

42. It seems from these arguments (paras.38–41) that in respect of some of their acts, spirits are in time, and thus are not entirely in everlastingness.

43. Solution. A distinction should be made, for there are three ways of being in time. (i) One way is to be in an indivisible part of time, as for example

---

24. *Lib. de causis*, prop.30 (31), 210; ed. Pattin, p.198 (43–48)
25. Ps.-Dionys.*De div.nom.*, 10; ed. Chevallier, 1, 493
26. *Conf.*, 12, 15, 19; *CCSL* 27, 225 (21–25)
27. *Proslog.*, 20; ed. Schmitt, p.115 (26)–116 (2)
28. *Ps.*72, 23 (74, 23 in *NEB*)

with a sudden change which is in time, as Aristotle says.[29] (ii) Another way is to be in time like the interrupted, and not continuous, changes of a thing, changes which exist in different instants of time. For example, suppose that an angel conceives a desire, and that first the desire is stable, and then increases. Though these desires are interrupted, they are nevertheless said to be in time since they occur at different instants of time, and in this way are in time in so far as time is a number, but not in so far as it is continuous. (iii) A third way of being in time is to be with the succession of time, as continuous motion is in time. And this is properly to be in time.

44. Furthermore, another distinction should be made. For spirit can be considered in respect of substantial existence, and as such it is in everlastingness; and it can be considered in respect of its acts or its active existence, and this act is either perpetual or transitory. If it is perpetual, as for example is the contemplation of God, then either it can be considered in itself, and in that case is in everlastingness, since its contemplating always remains and is stable; or it can be considered in respect of its circumstance, for example, in respect of the intension or remission[30] of the act. And then, according to those who claim that angels increase in knowledge and blessedness, there is motion and alteration there, as Jerome seems to claim,[31] and thus they can be said to be in time. Augustine however, seems to claim the opposite.[32] But if the act of the spirit is considered as transitory, then either the act is sudden, as is, for example, the sudden forming of a conception of something, and in that case it can be said to be in time in the first or second way of being in time. If the spirit's act is considered as successive, as for example, when it is sent to perform some task, such acts are, properly, in time.

45. On the basis of these distinctions (paras.43–44) the reply to all the foregoing objections made on either side (paras.37–41) is very plain. But you might say: Aristotle says that the continuity of motion arises from the

---

29. *Phys.*, iv, 13 (222b14–17); *U* fol.54ᵛ: 'Although suddenly exists in imperceptible time, it is remote on account of its smallness.'
30. 'intension' and 'remission', technical terms for phenomena closely investigated in the thirteenth and fourteenth centuries. Light and sound are equally good models. Each is more intense when closer to its source, and more remiss when further from it. 'Strength' and 'weakness' would serve as well.
31. Hieron.*In Epist.ad Ephes.*, 3, 3, 9–10, according to Peter Lombard *Sent.*, ii, 11, 2; ed. Grottaferrata, 1971, 1, 2, p.382 (10–16): '...Jerome says [cf.*PL* 26: 514B–515A] that the angels on high did not fully understand the aforementioned mystery until the passion of Christ was completed and the apostles' preaching spread through the gentile peoples.'
32. *De Gen.ad litt.*, v, 19, according to Peter Lombard *Sent.*, ii, 11, 2; ed. Grottaferrata, 1971, 1, 2, p.382 (18–22): 'Augustine seems to contradict this, when discussing the same passage in the Epistles, when he says: "The mystery of the kingdom of heaven did not lie hidden from the angels, a mystery which was revealed at the proper time for the sake of our salvation. That mystery, therefore, was known to them from the ages, for every creature is not before the ages but from them.'

continuity of magnitude;[33] but there is no magnitude in spirits. Their act therefore cannot be continuous in any way, and hence is not in time.

46. The reply is as follows. It should be said that what Aristotle says should be taken to refer only to magnitude which is corporeal and to magnitude in local motion, and in that case does not touch upon the issue at hand. Alternatively it can also be generally conceded that there is no motion without magnitude. But there are two sorts of magnitude, magnitude of mass and magnitude of power, and necessarily motion requires magnitude of one or the other of these sorts. But in the case of the motion of spirits the magnitude required is the magnitude of power. That motion can be based upon magnitude of power is obvious in the case of change from sickness to health, for there is motion there, not based upon magnitude of mass but of power, which loses some of one of a pair of contraries when it acquires more of the other.

47. Reply to the first objection (para.37) concerning angels. It should be said, in accordance with Augustine's teaching, that in contemplation by those spirits no change or alteration occurs. But for the sake of those who claim the opposite, make a distinction regarding the act of those spirits. Either it is an inner act, and in it there is, according to Augustine, no change, but their contemplating remains always the same; or it is outer, and such an act is in time, as is obvious from Augustine's words.[34]

48. Reply to the second objection (para.38). If Anselm is speaking about an inner act by angels in itself, an act such as contemplation, then such an act is in eternity, but if he is speaking about such an act in respect of its circumstances then it is in time. If he is speaking about an outer act then it is obvious that the act is, again, in time.

49. Reply to the subsequent objections (paras.39–41). It should be said that if the desire is continuous then it is in time in the third way of being in time (para.43–iii). It is now obvious which things are in time and which in everlastingness.

Question Twelve: ⟨In what way are things in everlastingness?⟩

50. Thirdly it is now asked in what way things are in everlastingness. Do all things which are in everlastingness have one everlastingness, or do different things have a different one? It seems that there is only one everlastingness, since on the lower side there is only one time, and on the upper side there is only one eternity. So in the middle there will be only one everlastingness.

---

33. *Cf. Phys.*, iv, 11 (219a12–13); *U* fol.51ᵛ: 'For it is because magnitude is continuous that motion is continuous.'
34. *Cf.*Aug.*De Gen.ad litt.*, viii, 24; *CSEL* 28, 3, 2, p.263 (7–14)

51. Moreover, where there is greater simplicity there should be greater unity. But there is greater simplicity in everlastingness than in time, since in everlastingness there is permanent existence, and in time existence is successive. But there is one time for all temporal things. Therefore there will be one everlastingness for all everlasting things.

52. Moreover, that everlastingness is one, follows from this argument. Greater unity follows from more perfect existence. If therefore perpetual existence is more perfect than temporal existence, perpetual existence will have greater unity. Therefore the duration measuring perpetual existence will be one to a greater degree. Since therefore the duration measuring the existence of all temporal things is one, how much more will that other duration be one.

53. Against this: If everlastingness were one there would be an earlier and a later within it, just as there is in time, since the angelic nature was created before the firmament, and each of these exists in everlastingness as has been said (paras.27, 30, 36).

54. Moreover, first one soul is created, then another. If they are in everlastingness in respect of their substance, as has been said (para.44), there will be an earlier and a later there. This is absurd, since Dionysius says that everlastingness measures an unchanging whole existence.[35]

55. Moreover, there is the following argument. Whenever two things are related as earlier to later in nature only, as are the sun and its rays, whatever precedes one of these in time, also precedes the other in time. As regards their substance, if Adam's soul and my soul are in everlastingness, the relation of earlier and later between them is a relation of earlier and later in nature only. Therefore whatever precedes my soul in time precedes Adam's soul in time. But my body preceded my soul in time, and therefore it also preceded Adam's soul.

56. Reply. These souls can be considered in respect of their substances, and in that case they are simultaneous in everlastingness. And they can be considered in respect of their beginnings, and in that case since the beginning of one was in a preceding time, then in this respect it preceded.

57. In reply to this some say that there is not one everlastingness.[36] And as regards the first objection (para.50) they reply that though there is a lower extreme and an upper, it does not follow that there is just one thing which is intermediate, as is obvious in the case of colours.

58. Reply to the second objection (para.51). We say that a unity is

---

35. Ps.-Dionys. *De div.nom.*, 10; ed. Chevallier, 1, 496: 'It is an inseparable characteristic of an age that it measures an ancient and immutable existence taken as a whole.'
36. Bonaventure denies the unity of everlastingness. See *In Sent.*, ii, 2, 1, 1, 2; ed. 'to clear waters' (Quaracchi), 1882, 2, 58-60. But the reply that Kilwardby cites is not there.

essential in respect of essence or in respect of existence. Therefore in respect of its essence and in itself everlastingness is one. But in respect of its existence which it has in many subjects it is not one. There is no comparison with time. For time is in one subject, the sky, and it is in relation to that that all temporal things have their existence. But everlastingness has not one subject but many, not one of which is dependent upon any other.

59. Against this, Aristotle says that even if there were many heavens, there would nevertheless be one time.[37] Likewise, therefore, though in everlastingness there are many things, none of which depends upon any other, there could nevertheless be one everlastingness.

60. Moreover, in all these things which are in everlastingness there is a unity, at any rate a unity by analogy, for existence is one in all everlasting things. In virtue of this fact, therefore, there can be unity in everlastingness. Hence there seems no reason to claim that there are many everlastingnesses.

61. It can therefore be said, and perhaps better said, that in all everlasting things there is one everlastingness. But a distinction should be made. For either it is considered in itself, and in that case it is a one which is one as a genus of entities. Alternatively it can be considered in respect of its particularization in the things which are in it, and in that case it is multiple, just as are those many things, and it is one just as they also are. But all those things come together in one genus and one substance, which is a unity by analogy. Thus everlastingness will be one by analogy and by genus, but not numerically one.

62. The subsequent objection (para.53) should be dealt with in terms of this distinction: in everlastingness considered in itself there is no earlier and later, for it is a permanent unchangeable existence. But considered in its particularization in those things of which it is the measure, either it is considered in its particularization in single individuals (in which case there is no earlier and later in everlastingness, since these things are unchangeable), or in its particularization in all things at the same time. And since some of these things are earlier and some are later, there is an earlier and a later in everlastingness — not everlastingness in itself, but in respect of the individuals taken simultaneously, and this is a merely accidental earlier and later.

---

37. *Phys.*, iv, 10 (218b3–5): *U* fol.50^v: 'But furthermore, if there were several heavens, there would likewise be a time for the motion of all of them. There will, therefore, be many times simultaneously.'

Question Thirteen: What is everlastingness?

63. The fourth question is: What is everlastingness? It can be said, on the basis of the foregoing, that everlastingness is the measure of the unchanged existence of a perpetual thing.

64. A fifth thing is obvious here, namely the difference between an instant and everlastingness. For the unchanged existence of a perpetual thing, of which everlastingness is the measure, can be considered (i) absolutely and without qualification, that is, without duration, in so far as this existence is only present to a thing which exists in this way, and in that case its measure is an instant; or it can be considered (ii) with duration, and as such it falls under the heading of 'everlastingness'. For everlastingness is the measure of that existence in so far as it has duration, but the instant is the measure of the same existence in so far as it is present.

65. But there is a question about what it is of which everlastingness is essentially the measure. It should be said that essentially it is the measure of that unchanged existence. For just as Aristotle says that time is essentially the measure of the existence of moveable things, that is, of motion, and is accidentally the measure of the moveable things themselves, since they are measured only by their motion,[38] so also everlastingness is essentially the measure of that ⟨unchanged⟩ existence; and by means of that existence it is the measure of everlasting things.

66. To someone who objects that it seems absurd that everlastingness should essentially measure duration, since it would thereby be measuring itself, it should be said that that is not absurd. For it is universally the case as regards simple things that they give their name to, and measure, themselves. For example, motion is measured by time, but time is measured by itself.

---

38. *Ibid.*, 12 (221b19–20); *U* fol.53^v: 'For this reason what is in motion will be measurable by time not simply according as it has a quantity, but according as its motion has a quantity.'

Bibliography

Abbreviations

AL   *Aristoteles latinus*, eds. G. Lacombe, L. Minio-Paluello *et al.*, 1939–.
CCSL *Corpus christianorum. Series latina*, (Turnhout, 1953–).
CSEL *Corpus scriptorum ecclesiasticorum latinorum*, (Vienna, 1866–).
PL   *Patrologiae cursus completus...Series latina*, ed. J.P.Migne, 221 vols. (Paris, 1844–64).
U   See: Aristotle, *Physica*.

Alexander of Hales, *Summa Theologica*, ed. Quaracchi, 4 vols. and index 1924–79.
[Alhazen] 'auctor *Perspective*', *Optica*, ed. Risner, (Basel, 1572).
Anselm of Canterbury, *Monologion*, ed. F.S.Schmitt, *Opera Omnia*, 1, (Seckau, 1938)
—— *Proslogion*, ed. F.S.Schmitt, *Opera Omnia*, 1, (Seckau, 1938).
Aristotle, *Analytica Posteriora*, tr. Iacobi, ed. L.Minio-Paluello and B.G.Dod, *AL* 4, 1–4, (Leiden, 1968).
—— *De anima*, tr. Vetus, ed. C.Stroick, *S.Alberti Magni Opera Omnia,* 6, 1, *De anima*, (Munster, i.W,1968).
—— *De generatione animalium*, transl. Arab.-lat. MSS British Library, Royal 12. C. XV [*R*] and Harley 4970 [*H*].
—— *Historia animalium*, trans. Arab.-lat., MSS *R* and *H*.
—— *Physica*, transl. Vetus, MS Vat., Urb. lat.206 = *U*
—— *Metaphysica*, transl. Arab.-lat., *Aristotelis opera cum Averrois Cordubensis in eosdem commentariis*, 8, Venice, 1574.
—— *De insomniis* (*De somno et vigilia*), tr. Vetus, ed. H.J.Drossart Lulofs, *Philosophia antiqua*, 2, 1–2, (Leiden, 1947).
—— *De partibus animalium*, tr. Arab.-lat., MSS *R* and *H*.
—— *Praedicamenta*, tr. Boethius, editio composita, ed. L. Minio-Paluello, *AL* 1, 1–5, (Bruges-Paris, 1961).
Augustine, *Confessiones*, ed. L. Verheijen, *CCSL* 27, (Turnhout, 1981).
—— *De civitate Dei*, eds. B.Dombart and Kalb,A., 2 vols., *CCSL* 47, 48, (Turnhout, 1955).
—— *De diversis quaestionibus* 83, ed. A.Mutzenbecher, *CCSL* 44A, (Turnhout, 1975).

―― *Epistulae*, ed. A.Goldbacher, CSEL 34, (Vienna, 1895).
―― *De Genesi ad litteram*, ed. J. Zycha, *CSEL* 28, 3, pt.2, (Vienna, 1894).
―― *De musica*, *PL*, 32.
―― *De quantitate animae*, *PL* 32.
―― *Retractationes*, ed. P.Knöll, *CSEL* 36, (Vienna, 1902).
―― *Soliloquia*, *PL* 32.
―― *De Trinitate*, ed. W.J.Mountain, 2 vols., *CCSL*, 50, 50A, (Turnhout, 1968).
―― *De vera religione*, ed. K.-D. Daur, CCSL 32, (Turnhout, 1962).
Averroes, *In metaphysica*, *Opera*, 8, (Venice, 1574).
―― *In Physica*, *Opera*, 4, (Venice, 1574).
Avicenna, *Liber de anima*, ed. S. van Riet, 2 vols. (Louvain-Leiden, 1968–72).
Boethius, *Philosophiae consolatio*, ed.L.Bieler, *CCSL* 94, (Turnhout, 1957).
Bonaventura, *Commentaria in quatuor libros Sententiarum*, 4 vols., *Opera Omnia*, 1–4, (Quaracchi, 1882–89).
Callus, Daniel A., O.P., 'The "Tabulae super originalia patrum" of Robert Kilwardby, O.P.' in *Studia Mediaevalia in Honorem R.J.Martin* (Bruges, 1948), 243–52.
Clagett, M., *The Science of Mechanics in the Middle Ages*, (Madison, 1961).
[Costa ben Luca], *De differentia animae et spiritus*, ed. C.S.Barach, *Bibliotheca philosophorum Mediae Aetatis*, 2, (Innsbruck, 1878).
Euclid, *Elementa geometriae*, tr. Adelhard II: M.Clagett, 'The Medieval Latin Translations from the Arabic of the *Elements* of Euclid with Special Emphasis on the Versions of Adelhard of Bath', *Isis* 44, (1953), 16–42.
Gelber, H.G., 'The fallacy of accident and the Dictum de Omni', *Vivarium* 25, 1987, 110–145.
Hamblin, C.L., *Fallacies*, (London, 1970).
Hammond, E.A., *The Medical Practitioners in Medieval England: A Biographical Register*, (London, 1965).
Hieronymus, *In Epistola ad Ephesios*, *PL* 26.
Isidore, *Etymologiae*, ed. W.M.Lindsay, 2 vols., (Oxford, 1911).
Jerome, see Hieronymus.
Judy, Albert G., O.P. (ed.) *Robert Kilwardby, O.P., De Ortu Scientiarum* (Auctores Britannici Medii Aevi IV), (Oxford, 1976).
Kilwardby, Robert, see Judy, Albert G., and Lewry, P.Osmund (ed.).
Kneepkens, C.H., '"Mulier quae damnavit, salvavit": A note on the early development of the Relatio Simplex', *Vivarium*, 14 (1976), 1–25.
John of Damascus (Johannes Damascenus), *De fide orthodoxa*, tr. Burgundy, ed. E.M.Buytaert, (St Bonaventure, N..Y., 1955)
Lewry, P. Osmund, O.P., 'The Oxford Condemnations of 1277 in grammar and logic' in *English Logic and Semantics from the End of the Twelfth Century to the Time of Ockham and Burleigh: Acts of the Fourth European*

Symposium on Medieval Logic and Semantics, eds. H.A.G.Braakhuis, C.H.Kneepkens, L.M. de Rijk; (Nijmegen, 1981), Artistarium Supplementa 1, 235–278.

—— 'Robert Kilwardby on meaning: A Parisian course on the "Logica vetus"', in *Sprache und Erkenntnis im Mittelalter,* ed. A.Zimmermann, (Berlin-New York, 1981), Miscellanea Mediaevalis, 13/1, 376–384.

—— 'Robert Kilwardby on imagination: The reconciliation of Aristotle and Augustine' in *Medioevo,* 9, 1983, 1–42.

—— (ed.) *Robert Kilwardby O.P. On Time and Imagination: De Tempore, De Spiritu Fantastico* (Auctores Britannici Medii Aevi IX), (Oxford, 1987).

Liber de causis, ed. A.Pattin, Tijdschrift voor Filosofie, 28 (1966).

Liber sex Principiorum, Minio-Paluello, L. and Dod, B.G. (eds.), (Leiden, 1966).

Pattin, A. See *Liber de causis.*

Peter Lombard, *Sententiae,* 3rd ed., prolegomena and 2 vols. (Grottaferrata, 1971–81).

Plato, *Timaeus,* tr. Calcidius, ed. J.H.Waszink, (Leiden, 1962).

Pseudo-Augustine [Alcher Clarevallensis?], *De spiritu et anima,* PL 40.

Pseudo-Augustine [Fulgentius Ruspensis], *De fide ad Petrum,* ed. J.Fraipont, *CCSL* 91A, (Turnhout, 1968).

Pseudo-Dionysius, *De caelesti hierarchia,* transl. Robert Grosseteste, ed. P.Chevallier, *Dionysiaca,* 2, (Paris, 1950).

—— *De divinis nominibus* (transl. Saracen and Robert Grosseteste), ed. P. Chevallier, *Dionysiaca,* 1 (Paris, 1937).

Pseudo-Galen [Pseudo-Richard Anglicus], *Anatomia vivorum,* ed. R. von Töply, (Vienna, 1902).

Richard de St. Victoire, *De Trinitate,* ed. J.Ribailler, (Paris, 1958).

Richard Fishacre, *Commentaria in quatuor libros Sententiarum,* MS Oxford, Balliol College 57.

Thomas Aquinas, *In octo libros Physicorum Aristotelis expositio,* ed. M.Maggiolo, (Marietti, 1954).

—— *Summa Theologiae,* 60 vols., Blackfriars, with Eyre and Spottiswoode, (London, 1964–76).

Index

T = On Time I = On Imagination A = Appendix
Numerals prefixed by **T**, **I** or **A** refer to numbered paragraphs of *On Time*, *On Imagination* or of the *Appendix* respectively. Numerals not thus prefixed refer to the page of the *Introduction*

Albert the Great 1–2
Alexander of Hales
  on 'an age' **T** 122, n. 83
  angels have a higher existence than bodies **I** 56
  on 'now' **T** 105, n. 67, **T** 107, **T** 109, **T** 118
  on the punishment of Hell **T** 121, n. 82
  on the unity of time **T** 67, n. 43
Alhazan
  on optic nerves **I** 298, n. 209
angels
  creation of **T** 111–12, **T** 115, **A** 14
  desires of, in time **A** 43
  everlastingness and 8, **A** 14, **A** 27, **A** 37
  inner acts by **A** 44, n. 31–2, **A** 47, **T** 131
  mutable by nature **A** 16
  nature of 18
  the now of **T** 105, **T** 109–110
animals
  common sense in **I** 254
  and desirable things **I** 209–10
  mind and soul in **I** 2
  two souls in **I** 182
Anselm
  on acts in time and eternity **A** 48
  on eternity **A** 38
  on the existence of God in all time **T** 128, **T** 132–3, **T** 136, **T** 140, **T** 143
Aquinas 1–2
  on time **T** 3, n.3
Aristotle
  on blood **I** 260, **I** 276–7, **I** 294, **I** 309
  on the brain **I** 225–8, **I** 230, **I** 233–4, **I** 236, **I** 250, **I** 252, **I** 259, **I** 261, **I** 264, **I** 267, **I** 275–8, **I** 288
  on continuity of motion **A** 45–6
  on the countability of motion 4
  on defective sense **I** 76
  on dreaming as a passivity of the common sense **I** 151
  on efficient cause **I** 83
  on the fallacy of the argument **I** 122, n. 91
  on fantasy as a motion made by sense **I** 150, **I** 193
  on the flux of time **T** 106
  on the heart **I** 242–9, **I** 253, **I** 256–8, **I** 267, **I** 269, **I** 275–8
  on images **I** 26, **I** 269
  on images of sensible things **I** 69, **I** 159
  on imagination **I** 32, **I** 144
  on imperceptible time **A** 43
  on intelligible things **I** 15, **I** 26
  on an intermediary **A** 8
  on 'lesser genus of being' **I** 96
  on likenesses **I** 4
  on local motion **T** 14–16, **T** 96
  on a measure of knowable things **A** 24
  on measure of a quantity **A** 19–20, **A** 23
  on mind in relation to soul **I** 1–2
  on motion and matter **T** 65
  on motion of the mind **I** 167
  on motion of the sphere **T** 50–1
  on nerves in the head **I** 262, **I** 314
  on the now and when of time **T** 89–90
  on one time **A** 59
  on the organ of common sense **I** 159, **I** 194, **I** 201, **I** 269
  on permanence of images **I** 159, **I** 194, **I** 201, **I** 269
  on pure blood **I** 256, **I** 304
  on sense **I** 112, **I** 254, **I** 260, **I** 264
  on sense of hearing **I** 191, **I** 250
  on sense of touch **I** 236–8, **I** 249
  on sensible things **I** 15, **I** 69
  on the sentient soul **I** 69
  on sight **I** 212, **I** 250
  on things agreeable to the mind **I** 207
  on things not in time **T** 129–30
  on three causes and matter **I** 80–1, **I** 129–32
  on time and motion **T** 10, **T** 13, **T** 21, **T** 27, **T** 30–1, **T** 39–45, **T** 50–1, **T** 73–75, **T** 77, **T** 85, **A** 65
  on time as a cause of decay **T** 5
  on time as a measure **T** 71, **T** 86

on time outside the mind 3, 7
on two modes of change I 61–2
Augustine
  on acts of nature I 127
  on bodily sense I 118–19, I 172
  on body and mind I 49–50, I 84, I 102, I 118, I 120, I 171, I 177–8
  on body and soul 12, I 47–8, I 52–5, I 64, I 89–91
  on the brain and the senses I 170, I 291
  on corporeal seeing I 106–7
  on everlastingness A 15, A 29, A 34
  on existence in time T 4, T 10
  on false images I 33–5
  on four kinds of 'earlier' A 1
  on God I 164
  on images I 4, I 6–7, I 18, I 24, I 30, I 36–7, I 45, I 64, I 67, I 72–4, I 78, I 80–1, I 145–6
  on images in and from the mind 14
  on images of sensible things 13, I 128, I 148
  on imagination I 24, I 29, I 37, I 144, I 193
  influence on Kilwardby 1
  on informing of sense I 160, I 205
  on inner acts by angels A 44, n. 32, A 47
  on the intellect I 18–19, I 35, I 43
  on intelligible things I 26
  on mind acting on itself I 120–1, I 134
  on mind common to man and beasts I 84–5, I 140–1
  on mind in relation to soul I 1–2
  on motion of the mind I 167
  on the organs of sense I 170–1, I 191
  on phantasms I 66, I 72, I 115
  on quantity A 23
  on sense I 184
  on sense of taste I 294
  on sense of touch I 297
  on the senses I 8–9, I 24, I 37, I 54, I 71
  on 'sensing' I 102, I 105
  on the soul as a visual organ I 174
  on the soul as the primary organ of hearing I 175
  on time and the actions of the spirits T 71
  on time counted by the mind T 73, n. 50
  on time in the mind T 4, T 10
  on trinities I 107, I 109
Averroes
  on acts of nature I 127
  on forming of images I 127
  on measuring motion 5–6
  on natural motion I 166
  on 'number' T 37–8
  on time and mind 7
  on time and motion T 34–6, T 39, T 41, T 45, T 62, T 75–7
Avicenna
  on common sense and the soul I 168, n. 114
  on imagination I 152, n.106

beasts
  images in the sensory soul of 12
  imagination of I 13
  intellect of I 44
  mind common to man and I 84–7, I 109, I 139–41
blood I 256, I 260, I 268, I 276–7, I 294, I 304, I 307–10
body
  and corporeal things I 120
  and efficient cause I 62, I 121
  five senses of I 176
  health of the I 99–101
  and intellect I 51
  and images I 47, I 60, I 63–4, I 66–7, I 73–4, I 78, I 80, I 85–6, I 119, I 134, I 145, I 165
  and images of sensible things 12–13
  and imagination I 52
  and mind I 49–50, I 54, I 65, I 75, I 84, I 100, I 118, I 120–1, I 123, I 125, I 166, I 171, I 174, I 178–9, I 217
  next to the incorporeal I 177
  passivity of the I 54, I 102–3, I 119–20, I 123, I 136, I 150–1, I 166, I 171, I 185
  and sense I 119, I 264
  and the sensory soul I 99
  and soul 12, I 3, I 47–8, I 53, I 55, I 60–1, I 89–91, I 101, I 103, I 165
Boethius
  on images I 20–2
  on intellect I 20–2, I 27
  on the order of creation T 111
Bonaventure
  denies the unity of everlastingness A 57, n. 36
  on time T 68, n. 45, T 71, n. 46
brain
  and animal soul I 270, I 301
  blood around the I 277
  is bloodless I 261
  is cold I 223, I 259, I 274–6
  and common sense I 169, I 201, I 220, I 227, I 229–30, I 232, I 234, I 238–41, I 259, I 263, I 265–6, I 268, I 274, I 280–6, I 285, I 288–9, I 298, I 302, I 315
  composition of the I 169–70, I 196, I 201, I 221–3, I 225–6, I 228, I 230, I 259, I 286, I 289, I 300–1, I 312
  and the corporeal soul I 239, I 280
  imagination in the I 169, I 201, I 284–6
  and memory I 201

INDEX

opposite the heart I 276, I 278
is the organ of thought I 224
and the proper senses I 169–70, I 251, I 266, I 271, I 288, I 299–302
rational chamber in the I 201, I 221
and sense I 264
and sense of hearing I 291, I 298
and sense of sight I 315
and sense of smell I 315
and sense of taste I 289–95
and sense of touch I 236, I 297
and the sense organs I 231–3, I 250–2, I 267
is the spiritual organ I 239
and the vital soul I 301

cognition
  and desire I 163
  and imagination I 151, I 164
  produced by light I 164
common sense
  in the brain I 169, I 201, I 220, I 227, I 229–30, I 232–4, I 238–41, I 259, I 263, I 265–6, I 268, I 274, I 280–6, I 298–9, I 302, I 315
  brain is an organ of I 288
  common to sight and hearing I 227
  and the corporeal soul I 205
  and dreaming I 151
  in the heart I 242–9, I 251, I 255–7, I 259, I 263, I 265–6, I 274, I 280–3, I 285, I 288, I 299, I 311
  and images of sensible things I 151–7, I 168, I 183–6, I 219
  and imagination I 151, I 168, I 285
  the imaginative soul is I 239
  is a natural operation of the brain I 229, I 232
  organ of 16–17, I 152–3, I 156, I 219–20, I 234
  is the primary power I 254
  and the proper senses I 156, I 168, I 173, I 183–6, I 191, I 219, I 251–2, I 254
  and pure blood I 256, I 304
  relation to imagination I 151
  and sensible things I 151, I 154–6
  and the sensory soul I 154, I 156, I 185
  and the soul I 168
  two organs corresponding to I 271–4
  and warm blood I 309
corporeal things
  and bodily sense I 172
  and the body I 120
  images of 11–12, I 5–7, I 9–13, I 23, I 25, I 28–9, I 31, I 41, I 45, I 68, I 134, I 140, I 150, I 166, I 191
  measured by time T 72

and the mind I 140
Costa ben Luca
  on animal and vital soul I 270, n. 197
  on the brain I 201, I 288, n. 203
  on common sense and imagination I 169
  on the mind I 262
  on motion and the brain I 285
  on the organ of sense I 173
  on the place of soul in the brain I 152, n. 106, I 301
  on sense of taste I 290, I 294–5

desire
  and cognition I 163
  confused I 162, I 209–10
  and images 16, I 162–3
  and imagination I 207–9
  and memory I 209, I 211
divine knowledge as the cause of things I 77

efficient cause
  of cognition I 123
  and a form I 82–3, I 138
  and images 13–15, I 60, I 62–3, I 66, I 80, I 103, I 115–17, I 129
  and the mind I 121
eternity
  durationless 8
  and everlastingness A 18, A 50
  as a measure of existence A 16
  and non-existence A 5, A 9, A 11
  the now of T 107
  and prime matter A 29
  and time 7–8, 18, T 69–70, T 79, T 84, A 1, A 6, A 11–16, A 38, A 48
  two ways of being in 7
everlastingness
  of angels 8, A 14, A 27, A 37
  between time and eternity 19, T 68, A 14–26, A 28
  the elements in A 31
  essence of everything in A 32
  and eternity A 18, A 21, A 50
  and existence A 21, A 62, A 65
  existence of angels in T 131
  God is T 108, A 21
  many subjects in A 58–9
  is a measure A 14–17, A 19–20, A 25–6, A 63–6
  measures stable existence T 124, A 23
  minds not in A 33
  nature of A 63–6
  now of T 102–4, T 107, T 110, T 117–19, T 122
  one A 50–3, A 57, A 59–62

precedence in **A** 55–6, **A** 62
prime matter exists in **A** 29
simplicity in **A** 51
the sky in **A** 30
spirits in **A** 42, **A** 44, **A** 54
as stable duration 8, **A** 15
taken in several ways **A** 21
things in **A** 50
and time 19, **T** 70–2, **T** 101–7, **T** 110–11, **T** 113–14, **T** 116–20, **T** 122, **T** 127, **A** 18–22, **A** 25–6, **A** 28, **A** 32–7, **A** 48–51, **A** 53
existence
of angels 8, **T** 131
changeable **T** 97, **T** 104, **T** 111, **T** 117, **T** 124
of everlastingness **A** 21, **A** 62
everlastingness as a measure of **A** 65
of God in eternity **A** 18
of God in time 8–10, **T** 128–43,
indeterminate **T** 98
mode of 3
more perfect **A** 52
and motion 4, **T** 94–6, **T** 120–1
of a moveable object **T** 95–6
mutable and immutable **A** 16, **A** 26
and non-existence 17–18, **T** 119, **T** 147, **T** 150, **A** 1–13
of parts **A** 25
permanent and successive **A** 51
of perpetual things **A** 63–4
and quality **A** 25
and spirits **T** 123
stable **T** 104, **T** 111, **T** 117, **T** 124
substantial and active **A** 36
of temporal things **A** 58
third kind of **A** 17
and time **T** 4, **T** 10, **T** 78–87, **T** 120, **T** 127
unchanging whole **A** 54
unity in **A** 58, **A** 60
of what cannot exist **T** 148

fallacy of the accident **I** 122, **A** 10

God
between eternity and everlastingness **A** 15
contemplation of **A** 44
and creation of the world **T** 146, **T** 149, **T** 151
and eternity 19, **T** 145–6, **A** 18, **A** 28
and everlastingness **T** 108, **A** 21
existence of **A** 16, **A** 18
existence of, in time 8–10, **T** 128–43
the now of **T** 109
and spiritual motion 8
Gregory of Nazianzen
on the order of creation **T** 111

hearing, sense of
and the brain **I** 315
and common sense **I** 227
and its image in the soul **I** 64
organ of **I** 191, **I** 298
and passivities of the body **I** 54
and its sensible object **I** 188–90
heart
and common sense **I** 242–9, **I** 251, **I** 255–7, **I** 259, **I** 263, **I** 265–6, **I** 274, **I** 280–3, **I** 285, **I** 288, **I** 299, **I** 311
and the corporeal soul **I** 239, **I** 270, **I** 280
desiderative power in the **I** 257, **I** 284–6, **I** 311
heat of the **I** 274–7
images toward the **I** 269
imaginative power in the **I** 257, **I** 284–5, **I** 311
and motions of every sense **I** 258
opposite the brain **I** 239, **I** 267, **I** 276, **I** 278
is the primary organ **I** 253, **I** 268, **I** 303
and the proper senses **I** 266, **I** 271, **I** 281, **I** 299–302
and sense of taste **I** 294–5
and sense of touch **I** 297
source of motion **I** 285
and the vital soul **I** 270

images
of bodies **I** 47, **I** 60, **I** 63–4, **I** 66–7, **I** 73–4, **I** 77–8, **I** 80, **I** 85–6, **I** 119, **I** 134, **I** 145, **I** 165
and common sense **I** 151, **I** 168
and the corporeal soul *see* soul, corporeal
of corporeal things *see* corporeal things
of desirable things **I** 211
and desire **I** 162–3
duplicate **I** 4
forming of **I** 126
have matter **I** 135
in the imagination *see* imagination
impressed by sensed things **I** 72–3, **I** 115
are knowledge dispositions **I** 95
and memory **I** 74, **I** 197, **I** 206, **I** 217
mental **I** 150
and the mind 14, **I** 125, **I** 147–8
and motion **T** 58, **T** 62–3, **T** 65
pass from sense to the imagination **I** 157
permanence of **I** 158, **I** 161, **I** 194, **I** 198, **I** 269

INDEX 175

in the sense organ *see* sense organ
sensible **I** 78
of sensible things *see* sensible things
sensing of 11
and the sensory soul *see* soul, sensory
and the soul *see* soul
of sound **I** 71
are substances and accidents **I** 82, **I** 88, **I** 96, **I** 142
and thought **I** 40
of time **T** 54–5, **T** 59–60
imagination
  act of **I** 78
  of beasts **I** 13
  and body **I** 52
  in the brain **I** 169, **I** 201, **I** 284–6, **I** 288
  and cognition **I** 164
  and common sense **I** 151, **I** 168, **I** 285
  and the corporeal soul **I** 193, **I** 205
  and desire **I** 207–9
  and dreaming **I** 151
  in the heart **I** 257, **I** 284–5, **I** 311
  images in the 11–12, **I** 5–7, **I** 10–11, **I** 13, **I** 15–18, **I** 24–5, **I** 28, **I** 33, **I** 36, **I** 41–2, **I** 143, **I** 149–51, **I** 157, **I** 192
  and images of sensible things 12–13
  imitation of sense **I** 35
  and intellect **I** 25, **I** 33, **I** 36–7, **I** 39–40
  is motion **I** 2
  phantasms in **I** 66
  position in the soul 10
  and the proper senses **I** 219
  relation to desire 16
  relation to memory 16, **I** 207–8
  and the sensory soul **I** 2, **I** 52
intellect
  of beasts **I** 44
  and body **I** 51
  in the cognitive power **I** 1
  and doctrine **I** 27
  and images of sensible things 12–13, **I** 42–3, **I** 63
  and imagination **I** 25, **I** 33, **I** 36–7, **I** 39–40
  inner **I** 30
  has intellectual objects **I** 18–19
  and intelligible things **I** 15, **I** 35–6
  liberal arts in the **I** 34–5
  in the mind **I** 85
  position in the soul 10
  potential **I** 14
  rational **I** 84
intelligible things
  and imagination **I** 36, **I** 40
  in the intellect **I** 15, **I** 35–6
  seen by intellectual vision **I** 25
  and sensible things **I** 14–15, **I** 26, **I** 30
  two kinds of **I** 26
Isidore **A** 17, **A** 21–2

Jerome **A** 44
Job **T** 121
John of Damascus **T** 111, **A** 21
John of Vercelli 1–2

Liber de Causis **A** 21, **A** 36
light
  and bodily sense **I** 172
  and colour **I** 188
  and images **I** 7, **I** 213
  as an organ **I** 174
  reflected **I** 40
  and seeing **I** 164, **I** 212–13
  and sense of sight **I** 191

magnitude
  and motion **T** 13–14, **T** 17–18, **A** 45–6
matter
  and accidents and substances **I** 81, **I** 133
  and efficient cause **I** 82
  from which things come **I** 133
  and images **I** 135
  and motion **T** 65–6, **T** 68
  and the sensory soul **I** 99
  three causes and **I** 129–32
  and time **T** 57–8, **T** 64
measurable things
  four kinds of **T** 144, **T** 147
measure
  continuous **T** 47–8, **A** 20
  everlastingness is a **A** 14–17, **A** 19–20, **A** 23, **A** 25–6, **A** 63–6
  of existence **A** 54, **A** 64
  of God **A** 16
  intermediate **A** 28
  of knowable things **A** 24
  of motion 5, **T** 49–50
  proper **A** 12
  of a quantity **A** 19–20, **A** 23
  things of the same **A** 6–8
  and time **T** 71–2, **T** 86, **A** 66
memory
  and the corporeal soul **I** 217
  and desire **I** 209
  and images 15, **I** 74, **I** 78, **I** 145, **I** 148, **I** 197, **I** 199, **I** 203, **I** 206, **I** 217
  and the incorporeal soul **I** 217
  position in the brain **I** 201
  and the recollective power **I** 200
  relation to imagination 16, **I** 207–9
  and the sense organ **I** 189
  and the sensory soul 15
  and soul **I** 205–6, **I** 215, **I** 217
mind
  acted upon by itself **I** 120–2, **I** 125

INDEX

afflicted **I** 75, **I** 120
and body **I** 49–50, **I** 54, **I** 65, **I** 75, **I** 100, **I** 118, **I** 120–1, **I** 123, **I** 166, **I** 171, **I** 174, **I** 178–9, **I** 217
  human **I** 56
and images **I** 6, **I** 20–2, **I** 65, **I** 67, **I** 78, **I** 82, **I** 84–5, **I** 121, **I** 139–40, **I** 198
and images of bodies **I** 81, **I** 84–6
and imagination **I** 192
and indeterminate existence **T** 98
and memory **I** 197, **I** 199–200
motion of the **I** 121, **I** 150–1, **I** 166–7
and the sense organ **I** 121
and soul **I** 1–2, **I** 85–6, **I** 140, **I** 174, **I** 199
and time 2–3, 6–7, **T** 4, **T** 10, **T** 73, **T** 75–7, **T** 92
motion
  of the appetites **I** 210
  continuous **T** 12–18, **T** 22, **A** 45–6
  controlled by the brain **I** 284–5
  and corporeal nature **T** 123
  and the corporeal soul **I** 179, **I** 204
  countability of 4
  of the damned **T** 125
  and the desiderative power **I** 284–5
  diurnal 5–6
  and everlastingness **T** 120–1
  existence of 4, **T** 94–6, **T** 120–1
  heart is the source of **I** 242, **I** 285
  and images **T** 58, **T** 62–3, **T** 65
  and imagination **I** 2, **I** 144
  leads back to matter **T** 65
  local **T** 11, **T** 14–16, **T** 90, **T** 96
  and magnitude **T** 13–14, **T** 17–18
  measurement of 4–6
  natural **I** 166
  perpetual **T** 121
  progressive **I** 207
  quantity of **T** 19–25, **T** 27–8, **T** 34, **T** 49
  and sensing 14
  and time **T** 3, **T** 6–7, **T** 9–10, **T** 13, **T** 19, **T** 21, **T** 24, **T** 27, **T** 29–31, **T** 34–6, **T** 39–45, **T** 49–52, **T** 55–6, **T** 58, **T** 62, **T** 64, **T** 66–8, **T** 72–7, **T** 83, **T** 85, **T** 87, **T** 94, **T** 105, **T** 109–10, **T** 126, **A** 65–6

nature
  forming of images in **I** 125–8
Nebridius
  on images **I** 18
  on intelligible things **I** 26
now
  of eternity **T** 107
  of everlastingness **T** 102–4, **T** 107, **T** 110, **T** 117–19, **T** 122
  indivisible **T** 81

and motion **I** 109
three kinds of **T** 122
of time **T** 88–92, **T** 97, **T** 102, **T** 104, **T** 106–7, **T** 110, **T** 117–18, **T** 122
numerus motus
  note on the translation of 4

Peter Lombard
  on Augustine on angels **A** 44, n. 32
  on the creation of angels **A** 14
  on Jerome on angels **A** 44, n. 31
  on simultaneous creation **T** 112, **T** 115
phantasms *see* images
Plato
  on everlastingness and time **A** 18, **A** 21–2, **A** 35
  on time as coeval with heaven **T** 120
Psalms **T** 125, **A** 41
pseudo-Augustine (Alcher Clarevallensis?)
  on the brain **I** 201, **I** 221
  on the corporeal soul **I** 193
  on fire and air **I** 179, n. 125, **I** 180
  on the five senses of the body **I** 176
  on imagination **I** 193
pseudo-Augustine (Fulgentius Ruspensis)
  on everlastingness **A** 27, **A** 33
pseudo-Dionysius
  on everlastingness **A** 54
  on God as everlastingness **T** 108
  on intermediate things **A** 36
  on nothing **A** 32
pseudo-Galen (pseudo-Ricardus Anglicus)
  on the brain **I** 196, **I** 222–3, **I** 301

Richard of Saint Victor
  on everlastingness and time **T** 113
Richard Fishacre
  on the now of time **T** 91, n. 64

seeing
  bodily **I** 164, **I** 212
  corporeal **I** 106–9
  and the corporeal soul **I** 213
  imaginative **I** 164–5, **I** 218
  and inner light **I** 213
  intellectual **I** 164, **I** 212
  spiritual **I** 212, **I** 214–16
sense
  bodily **I** 66–7, **I** 118–19, **I** 172
  and the corporeal soul **I** 193
  defective **I** 76
  and images 12, 14, **I** 41–2, **I** 46, **I** 150
  and imagination **I** 35, **I** 78, **I** 144, **I** 157, **I** 192

informing of I 73
position in the soul 10
and sensible things 11, I 15, I 69, I 154, I 192
and the sensory soul I 79
sense organ
  in the brain I 231–3, I 250, I 267
  is called 'soul' I 173
  and cognition I 59, I 123
  consists of two parts I 3
  and corporeal soul I 181, I 183–4, I 193
  effect of the sensible object on the 13–14
  health of the I 100
  and images 13–14, I 41–2, I 46, I 60, I 79, I 102–4, I 113, I 115–17, I 140, I 149, I 183, I 185
  and the imaginative soul I 140
  and motion I 189
  position of the I 171
  purpose of the I 59, I 70
  sense of sight in the I 126
  and the senses I 189, I 202
  sensible species in the I 58
  and sensible things 13–14, I 4, I 59, I 102–6, I 109, I 111–12, I 121, I 124
  and the sensory soul *see* soul, sensory
senses
  and body and mind I 54
  in the brain I 278
  and images I 7–9, I 22–4, I 41, I 143, I 151, I 190
  and imagination I 144
  mode of imagining in the I 39–40
  motion of the I 188–9
  organs of the I 152–4
  and sensible things I 76, I 154
  and the sensory soul I 100
senses, proper
  and the brain I 169–70, I 266, I 271, I 288, I 299–302
  and common sense I 156, I 168, I 173, I 183, I 186, I 191, I 219, I 252
  and the heart I 266, I 271, I 281, I 299
  and images of sensed corporeal things I 191
  and images of sensible things I 183–5, I 219
  material passivity in the I 205
  organs of the I 168–70, I 173, I 251, I 296
sensible things
  and the brain I 266
  causing a change I 112
  and cognition I 76, I 123
  and common sense I 151, I 154–6
  and the heart I 266
  images of 11–13, 15, I 4–5, I 10, I 25, I 28–9, I 31–2, I 36, I 41, I 43–5, I 57–9, I 63, I 68, I 94, I 96–7, I 103, I 105, I 112, I 124, I 128–9, I 140, I 143, I 148–9, I 152–7, I 166, I 168, I 183–6, I 203–4, I 219, I 268, I 270–1, I 280
  and imagination 11, I 36, I 192
  and the imaginative soul I 5, I 15, I 29, I 143
  and intelligible things I 14–15, I 26, I 30
  knowledge of I 3
  in the mind I 22
  motion of I 187–8, I 190
  and 'seeing' I 108
  and sense 11, I 15, I 69, I 76, I 154, I 192
  and the sense organ 13–14, I 4, I 59, I 102–4, I 105–6, I 109, I 111–12, I 121, I 124
  and the sensory soul *see* soul, sensory – and sensible things
  three kinds of I 32
sensing
  mechanics of 14
  as a motion of the mind I 150
  organ of I 168, I 181, I 220
sight, sense of
  and the brain I 315
  and common sense I 227
  forming of images in the I 126
  and images I 268
  and its sensible object I 188–90
  and light I 191
  one of the shining things, according to Aristotle I 212
smell, sense of
  and the brain I 315
  and its sensible object I 188–9
  is material I 190
  organ of I 191
soul
  and body 12, I 3, I 47–8, I 53, I 55, I 60–1, I 64, I 89–91, I 101, I 103, I 165
  and common sense I 168
  composition of the 10, I 174, I 176
  and efficient cause I 62
  and images 15, I 64, I 80–4, I 93, I 126–7, I 133, I 135, I 149, I 161–2, I 165, I 216
  and images of sensible things I 103, I 105, I 128
  organ of the mind I 174
  as the primary organ of hearing I 175
  relation to mind I 1–2, I 85, I 140
  and the sense organ I 56, I 103–4
  and sensible things I 96, I 138
soul, animal
  part of the corporeal soul I 270
  as the possible organ of common sense I 274, n. 197, I 302
  produced in the brain I 239, I 270, I 301
soul, cognitive I 87, I 141
soul, corporeal

in the brain and the heart I 239, I 262, I 270, I 280
and common sense I 205
divided into vital and animal I 270
and fire and air I 176, I 179–80
and images I 185, I 194, I 196, I 198–200, I 203–4, I 213, I 215–17
is imagination I 193
and the incorporeal soul I 182, I 216–17
and light I 213
light and air in the I 175
is luminous I 212
and motion I 179
is one of two souls in an animal I 182
is sense I 193
is the sense organ I 181, I 183–5, I 191, I 193
spiritual passivity in I 205
is vitalized I 182, I 185
and the vitalizing soul I 215
soul, imaginative
is common sense I 239
images in I 165
and imaginative acts I 214
inner light in the I 213
relation to the sensory soul 15, I 2, I 150–1
and the sense organ I 140
and sensible things I 5, I 15, I 29, I 143
soul, incorporeal
and the corporeal soul I 182, I 216–17
and images I 198, I 216–17
and images of sensible things I 185
and memory I 217
is one of two souls in an animal I 182
vitalizes I 182
soul, sensory
acted upon I 56–7
of a beast 12
and bodily sense I 66
and body I 47–8, I 51–2, I 54–5, I 61, I 99, I 136
and the cognitive soul I 87
and common sense I 154, I 156, I 185
is a form I 99
and images 12–15, I 15–16, I 41, I 43, I 46, I 54, I 63, I 68, I 78–81, I 97, I 104, I 117, I 125, I 136, I 154
and images of sensible things I 105, I 112, I 124, I 128, I 145
and imagination I 52
and the imaginative soul I 2, I 150
and memory 15
and the sense organ 13–14, I 41, I 55–7, I 70, I 97, I 100–1, I 103, I 110–13, I 116, I 140
and sensible things 15, I 4–5, I 15, I 57, I 63, I 69, I 80, I 97, I 105, I 111, I 128, I 140, I 143, I 154, I 206
vitalizing I 185

soul, vital
becomes the animal soul I 301
in the brain I 301
in the heart I 270
part of the corporeal soul I 270, I 274, n. 197
produced in the heart I 239
soul, vitalizing
images in I 215, I 268
and spiritual seeing I 215
species *see* images
spiritus fantasticus
note on the translation of 10

taste, sense of I 237, I 248–9, I 251, I 289–95
time
actions subject to A 36
acts of the spirits in A 44–5
angels not in A 27
beginning of 7
being in 8
between existence and non-existence A 4
change in A 33
and eternity 7, A 1, A 6, A 8–16, A 48
and everlastingness 19, A 15–16, A 18–19, A 21–2, A 25–6, A 28, A 32–7, A 48–51, A 53
existence of God in 8–10
imperceptible A 43
intermediate 18
location of 2–3
as a measure 8, 19, A 20, A 25–6, A 65
and the mind 2–3, 6
nature of 4
in one subject A 58
precedence in A 55–6
prime matter is above A 29
as a quantity 4, 7, 19
rational nature in A 34
sensible world in A 18, A 35
sky not in A 30
spirits are in A 38–42
as successive duration 8
three ways of being in A 43, A 49
unity of T 44–6, T 51–2, T 54, T 67, T 70
touch, sense of I 235–8, I 248–9, I 251, I 297

universals 3

when
and time T 61, T 78, T 88, T 93, T 99, T 141
world, created
existence of 17–18

DATE DUE